Praise for
NEHEMI

T0243548

"This commentary by T. J. Betts will serve well any person who wants to understand clearly and expound faithfully the book of Nehemiah. It has a beautiful balance expositionally, theologically, and homiletically. I will be sure to consult it each and every time I study and proclaim this pivotal Old Testament book."

—Daniel L. Akin, president,
Southeastern Baptist Theological Seminary

"T. J. Betts is a scholar-practitioner—a student and teacher of the word who loves to proclaim that word. He is a pastor at heart, and he writes this commentary with the church in mind. T. J. helps us understand some of the technical issues of the book of Nehemiah, but he doesn't land there. Instead, he uses exposition, summaries, outlines, illustrations, applications, and reflection questions to guide us in knowing and teaching the word. This commentary is insightful, practical, challenging, and convicting. It will inform your mind while also moving your heart."

—Chuck Lawless, dean of doctoral studies and vice president of
spiritual formation and ministry centers,
Southeastern Baptist Theological Seminary

"The beauty of T. J. Betts's *Nehemiah: A Pastoral and Exegetical Commentary* is that it genuinely lives up to its name. This engaging work is astute technically but also so focused on the emotional content of the text that it connects the heart of the reader to the divine Author's heart as well as Nehemiah's. I found myself not just informed but stirred, particularly by the way this work moves from the ancient walls of Jerusalem to my own life in the twenty-first century."

—Hershael York, dean of the School of Theology,
The Southern Baptist Theological Seminary

NEHEMIAH

A Pastoral & Exegetical
Commentary

NEHEMIAH

T. J. BETTS

LEXHAM PRESS

Nehemiah: A Pastoral and Exegetical Commentary

Lexham Press, 1313 Commercial St., Bellingham, WA 98225
LexhamPress.com

Print ISBN 9781683593935
Digital ISBN 9781683593942
Library of Congress Control Number 2020932109

Lexham Editorial: Elliot Ritzema, Justin Marr, Ronald van der Bergh
Typesetting: Sarah Vaughan, Abigail Stocker

CONTENTS

PREFACE

The book of Nehemiah speaks of a time when God's people were in distress and in need of spiritual leadership. It shows how God is faithful to keep his word and how he is faithful to care for his people when from their perspective the present is difficult and the future appears to be grim. The book of Nehemiah shows how God called a leader and used this leader to encourage the people to trust in God and act on that trust. The message and principles of this book are relevant today for the people of God, especially those who lead them.

The preaching, teaching, and understanding of Old Testament narrative and historical literature is a continual challenge. Many times preachers and teachers boil down the text to a number of life lessons without considering the literary, canonical, historical, or theological contexts of the message, much less its exegetical and expositional concerns. They are like extended daily devotions. On the other hand, others are adept at understanding exegetical and expositional works that do give adequate attention to these various concerns pertaining to a passage, but have difficulty translating that information into an adequate sermon that not only reflects careful exposition of the text but also communicates it in a way that is relevant to contemporary audiences by providing illustrations and applications to the text. What's more, while evangelicals recognize the Old Testament anticipates, speaks of, and is fulfilled in the person and work of Jesus Christ, most struggle with *how* it does so and therefore how Christians may benefit from its study today. What is needed for pastors, teachers, and serious Bible students are works that, through careful exegesis and exposition, help them clearly understand the message of Old Testament books, taking the books and communicating them in relevant, readable, user-friendly formats that relate to contemporary life and provide a model to use and hopefully improve on for Bible study and the ministry of proclamation to the church. Such works contain illustrations and quotes in order to provide preachers and teachers with material that will hopefully serve as a catalyst for finding ways to communicate the message. This work is neither altogether devotional (although it speaks to devotional concerns) nor altogether technical (although it addresses some technical concerns). Landing somewhere in the middle, this work is intended to help those who preach and teach the Bible along with laypeople who wish to better understand the message of Nehemiah and who would benefit from a work that bridges the gap between the two.

THE BOOK OF NEHEMIAH IN ITS
BIBLICAL AND HISTORICAL CONTEXT

One may begin to understand the significance of the events in the book of Nehemiah only when one looks at God's words to the children of Israel in Moab through his servant Moses just before the nation entered into the promised land. Moses foretells of exile and return in Deuteronomy. Moses says to the people,

> All these curses shall come upon you and pursue you and overtake you till you are destroyed, because you did not obey the voice of the LORD your God, to keep his commandments and his statutes that he commanded you. They shall be a sign and a wonder against you and your offspring forever. Because you did not serve the LORD your God with joyfulness and gladness of heart, because of the abundance of all things, therefore you shall serve your enemies whom the LORD will send against you, in hunger and thirst, in nakedness, and lacking everything. And he will put a yoke of iron on your neck until he has destroyed you. The LORD will bring a nation against you from far away, from the end of the earth, swooping down like the eagle, a nation whose language you do not understand, a hard-faced nation who shall not respect the old or show mercy to the young. It shall eat the offspring of your cattle and the fruit of your ground, until you are destroyed; it also shall not leave you grain, wine, or oil, the increase of your herds or the young of your flock, until they have caused you to perish. They shall besiege you in all your towns, until your high and fortified walls, in which you trusted, come down throughout all your land. And they shall besiege you in all your towns throughout all your land, which the LORD your God has given you. (Deut 28:45–52 ESV)

And the LORD will scatter you among all peoples, from one end of the earth to the other, and there you shall serve other gods of wood and stone, which neither you nor your fathers have known. And among these nations you shall find no respite, and there shall be no resting place for the sole of your foot, but the LORD will give you there a trembling heart and failing eyes and a languishing soul. (Deut 28:65–66 ESV)

All the nations will say, "Why has the LORD done thus to this land? What caused the heat of this great anger?" Then people will say, "It is because they abandoned the covenant of the LORD, the God of their fathers, which he made with them when he brought them out of the land of Egypt, and went and served other gods and worshiped them, gods whom they had not known and whom he had not allotted to them. Therefore, the anger of the LORD was kindled against this land, bringing upon it all the curses written in this book, and the LORD uprooted them from their land in anger and fury and great wrath, and cast them into another land, as they are this day." (Deut 29:24–28 ESV)

And when all these things come upon you, the blessing and the curse, which I have set before you, and you call them to mind among all the nations where the LORD your God has driven you, and return to the LORD your God, you and your children, and obey his voice in all that I command you today, with all your heart and with all your soul, then the LORD your God will restore your fortunes and have compassion on you, and he will gather you again from all the peoples where the LORD your God has scattered you. If your outcasts are in the uttermost parts of heaven, from there the LORD your God will gather you, and from there he will take you. And the LORD your God will bring you into the land that your fathers possessed, that you may possess it. And he will make you more prosperous and numerous than your fathers. (Deut 30:1–5 ESV)

The first of these deportations into exile happened in the eighth century at the hands of the Assyrians when they deported the northern ten tribes of Israel to the east after their capture of Israel's capital, Samaria, in 722 BC. After that, only Judah was left. In its last days of monarchy, Judah found itself in a precarious position, with four superpowers of that day vying for power and determining the political landscape in which Judah found itself. These nations were Egypt, Assyria, Babylon, and Media. At the battle of Carchemish in 605 BC Babylon, along with it Median allies, handily defeated both Assyria and Egypt. Assyria ceased to exist, and Egypt retreated back home. Babylon emerged as ruler over "the whole of the land of Hatti," the name the Babylonians called all of Syria and

Palestine, including Judah.[1] Before Nebuchadnezzar went back to Babylon, he
made Jehoiakim, Judah's king, swear allegiance to Babylon. It was somewhere
near that time that Daniel and his companions were taken into Babylonian captivity (Dan 1:1–2).[2] Jehoiakim remained loyal to Nebuchadnezzar for three years,
but in 601 BC Jehoiakim decided to rebel. Nebuchadnezzar responded decisively
and quickly with auxiliary troops from the nations nearest to Judah (2 Kgs 24:1–
7). However, Nebuchadnezzar's main objective was the subjugation of Egypt.
Once again he met Pharaoh Neco in battle at Migdol on Egypt's border.[3] Both
sides suffered heavy casualties, and Nebuchadnezzar was forced to retreat back
to Babylon.[4] Jehoiakim saw this as another opportunity to withhold tribute from
Nebuchadnezzar and pursue friendly relations with Neco.

Nebuchadnezzar took about two years to gather his forces, but in 598 BC
his army began the march west to deal with the treachery of Judah.[5] As the
Babylonians started their journey, Jehoiakim died, and his eighteen-year-old son,
Jehoiachin, became king of Judah.[6] After a month's siege, Jerusalem capitulated
to the Babylonians.[7] According to 2 Kings 24:14–16,

> [Nebuchadnezzar] led away into exile all Jerusalem and all the captains
> and all the mighty men of valor, ten thousand captives, and all the crafts-
> men and the smiths. None remained except the poorest people of the land.
> So he led Jehoiachin away into exile to Babylon; also the king's mother
> and the king's wives and his officials and the leading men of the land, he
> led away into exile from Jerusalem to Babylon. All the men of valor, seven

1. Walter C. Kaiser Jr., *A History of Israel* (Nashville: Broadman & Holman, 1998), 401.

2. See D. J. Wiseman, *Chronicles of Chaldaean Kings, 626–556 B. C.* (London: British Museum Press, 1956); Wiseman, *Notes on Some Problems in the Book of Daniel* (London: Tyndale, 1956), 16–18.

3. Thomas Brisco, *Holman Bible Atlas* (Nashville: Broadman & Holman, 1998), 160.

4. Wiseman, *Chronicles of Chaldaean Kings*, 131.

5. Wiseman, *Chronicles of Chaldaean Kings*, 31, 70.

6. According to 2 Chr 36:9 in the Masoretic Text, he was eight years old, yet according to 2 Kgs 24:8 and the LXX, he was eighteen years old. The Babylonian records indicate that in 592 BC Jehoiachin had five sons, that is, five years after he went into Babylonian exile. Therefore, he must have been eighteen years old when he took the throne of Judah; see Wiseman, *Chronicles of Chaldaean Kings*, 220. (The Masoretic Text is the completed Hebrew text that sought to preserve the Hebrew Bible through a system of accents, vocalizations, and notes called the Masorah, compiled by scribes called the Masoretes from about AD 600 to 900. The LXX refers to the Septuagint, the Greek translation of the OT.)

7. A. Malamat, "Last Kings," *Israel Exploration Journal* 18 (1968): 144.

thousand, and the craftsmen and the smiths, one thousand, all strong and fit for war, and these the king of Babylon brought into exile to Babylon.[8]

Jeremiah 52:28 indicates that only 3,023 captives were taken, but the smaller figures of Jeremiah probably represent only men of the most influential families.[9] Furthermore, Nebuchadnezzar made Jehoiachin's uncle Zedekiah king in his place.

Contrary to Jeremiah's instruction, Zedekiah involved himself in plans to rebel against Babylon, and with the promise of Egyptian support he withheld tribute from Nebuchadnezzar in 589 BC (see Jer 38:14–23). Nebuchadnezzar acted quickly, dividing his army, sending one part to the Mediterranean coast to meet the Egyptians and sending the other part to Jerusalem to begin a siege on the city. The Egyptians attempted to help Judah, but they were outnumbered, forcing their withdrawal. In 588 BC the siege began, and Jerusalem fell in 587/586 BC.[10] Zedekiah attempted to flee but was captured and forced to watch the execution of his sons before his eyes were gouged out. Zedekiah was taken into captivity along with the people who had deserted to the Babylonians and those who were left in Jerusalem (2 Kgs 25:8–21).

THE RISE OF THE PERSIAN EMPIRE

In 539 BC, Cyrus the Great invaded Babylon. A major battle took place at Opis on the Tigris, with a Babylonian defeat. Then Cyrus ordered the conquest of the city of Babylon, and it fell quickly in late October. King Nabonidus of Babylon came to lead the defense, but he was too late.[11] Daniel describes how Babylon fell while Belshazzar, the king's son, was having a feast (Dan 5). The historian Xenophon corroborates Daniel, saying the attack happened at a time when "all Babylon was accustomed to drink and revel all night long."[12] Herodotus

---

8. Being from a priestly family, Ezekiel was taken into captivity at this time.

9. Edwin M. Yamauchi, "Ezra-Nehemiah," in *The Expositor's Bible Commentary*, ed. Frank E. Gaebelein (Grand Rapids: Zondervan, 1988), 4:567.

10. It is difficult to know which year Jerusalem fell with certainty because historians are not sure which dating system was being used in Judah. See A. Malamat, "The Last Years of the Kingdom of Judah," in *The Age of the Monarchies: Political History*, vol. 4 of *World History of the Jewish People* (Jerusalem: Massada, 1979), 218–20.

11. A. Kirk Grayson, *Assyrian and Babylonian Chronicles* (Locust Valley, NY: J. J. Augustin, 1975), 109–11.

12. Xenophon, *Cyropaedia* 7.5.15, in *Xenophon in Seven Volumes*, trans. Walter Miller (Cambridge, MA: Harvard University Press, 1914).

states, "The Babylonians themselves say that owing to the great size of the city the outskirts were captured without the people in the center knowing anything about it; there was a festival going on, and even while the city was falling they continued to dance and enjoy themselves, until hard facts brought them to their senses."[13] Belshazzar was killed, and Nabonidus was imprisoned.

THE RETURN OF THE EXILES

Cyrus had the policy of allowing conquered peoples to worship their own gods and establish some semblance of autonomy as long as they paid their taxes to the empire and remained loyal citizens. He encouraged people who had been uprooted from their homelands and religions to return home and reestablish the worship of their gods with the blessing and support of his government. The Edict of Cyrus as recorded in Ezra 1:2–4 occurred in 539 BC and demonstrates this Persian policy. Cyrus had this policy along with his achievements in Babylon recorded on what scholars and archaeologists call the Cyrus Cylinder.[14] Probably not long after this edict, a group of close to fifty thousand exiles returned to Judah under the leadership of Sheshbazzar (Ezra 2:64–65). The actual date of this return is unknown. One can safely say that it happened sometime after Cyrus' edict and sometime before the end of his reign in 530 BC, since Ezra 4:5 indicates that efforts to reconstruct the temple stalled during his reign. The best guess is probably 537 BC.[15] Zerubbabel became their governor, while Joshua served as the high priest.

Cambyses II (530–522 BC) became king when his father, Cyrus, died from wounds inflicted in battle. While involved in a military campaign, Cambyses received word that someone had usurped the throne, but on his way back home to deal with the treachery he died.[16] Darius I (522–486 BC), one of Cambyses' officers, dealt with the insurrection and became the next king of Persia. Cambyses must have been the king who supported the enemies of the returnees and put a stop to the reconstruction of the temple. However, Darius I upheld the Edict of Cyrus, and under his rule the returnees completed the reconstruction of the temple in Jerusalem (Ezra 4–6; see Hag 1:1, 15; 2:10; Zech 1:1, 7; 7:1). The next

---

13. Herodotus, *Histories* 1.191, trans. Aubrey de Sélincourt (New York: Penguin Books, 2003).

14. Antoine Simonin, "The Cyrus Cylinder," Ancient History Encyclopedia, https://www.ancient.eu/article/166/the-cyrus-cylinder/ (accessed February 18, 2019).

15. See Andrew E. Steinmann, *Ezra and Nehemiah*, Concordia Commentary (St. Louis: Concordia, 2010), 29–30; Yamauchi, "Ezra-Nehemiah," 595.

16. Edwin M. Yamauchi, *Persia and the Bible* (Grand Rapids: Baker, 1996), 125–26.

Persian king was Xerxes (biblical Ahasuerus, 486–465 BC). He was the Persian king to whom Esther was married.[17] He was assassinated in his bedchamber in 465 BC by an influential courtier named Artabanus.[18]

Artaxerxes I followed Xerxes (464–424 BC). Artaxerxes was the third son of Xerxes, and Damaspia his queen. He was nicknamed Longimanus. Plutarch says, "The first Artaxerxes, among the kings of Persia the most remarkable for a gentle and noble spirit, was surnamed the Long-handed, his right hand being longer than his left, and was the son of Xerxes."[19]

NEHEMIAH THE ROYAL CUPBEARER

Nehemiah served as cupbearer to Artaxerxes I (Neh 1:1; 2:1), and it was in Artaxerxes' seventh year on the throne that Ezra returned to Jerusalem, in 458/457 BC according to the traditional view (Ezra 7:7).[20] Yamauchi cites various sources indicating what traits Nehemiah had as a royal cupbearer:

> He would have been well trained in court etiquette (compare Dan 1:4, 13, 15; Josephus, *Antiquities* 16.230). He would certainly have known how to select the wines to set before the king. A proverb in the Babylonian Talmud (Baba Qamma 92b) states: "The wine belongs to the master but credit for it is due to his cupbearer." He would have been a convivial companion with a willingness to lend an ear at all times. Robert North is reminded of Saki, the companion of Omar Khayyam, who served wine to him and listened to his discourses. Nehemiah would have been a man of great influence as one with the closest access to the king, and one who could well determine who got to see the king (Xenophon, *Cyropaedia* 1.3.8–9). Above all Nehemiah would have enjoyed the unreserved confidence of the king. The great need for trustworthy attendants is underscored by the intrigues that were endemic to the Achaemenid court.[21]

---

17. Robert Dick Wilson, *A Scientific Investigation of the Old Testament* (Chicago: Moody, 1959), 69n25, has shown that "Ahasuerus" is the proper Hebrew rendering of the Greek "Xerxes."

18. Wilson, *Scientific Investigation*, 248.

19. Plutarch, *Artaxerxes* 1.1, in *Plutarch's Lives: The Translation Called Dryden's*, corrected from the Greek and revised by A. H. Clough, in 5 vols (Boston: Little Brown, 1906).

20. For arguments concerning the chronological order of Ezra and Nehemiah, see F. Charles Fensham, *The Books of Ezra and Nehemiah*, New International Commentary on the Old Testament (Grand Rapids: Eerdmans, 1982), 5–9; Yamauchi, "Ezra-Nehemiah," 583–86.

21. Yamauchi, *Persia and the Bible*, 259–60.

At least four of the Persian kings had been murdered, and at least a half-dozen of them reached the throne by way of some conspiracy.[22] Therefore, a most trusted individual had to fill the position of royal cupbearer.

NEHEMIAH THE GOVERNOR OF JUDAH

In 460 BC, Egypt revolted against the Persians with the help of the Greeks from Athens. They defeated and killed the Persian satrap who happened to be Artaxerxes' uncle and gained control of most of Lower Egypt in the north by 462 BC. In 459 BC, the Athenians sent two hundred ships to Egypt and helped the Egyptians capture Memphis, the administrative center of the delta region. In 456 BC, the Persians responded by sending Megabyzus, the satrap of Syria, with a large fleet and army to Egypt. By the end of eighteen months he was able to trap the Athenian fleet, capture Inarus, the leader of the revolt, and restore Persian rule in the region. Megabyzus had promised to spare the life of Inarus, but at the instigation of Amestris, the mother of Artaxerxes, he was impaled. Megabyzus was so angered by the deed that he revolted against the king from 449–446 BC but then was reconciled with him.[23]

The instability in the region may account for the reason Artaxerxes was in favor of Ezra's reforms and Nehemiah's appointment to be the governor of Judah. The province of Judah was much smaller than the nation of Judah had been, but Artaxerxes probably thought he could use some loyal supporters in the area given the instability in that region of the empire.[24] Ezra's commission to administer the Torah and return to his people in 458/57 BC was in line with Persian policy. The Persians hoped it would bring order to the people and pacify their religious concerns.[25] Nehemiah was a perfect choice to go to Judah given his loyalty to the king. Nehemiah arrived in Jerusalem in 445/445 BC. Artaxerxes needed someone he could trust in the area, and he appreciated Nehemiah's service. Artaxerxes gives this impression when he wants to know when Nehemiah can return to him (Neh 2:6).

---

22. I. Gershevitch, ed., *The Cambridge History of Iran II: The Median and Achaemenian Periods* (Cambridge: Cambridge University Press, 1985), 22.

23. Yamauchi, "Ezra-Nehemiah," 571.

24. John M. Cook, *The Persian Empire* (New York: Schocken, 1983), 128.

25. See Eugene H. Merrill, *A Kingdom of Priests: A History of Old Testament Israel* (Grand Rapids: Baker Books, 1996), 514–18, for a discussion concerning the dating of Ezra's return to Jerusalem.

As governor, Nehemiah faced an economic crisis (Neh 5). Non-landowners were short of food, landowners had to mortgage their properties, many were forced to borrow money at extremely high interest rates, and some were compelled to sell their children into slavery. While the Persian kings were kind when it came to matters of faith and local administration, they were quite severe when it came to money and taxation. Their economic policies led to inflationary conditions in which the rich got richer, any middle class became poor, and the poor became poorer. The economic conditions Nehemiah faced were prevalent throughout the Persian Empire.[26] As governor, Nehemiah was in a position to enjoy the spoils that Persian aristocrats enjoyed at the expense of the people under them, but he refused to do so. Instead he lent money and grain to those in need without interest and did not take of the royal food allotted to him as an appointed governor of the king (Neh 5:10, 14). Most governors became very prosperous in their positions at the expense of the people (Neh 5:15), but by his example and leadership Nehemiah helped his people in a time of dire need and withstood any temptation to take advantage of them (Neh 5:17).

CONCLUSION

The events leading up to the exile, the exile itself, and the return all point to God's sovereignty and grace. The Lord God is not only the God of Israel, but he is the God of the nations. Kings and leaders plan their courses of action, but it is the Lord who raises them up and brings them down for his own glory and purposes. God has always been and always will be faithful to his word and to his people.

---

26. See M. Dandamyev, "Achaemenid Babylonia," in *Ancient Mesopotamia*, ed. I. M. Diakonoff (Moscow: Nauka, 1969), 309, for conditions described in Babylon that are similar to what Nehemiah describes in Jerusalem.

THE HEART OF A SERVANT

Nehemiah 1:1–11

INTRODUCTION

Second Chronicles 16:9 states, "For the eyes of the LORD move to and fro throughout the earth that He may strongly support those whose heart is completely His." Nehemiah had such a heart. The beginning of Nehemiah's book reveals something of his heart for God's glory and the reputation of God's people. It shows how Nehemiah was both a man of prayer and a man of action, ready to serve the Lord in any capacity. It also reveals some important truths about Nehemiah's God. He is a God who is at the same time both just and merciful. He is a faithful God who is ready to hear the prayers of those who love him and act on their behalf.

STRUCTURE

The structure of the passage is rather straightforward. It has two sections. The first section (1:1–3) introduces Nehemiah, the setting in which the events of the book take place, and the problem Nehemiah will address. The second section (1:4–11) is Nehemiah's prayer concerning the revival and restoration of the people of God in Jerusalem.

SUMMARY OF THE PASSAGE

A burden for the condition of the people of God leads to fervent intercessory prayer for them and a commitment to act on their behalf.

OUTLINE OF THE PASSAGE

I. The Predicament of the People of God (1:1–3)

    A. The context of the report concerning the people of God in Judah (1:1–2)

    B. The content of the report concerning the people of God in Judah (1:3)

II. The Prayer for the People of God (1:4–11)

A. The characteristics of Nehemiah's prayer
1. Nehemiah's response is emotional (1:4)
2. Nehemiah's response is serious (1:4)
3. Nehemiah's response is persistent (1:4)
B. The contents of Nehemiah's prayer
1. Nehemiah's prayer is confessional (1:5–7).
a. Confessional concerning God (1:5)
b. Confessional concerning Israel (1:6–7)
2. Nehemiah's prayer is founded on God's promises (1:8–9)
3. Nehemiah's prayer is based on the identity of Israel as the people of God (1:10)
4. Nehemiah's prayer recalls God's work of redemption on behalf of Israel (1:10)
5. Nehemiah's prayer is shared by others (1:11)
6. Nehemiah's prayer reveals his faith in God, his submission to God, and his dependence on God to give him success as God's servant (1:11)

DEVELOPMENT OF THE EXPOSITION

I. THE PREDICAMENT OF THE PEOPLE OF GOD (1:1–3)

[1] The words of Nehemiah the son of Hacaliah. Now it happened in the month Chislev, *in* the twentieth year, while I was in Susa the capitol, [2] that Hanani, one of my brothers, and some men from Judah came; and I asked them concerning the Jews who had escaped *and* had survived the captivity, and about Jerusalem. [3] They said to me, "The remnant there in the province who survived the captivity are in great distress and reproach, and the wall of Jerusalem is broken down and its gates are burned with fire."

A. *The Context of the Report concerning the People of God in Judah (1:1–2)*

The book of Nehemiah begins by answering questions just about any reader would ask and want answered in the introduction of a historical narrative. First, it identifies who wrote this historical record. Nehemiah's name means "Yahweh comforts." Verse 1 identifies Nehemiah's father as Hacaliah, and here is the only occurrence of this name in the Old Testament. It probably means "hope in Yahweh" or "wait on Yahweh."[1] Second, it indicates that the first encounter in the book happened in the month of Chislev in the twentieth year. On the Jewish calendar, the month of Chislev occurs during the months of November and December. However, there is some uncertainty as to what "in the twentieth year" refers. It possibly is a reference to the twentieth year of Nehemiah's service as the cupbearer, or it may be referring to the twentieth year of King Artaxerxes' reign.[2] It was probably the former, taking place in about 446/445 BC. Either way, it is at this time that Hanani, Nehemiah's brother, and some men from Judah came to Susa and gave Nehemiah a report of the situation back in Judah.

B. The Content of the Report concerning the People of God in Judah (1:3)

The report concerning Jerusalem is twofold: it gives a description of the people, and it provides a description of the physical condition of the structures of the city itself. Two words describe the people. The first, *rā'â*, usually translated "distress," is perhaps the strongest word in the Hebrew language that depicts danger, disaster, calamity, or misery. It basically describes a condition detrimental to life. The second word describing the people, *ḥerpâ*, depicts reproach, shame, disgrace, scorn, insult, contempt, and threat.[3] The situation is exactly what Ezekiel prophesied would happen as a result of Judah's sin and the Lord's judgment. In Ezekiel 5:13–15 the Lord says,

> Thus My anger will be spent and I will satisfy My wrath on them, and I will be appeased; then they will know that I, the LORD, have spoken in My zeal when I have spent My wrath upon them. Moreover, I will make you a desolation and a reproach among the nations which surround you, in the sight of all who pass by. So it will be a reproach, a reviling, a warning and an object of horror to the nations who surround you when I execute judgments against you in anger, wrath and raging rebukes. I, the LORD, have spoken.

1. Andrew E. Steinmann, *Ezra and Nehemiah,* Concordia Commentary (St. Louis: Concordia, 2010), 371.

2. For a comprehensive discussion of the issues concerning "the twentieth year" see H. G. M. Williamson, *Ezra, Nehemiah,* Word Biblical Commentary (Nashville: Thomas Nelson, 1985), 168–70.

3. John E. Hartley, "חָרַף," in *New International Dictionary of Old Testament Theology and Exegesis,* ed. W. VanGemeren (Grand Rapids: Zondervan, 1997), 2:280.

The news only gets worse as Nehemiah hears about the physical condition of the city itself as the men tell Nehemiah, "The wall of Jerusalem is broken down and its gates are burned with fire." Second Kings 25:8–10 gives a pointed description how this tragedy happened in 587/586 BC:

> Now on the seventh day of the fifth month, which was the nineteenth year of King Nebuchadnezzar, king of Babylon, Nebuzaradan the captain of the guard, a servant of the king of Babylon, came to Jerusalem. He burned the house of the LORD, the king's house, and all the houses of Jerusalem; even every great house he burned with fire. So all the army of the Chaldeans who *were with* the captain of the guard broke down the walls around Jerusalem.

Nearly 140 years later, Nehemiah receives word that the conditions in Jerusalem are as bad as they ever were since its destruction by the Chaldeans.[4] Such news surely is difficult for Nehemiah to absorb, given that the same prophet who prophesied of the eminent destruction of Jerusalem and the reproach of its inhabitants also proclaimed,

> Thus says the Lord GOD, "When I gather the house of Israel from the peoples among whom they are scattered, and will manifest My holiness in them in the sight of the nations, then they will live in their land which I gave to My servant Jacob. They will live in it securely; and they will build houses, plant vineyards and live securely when I execute judgments upon all who scorn them round about them. Then they will know that I am the LORD their God." (Ezek 28:25–26)

People from the house of Israel who had been scattered had indeed returned and reclaimed some of their land, including Jerusalem. Shortly after they arrived, they set out to repair the walls and rebuild the temple, but their efforts were thwarted by the false reports of their enemies, who claimed the returned exiles were planning to rebel against the king as soon as they were able. So the king put a stop to their efforts (Ezra 4:8–24). Now, about ninety years have transpired since the first exiles returned, and up to this point the prosperity and security of

---

4. The terms "Chaldeans" and "Babylonians" are interchangeable expressions describing the people from what is modern-day southern Iraq in OT historical and prophetic literature.

which Ezekiel spoke has yet to materialize. Nehemiah's reaction indicates how disturbed he is by the report he has received.

II. The Prayer for the People of God (1:4–11)

> [4] When I heard these words, I sat down and wept and mourned for days; and I was fasting and praying before the God of heaven. [5] I said, "I beseech You, O Lord God of heaven, the great and awesome God, who preserves the covenant and lovingkindness for those who love Him and keep His commandments, [6] let Your ear now be attentive and Your eyes open to hear the prayer of Your servant which I am praying before You now, day and night, on behalf of the sons of Israel Your servants, confessing the sins of the sons of Israel which we have sinned against You; I and my father's house have sinned. [7] We have acted very corruptly against You and have not kept the commandments, nor the statutes, nor the ordinances which You commanded Your servant Moses. [8] Remember the word which You commanded Your servant Moses, saying, 'If you are unfaithful I will scatter you among the peoples; [9] but *if* you return to Me and keep My commandments and do them, though those of you who have been scattered were in the most remote part of the heavens, I will gather them from there and will bring them to the place where I have chosen to cause My name to dwell.' [10] They are Your servants and Your people whom You redeemed by Your great power and by Your strong hand. [11] O Lord, I beseech You, may Your ear be attentive to the prayer of Your servant and the prayer of Your servants who delight to revere Your name, and make Your servant successful today and grant him compassion before this man." Now I was the cupbearer to the king.

Nehemiah is a man of prayer. This prayer is the first and longest prayer of nine prayers recorded by Nehemiah in this book. He is an example of a believer who truly prays without ceasing. At times it seems he is carrying on an ongoing conversation with God. It is very natural for Nehemiah to go to God in prayer when he hears the report from Jerusalem. Sometimes in dire situations people will say, "I guess all we can do is pray." It is as if prayer were a last resort, but it is no last resort for Nehemiah. For him, it is his first option. When prayer becomes the first option for a person, it is an indication that he or she is truly walking with and depending on God in all things. It is a true sign of humility. It is no wonder

God used Nehemiah as he did, knowing that "God is opposed to the proud, but gives grace to the humble" (Jas 4:6).

The structure of the prayer is straightforward: (1) Nehemiah begins by addressing God and acknowledging who God is, (2) he confesses the sins of Israel, (3) he asks God to restore his people, and (4) he asks God to give him success in serving the Lord toward this end. Nehemiah's words convey both a confidence in God's word and a commitment to God's work. The prayer's characteristics reveal its significant meaning.

A. The Characteristics of Nehemiah's Prayer

1. Nehemiah's Response Is Emotional (1:4)

After hearing of the report from his brother and the men from Judah, Nehemiah "sat down and wept and mourned." Nehemiah's response indicates he is a godly man who cares deeply for the reputation and well-being of the people of God, as both are a reflection of God's own reputation. Such concerns become apparent throughout the remainder of the book as Nehemiah demonstrates his commitment to God's glory and the flourishing of God's covenant people in Jerusalem. His reaction is more than just a reflection of his culture or religious tradition. He is deeply grieved by the great distress and reproach of the people and the broken-down condition of the holy city. Nehemiah sincerely empathizes with the misery his people are experiencing. The bold actions he takes to rectify the situation in Judah are born out of a deep burden for its people and commitment to his God. Furthermore, one should note that Nehemiah is not the only one to weep over Jerusalem and its people. Years later, Jesus also weeps over the poor spiritual condition of the people and the hardships that will come to them as a result of it (Luke 19:41–44), and he too takes extremely bold actions to remedy their situation.

2. Nehemiah's Response Is Serious (1:4)

Not only do Nehemiah's weeping and mourning indicate the seriousness of his concern, but so does his fasting. Simply put, biblical fasting is a believer's voluntary abstinence from food for spiritual purposes. If it is not for spiritual purposes it is nothing more than a diet. Fasting enhances fervent prayer. Fasting indicates the desire of our prayers is greater than any physical desire our body might have. Arthur Wallis writes, "Fasting is calculated to bring a note of urgency and importunity into our praying, and to give force to our pleading in the court of heaven. The man who prays with fasting is giving heaven notice that he is truly earnest."[5] Nehemiah's desire for the glory of God and the reputation of the people of God is greater than his concerns for his own body. He understands the power of prayer and fasting.[6]

3. Nehemiah's Response Is Persistent (1:4)

There is no indication of how long Nehemiah's weeping, mourning, and praying last, except that he does them "for days" (v. 4), "day and night" (v. 6). Nehemiah's response is more than just a mere whim. His perseverance in prayer and fasting is an indication of what his priorities are and the depth of his faith. He continues in his praying and fasting for days, day and night, because he is convinced only the Lord can answer his prayers. Speaking of persevering prayer, Andrew Murray writes,

> Don't let delay shake your faith, for it is faith that will provide the answer in time. Each believing prayer is a step nearer to the final victory! It ripens the fruit, conquers hindrances in the unseen world, and hastens the end. Child of God! Give the Father time! He is long-suffering over you. He wants your blessing to be rich, full, and sure. Give Him time, but continue praying day and night. And above all, remember the promise: "I say unto you, He will avenge them speedily."[7]

Nehemiah's faith is a consuming, persevering faith expressed by unceasing petition to the God of heaven. It is not until four months later that Nehemiah gets the opportunity to take further action and sees God begin to answer his prayer.

B. The Contents of Nehemiah's Prayer

1. Nehemiah's Prayer Is Confessional (1:5–7)

The Hebrew word *yādâ* often appears as "confess" in English translations, as it does in verse 6.[8] However, its basic meaning is "to know." Therefore, it often carries with it the idea of acknowledgment. In verse 6, the word actually occurs, but

---

5. Arthur Wallis, *God's Chosen Fast* (Fort Washington, PA: Christian Literature Crusade, 1968), 42.

6. For an informative discussion of the discipline of biblical fasting, see Donald S. Whitney, *Spiritual Disciplines for the Christian Life* (Colorado Springs: NavPress, 1991), 151–72.

7. Andrew Murray, *With Christ in the School of Prayer* (Springdale, PA: Whitaker House, 1981), 122.

8. As in the KJV, NASB, ESV, HCSB, NIV, etc.

verses 5–7 all are a part of Nehemiah's confession or acknowledgments. In verse 5, he acknowledges important truths about God, and in verses 6–7, he acknowledges important truths concerning him and his people, Israel.

a. Confessional concerning God (1:5)

Nehemiah prays because he believes in the God who is near to his people and answers their prayers (Deut 4:7). "Yahweh, God of heaven" indicates that the personal, covenant-keeping God of Israel reigns over all of creation. Nehemiah is addressing this God, the God who is "great"—the one and only God who is omnipotent and able to answer his prayer. Also, God is "fearsome." The God who is over all his creation is the God who judges the nations, the God who brought judgment on his own people Israel.

However, he is also the God who is faithful to keep his loving covenant with his people, even a sinful people such as Israel. The Hebrew word *ḥesed*, often translated "lovingkindness" or "steadfast love," points to God's faithfulness, favor, love, and mercy that God has demonstrated in his covenant to Israel. It is God's disposition toward his covenant people, Israel, his beloved. It is altogether unexpected and undeserved from the perspective of its recipient. J. G. McConville rightly observes, "The prayer, then, is essentially an appeal to God's mercy, based on a knowledge of his character expressed in his covenant with Israel."[9] Therefore, a proper perspective of who God is and of God's faithfulness and lovingkindness to his people in light of such might and majesty produces awe, utter respect, and a healthy sense of fear. It produces the faith of his people, who respond in love and obedience to him. They, whom he has loved, love him and keep his commandments. It is as Jesus later teaches his disciples (John 14:15).

Moreover, such an understanding of God produces repentance. Nehemiah's prayer is based on an intimate knowledge of who God is. Prayers of confession like the one Nehemiah prayed only come as a result of intimate knowledge of God and an honest assessment of oneself in light of that knowledge. All prayer must begin with being God-centered and not self-centered. Only when we have a proper perspective of God can we begin to gain a proper perspective of ourselves and the world around us. For some of us, it may be that a lack of prayer and a lack of answered prayers occurs because we fail in truly knowing the One to whom we pray. Hosea confronts people who identify themselves as God's

---

9. J. G. McConville, *Ezra, Nehemiah, and Esther* (Louisville: Westminster John Knox, 1985), 77.

people but who have no knowledge of God, and the result is tragic (Hos 4). However, Nehemiah knows the God to whom he prays, and such knowledge lays the groundwork for the remainder of what he says.

b. Confessional concerning Israel (1:6–7)

Nehemiah not only has a clear understanding of God, but he also knows himself and his people, Israel. They are corrupt, their sin is against God, and therefore they have broken their covenant with the Lord. The "commandments, statutes, and ordinances" is a reference to God's law, the Pentateuch (Deut 7). While God has been faithful to the covenant, Israel has been unfaithful. The terrible condition in which the people of God find themselves is the result of their own sin. Israel has become its own worst enemy.

But Nehemiah obviously knows God's word. He understands the truth that "He who conceals his transgression will not prosper, but he who confesses and forsakes them will find compassion" (Prov 28:13). Nehemiah knows he is addressing a compassionate God. Nehemiah's prayer echoes the words of Solomon when he dedicated the temple:

> Yet have regard to the prayer of Your servant and to his supplication, O LORD my God, to listen to the cry and to the prayer which Your servant prays before You; that Your eye may be open toward this house day and night, toward the place of which You have said that You would put Your name there, to listen to the prayer which Your servant shall pray toward this place. Listen to the supplications of Your servant and of Your people Israel when they pray toward this place; hear from Your dwelling place, from heaven; hear and forgive. (1 Kgs 8:28–30; 2 Chr 6:19–21)

Note God's reply to Solomon: "If … My people who are called by My name humble themselves and pray and seek My face and turn from their wicked ways, then I will hear from heaven, will forgive their sin and will heal their land. Now My eyes will be open and My ears attentive to the prayer offered in this place" (2 Chr 7:13–15). Solomon anticipates a day when Israel will fall away, so he asks God that when they come to their senses God would hear their prayer of repentance. Nehemiah trusts God to "remember" his promises, especially those concerning hearing from heaven, forgiving their sin, and healing their land.[10]

---

10. Steinmann, *Ezra and Nehemiah*, 392.

It is commendable of Nehemiah to acknowledge his own guilt and the guilt of his own forebears along with the rest of Israel in sinning against the Lord. Nehemiah probably had not been born when all the events happened that led to Babylonian exile, yet Nehemiah's personal identity in the Lord is bound to his identity with Israel, God's covenant people. One identity is impossible without the other. He recognizes both the personal and communal nature of God's covenant with Israel. It is similar to Paul's teaching concerning the body of Christ. We are members of one another, and the actions of one affect the whole (1 Cor 12:26). His attitude is "We are all in this thing together."

2. Nehemiah's Prayer Is Founded on God's Promises (1:8–9)

Speaking of Nehemiah's prayer, Raymond Brown says, "The words are a skillfully arranged mosaic of great Old Testament warnings and promises originally given to Moses and repeated by Solomon at the dedication of the temple."[11] Nehemiah recalls how God promised Moses to bring about judgment and finally exile for Israel's infidelity to God, and he recalls God's anticipation of Israel's repentance and promise to restore the nation when that happens (Lev 26:40; Deut 4:27; 12:11; 30:2, 4; 1 Kgs 8:28–30; 2 Chr 6:19–21). The first part of the promise, Israel's unfaithfulness and exile, has happened. Now Nehemiah is saying, "As we come to you in repentance, please fulfill the second part of your promise to restore your people and their land." Nehemiah recognizes the God who is faithful to carry out his judgment is also faithful to reconcile and restore his people.

The phrase "where I have chosen to cause My name to dwell" echoes passages in Deuteronomy, all connected to Israel worshiping Yahweh (Deut 12:5, 11; 14:23; 16:2, 6, 11; 26:2). Though Nehemiah cares about the economic conditions of his people, Nehemiah's concern is about more than that. He is concerned about God's people exalting God and serving God. It is about their fulfilling their purpose as a kingdom of priests (Exod 19:6). For that reason, it is no coincidence Nehemiah echoes Deuteronomy, the book that explains what it means for Israel to live as God's covenant people, and echoes Solomon's dedication of the temple in Jerusalem, the place where God designated his people to worship and serve him as a kingdom of priests. Just as Deuteronomy and Solomon's prayer of dedication demonstrate a concern for the reputation of the people of God before the

---

11. Raymond Brown, *The Message of Nehemiah*, The Bible Speaks Today (Downers Grove, IL: InterVarsity Press, 1998), 39.

nations, so Nehemiah wants Jerusalem no more to be a reproach (see Deut 4:6; 1 Kgs 8:41–43). Instead, he wants to see it become what it once was, the place where Yahweh chose for his name to dwell.

3. Nehemiah's Prayer Is Based on the Identity of Israel as the People of God (1:10)

Nehemiah understands that both he and his people were called to be servants of the Lord. Eight times the word "servant" appears in this prayer. He refers to himself, Moses, and to all of Israel as God's servants. When God's law was given to Israel by Moses, such an understanding was made clear: "For the sons of Israel are My servants; they are My servants whom I brought out from the land of Egypt. I am the LORD your God" (Lev 25:55). As he prays, Nehemiah may be remembering the words of the prophet Jeremiah that spoke of God's gathering his people from exile and bringing them back to the promised land: "'Fear not, O Jacob My servant,' declares the LORD, 'and do not be dismayed, O Israel; For behold, I will save you from afar and your offspring from the land of their captivity. And Jacob will return and will be quiet and at ease, and no one will make him afraid'" (Jer 30:10).

Nehemiah's emphasis on their identity as servants of the Lord reveals his submissive disposition before God and his sense of purpose in respect to God. Israel's existence as God's covenant people centers on their service to Yahweh. They were chosen to be his servants. Every believer should have this disposition and sense of purpose. Jesus demonstrates it when he washes the feet of his disciples (John 13:15–17), and he teaches that greatness in his kingdom comes through servitude (Matt 20:26; 23:11; Mark 9:35; 10:43; Luke 22:26). It goes against our nature, but it is evidence of our new nature in Christ.[12]

4. Nehemiah's Prayer Recalls God's Work of Redemption on Behalf of Israel (1:10)

Nehemiah recognizes Yahweh, Israel's covenant-keeping God, is Israel's Redeemer. The Hebrew verb pādâ, translated "redeemed," is closely associated with the redemption of the firstborn in Israel and with the idea of salvation. In Exodus 13, the Lord instructs Israel that every firstborn belongs to Yahweh. However,

---

12. In 1 Cor 14, Paul teaches that one of the reasons the Holy Spirit is given to believers is to serve Christ and his church through spiritual gifts.

the Lord allows for the redemption of firstborn sons and donkeys by way of a substitutionary sacrifice. By doing so, the people are to recall how the firstborn of every man and beast of the Egyptians perished, while the firstborn sons of Israel were redeemed.

In the book of Deuteronomy, Yahweh is the exclusive subject of the verb *pādâ*. The redemption of Israel from Egypt assures Israel God will continue to care for them. God's compassion for Israel is also to serve as an example of how the people should treat one another. In the Psalms, the cries for the Lord to redeem his people appear to be cries for his deliverance from some serious threat or burden (Pss 26:11; 69:18; 119:134). Several psalms use *pādâ* to affirm confidence and trust in Yahweh's readiness to rescue his people (Pss 31:5; 55:18; 71:23).

Moreover, in Jeremiah 31:11, the Lord states he "has ransomed Jacob and redeemed him from the hand of him who was stronger than he," Yahweh's assurance he will restore scattered Israel and bring her back home to Jerusalem on Mount Zion.[13] Following this statement, the Lord promises he will one day make a new covenant with Israel and Judah and that the city of Jerusalem will be rebuilt (Jer 31:27–40). Perhaps Nehemiah anticipates this day and sees this occasion as an opportunity to be involved in the fulfillment of God's promise. Nehemiah's confidence in God in his present situation rests on the assurance that Yahweh is Israel's Redeemer.

5. Nehemiah's Prayer Is Shared by Others (1:11)

Nehemiah recognizes there are others who are faithfully praying for the restoration of Jerusalem. He realizes the importance of ministering in the context of the community of faith. He knows he cannot do what God has laid on his heart alone, and neither is he meant to do it alone. The book of Nehemiah highlights the importance of God's people working together for God's purposes. On a number of occasions both the Old and New Testaments show how important the community of faith is to prayer and service. All too often believers underestimate the power of corporate prayer. It unifies, encourages, and inspires the people of God—all necessities for doing God's work, as seen in the book of Nehemiah.

---

13. J. A. Thompson and Elmer A. Martens, "פדה," in *New International Dictionary of Old Testament Theology and Exegesis*, ed. W. VanGemeren (Grand Rapids: Zondervan, 1997), 3:578–80.

6. Nehemiah's Prayer Reveals His Faith in God, His
Submission to God, and His Dependence on God
to Give Him Success as God's Servant (1:11)

Nehemiah's confidence in God is in the face of huge obstacles. His first is the Persian king. Artaxerxes will need to overturn his decree that put a stop to the rebuilding of Jerusalem (Ezra 4:21). The kings of Persia were not normally permitted to rescind a decree once they made it. For instance, King Darius is distraught when he discovers Daniel is to be put in a lion's den because of the king's edict. When Darius seeks to release Daniel, Daniel's enemies remind the king, "Recognize, O king, that it is a law of the Medes and Persians that no injunction or statute which the king establishes may be changed" (Dan 6:15). Esther's King Ahasuerus regrets listening to Haman and making a decree to slaughter the Judeans. Instead of rescinding the first decree, he issues a second decree encouraging the Judeans to defend themselves against their enemies. Even some of the king's princes and royal servants fight alongside the Judeans to help defend them (Esth 8:9–14; 9:1–3). No doubt, as cupbearer of the king, Nehemiah is very familiar with this law. King Artaxerxes needs to somehow rescind or circumvent his previous decree.

Nevertheless, Nehemiah understands the king is just a "man," while the Lord—he is God. All people are under God's authority, including the great king of Persia. As vast as the Persian Empire is and as powerful is its king, they pale in comparison to the "God of heaven, the great and fearsome God," and his entire kingdom. Nehemiah is willing to patiently wait on God to move the heart and mind of "this man." Even when believers pray about the right things with the right motives, God still sometimes delays in answering so that our perseverance in prayer may become a lesson in itself.

It is also noteworthy to recognize how God placed Nehemiah in this strategic position of cupbearer to the king.[14] Mark Throntveit correctly observes, "No menial servants, royal cupbearers were charged with tasting the king's wine (to prevent poisoning) and guarding the royal chambers. As such they became among the most trusted of officials and throughout the Near East enjoyed extensive influence with their masters."[15]

---

14. See the discussion of Nehemiah the royal cupbearer in chapter 1.

15. Mark A. Throntveit, *Ezra-Nehemiah*, Interpretation: A Bible Commentary for Teaching and Preaching (Louisville, KY: Westminster John Knox, 1992), 66.

The Lord not only moved in the heart of Nehemiah, but he providentially put Nehemiah in the proper place to act on behalf of Jerusalem. It is just one more instance in the Scriptures where one sees God at work on a grander scale while at the same time working in the lives of particular individuals in specific situations. Even though Nehemiah serves the Persian king, he is first and foremost a servant of the Lord.

CONCLUSION

Nehemiah's prayer is born out of an intense love for God and his people, Israel. Therefore, he perseveres in his praying and fasting day and night. He appeals to a great and merciful God who graciously made himself known to Israel through his covenant with them. He recognizes God is faithful to his promises both to discipline his people when they sin and to restore his people when they repent of their sin and return to him, their Redeemer. Nehemiah prays with confidence, knowing that God will hear his prayer because his prayer is founded on the promises of God. Nehemiah understands God's people were chosen to be God's servants, and it is with this humble spirit and sense of purpose he prays. He identifies with the people of God and knows he is not alone in his desire and prayers for the restoration of Jerusalem. Moreover, Nehemiah trusts in the power of God and the wisdom of God's timing to answer his prayer.

FINAL THOUGHTS

1. When was the last time you were deeply burdened and moved to prayer and fasting concerning the condition of the people of God today, the church?
2. Do you have a biblical understanding of who God is and who you are in relationship to him?
3. How naturally does prayer come to you in all situations?
4. How committed are you to intercessory prayer on behalf of other believers?
5. Do you see your identity as a servant of God?

WAITING FOR AN OPEN DOOR

Nehemiah 2:1–10

INTRODUCTION

Isaiah says, "Yet those who wait for the LORD will gain new strength; they will mount up with wings like eagles, they will run and not get tired, they will walk and not become weary" (Isa 40:31). In Nehemiah 2:1–10, Nehemiah demonstrates this truth. For four months Nehemiah grieves over the reproach Jerusalem has become and seeks the help and mind of God as he prays and fasts over the condition of his people. Finally, the Lord answers his prayers and gives Nehemiah the opportunity to take action on behalf of the people of God for the glory of God.

STRUCTURE

The two settings where events take place drive the structure of this passage. The first section, in verses 1–8, takes place in the palace of Artaxerxes, the Persian king. The second, shorter section, composed of verses 9–10, conveys what happened as a result of the interaction between Nehemiah and the king in the first section.

SUMMARY OF THE PASSAGE

In his grief concerning the condition of God's people and in the face of potential danger, depending on God, Nehemiah courageously voices his yearning to help his people and his desire for Artaxerxes to help him do it.

OUTLINE OF THE PASSAGE

I. The Emotions Nehemiah Feels (2:1–2)
    A. Nehemiah's sadness concerning the condition of Jerusalem (2:1–2a)
    B. Nehemiah's fear before the king (2:2b)
II. The Courage Nehemiah Displays (2:3–8a)
    A. Nehemiah's courage enables him to speak the truth (2:3)

B. Nehemiah's courage comes from a dependence on God (2:4)

C. Nehemiah's courage enables him to communicate his desire (2:5)

D. Nehemiah's courage results in pleasing the king (2:6)

E. Nehemiah's courage enables him to communicate his needs (2:7–8a)

III. The Favor Nehemiah Receives (2:8b–9)

IV. The Enemy Nehemiah Awakens (2:10)

DEVELOPMENT OF THE EXPOSITION

I. THE EMOTIONS NEHEMIAH FEELS (2:1–2)

1 And it came about in the month Nisan, in the twentieth year of King Artaxerxes, that wine was before him, and I took up the wine and gave it to the king. Now I had not been sad in his presence. 2 So the king said to me, "Why is your face sad though you are not sick? This is nothing but sadness of heart." Then I was very much afraid.

A. Nehemiah's Sadness concerning the Condition of Jerusalem (2:1–2a)

Ben Myers writes, "Where evangelical churches theologise happiness and ritualise the smile, sad believers are spiritually ostracised. Sadness is the scarlet letter of the contemporary church, embroidered proof of a person's spiritual failure."[1] While Myers's words might be a bit strong, many of us who are evangelicals tend to imply the Christian life is one happy day after another. When I was boy in church, we often sung "Happiness," which included the line, "I found happiness all the time."[2] I recall a favorite song of the church where I was a young pastor titled, "The Happy Side of Life." Some of the lyrics are, "I've found the happy side of life, With Jesus as my savior I've found a way. Rollin' along, singing a song, every single passing day."[3] However, sadness is a part of life, and godly people are sometimes grieved and experience very deep sadness. In fact, with this encounter happening in the month of Nisan, it appears Nehemiah has been in this state for about four months, fasting and praying on behalf of Jerusalem. Sadness and

---

1. Ben Myers, "On Smiling and Sadness: Twelve Theses," Faith and Theology, http://www.faith-theology.com/2010/11/on-smiling-and-sadness-twelve-theses.html (accessed February 7, 2017).

2. Bill Gaither, "Happiness," Gaither Music Company, 1968.

3. Eddie Smith, "The Happy Side of Life," Pilot Point Music, 1972.

grief are normal emotions for people who deeply care about others because pain, difficulties, and loss are a part of this fallen world. Nehemiah's emotions reveal he is just an ordinary man who experiences various emotions like anyone else.

However, Nehemiah apparently has concealed his grief from the king up to this point. It may be he concealed it because those who served kings were supposed to be a reflection of the king's radiance. It is also possible that the king could have interpreted Nehemiah's poor countenance as his having something against the king—not what a taste tester would want a king to think. Nehemiah could easily be executed if the king comes to the wrong conclusion. Nisan was the beginning of the new year for the Persians. It was a time of celebration. Perhaps the national festivities in Persia affected Nehemiah even more than he had already been affected up to this point, given the horrible condition of his people at home in Jerusalem and the fact that the beginning of Passover occurred just days after the Persian New Year's celebration.[4] Times of celebration sometimes accentuate the sting of personal sorrow. It was the time Israel normally celebrated the New Year too, but there appeared to be little to nothing for them to celebrate.

B. Nehemiah's Fear before the King (2:2b)

Some believe that Nehemiah's revelation of sadness was a calculated act, but his fear revealed at the end of verse 2 seems to dispel this notion.[5] Why would he be afraid when the king notices his sadness if Nehemiah purposely revealed his sadness to the king?[6] And while it appears Artaxerxes is genuinely concerned about Nehemiah, Nehemiah still has reason for concern. On the one hand, Artaxerxes had a record of shedding blood. Under the influence of the man who killed his father, Artaxerxes killed his own older brother in order to take the throne for himself. After that, he killed the man who had assassinated his father.[7] Persian kings were seldom reluctant when it came to killing, even when it concerned

---

4. Mahbod Khanbolouki, "Nowruz—The Persian New Year and the Spring Equinox," ancient-origins.net, https://www.ancient-origins.net/news-general/nowruz-persian-new-year-and-spring-equinox-002808 (accessed February 15, 2019).

5. Derek Kidner, *Ezra and Nehemiah*, Tyndale Old Testament Commentaries 12 (Downers Grove, IL: IVP Academic, 1979), 87; H. G. M. Williamson, *Ezra, Nehemiah*, Word Biblical Commentary (Nashville: Thomas Nelson, 1985), 178.

6. Andrew E. Steinmann, *Ezra and Nehemiah*, Concordia Commentary (St. Louis: Concordia, 2010), 399.

7. A. T. Olmstead, *History of the Persian Empire* (Chicago: University of Chicago Press, 1948), 289–90.

people who were close to them. Nehemiah's demeanor could have easily be construed as an affront to the king.

Another possible contributor to Nehemiah's fear could be the realization that the opportunity has presented itself for Nehemiah to inform the king of the plight of his people in Jerusalem and of his desire to help them. While Nehemiah wants this opportunity, there is no guarantee Artaxerxes will respond positively. When Artaxerxes became king, he almost immediately had to deal with major insurrections in Egypt and Greece. He succeeded in defeating his enemies but did so at great cost of lives and resources. Also, it was Artaxerxes who put an end to the rebuilding of Jerusalem when the Hebrews first returned to Judah out of exile. Ezra records what Jerusalem's enemies wrote Artaxerxes:

> "To King Artaxerxes: Your servants, the men in the region beyond the River, and now let it be known to the king that the Jews who came up from you have come to us at Jerusalem; they are rebuilding the rebellious and evil city and are finishing the walls and repairing the foundations. Now let it be known to the king, that if that city is rebuilt and the walls are finished, they will not pay tribute, custom or toll, and it will damage the revenue of the kings. Now because we are in the service of the palace, and it is not fitting for us to see the king's dishonor, therefore we have sent and informed the king, so that a search may be made in the record books of your fathers. And you will discover in the record books and learn that that city is a rebellious city and damaging to kings and provinces, and that they have incited revolt within it in past days; therefore that city was laid waste. We inform the king that if that city is rebuilt and the walls finished, as a result you will have no possession in *the province* beyond the River." (Ezra 4:11–16)

Note Artaxerxes' response to them:

> "Peace. And now the document which you sent to us has been translated and read before me. A decree has been issued by me, and a search has been made and it has been discovered that that city has risen up against the kings in past days, that rebellion and revolt have been perpetrated in it, that mighty kings have ruled over Jerusalem, governing all *the provinces* beyond the River, and that tribute, custom and toll were paid to them. So, now issue a decree to make these men stop *work*, that this city may

not be rebuilt until a decree is issued by me. Beware of being negligent in carrying out this *matter*; why should damage increase to the detriment of the kings?" (Ezra 4:17b–22)

So Artaxerxes believed Jerusalem to be a city of rebellion and put a stop to its being rebuilt. Given Artaxerxes' troubles with insurrection in his empire and given what he has already expressed concerning his sentiments about Jerusalem, Nehemiah may fear Artaxerxes' feelings about Jerusalem have not changed. But true courage is displayed in the midst of the greatest fears.

II. The Courage Nehemiah Displays (2:3–8a)

³ I said to the king, "Let the king live forever. Why should my face not be sad when the city, the place of my fathers' tombs, lies desolate and its gates have been consumed by fire?" ⁴ Then the king said to me, "What would you request?" So I prayed to the God of heaven. ⁵ I said to the king, "If it please the king, and if your servant has found favor before you, send me to Judah, to the city of my fathers' tombs, that I may rebuild it." ⁶ Then the king said to me, the queen sitting beside him, "How long will your journey be, and when will you return?" So it pleased the king to send me, and I gave him a definite time. ⁷ And I said to the king, "If it please the king, let letters be given me for the governors *of the provinces* beyond the River, that they may allow me to pass through until I come to Judah, ⁸ and a letter to Asaph the keeper of the king's forest, that he may give me timber to make beams for the gates of the fortress which is by the temple, for the wall of the city and for the house to which I will go."

A. Nehemiah's Courage Enables Him to Speak the Truth (2:3)

Even though gripped with fear, Nehemiah's response is both respectful and genuine. The expression "the king" in verse 3 is the equivalent of saying "His Majesty" in more contemporary terms, and even though the phrase "let the king live forever" may possibly have been the common way of addressing Persian kings, Nehemiah expresses a desire for the king to be blessed. No doubt what Nehemiah says had been backed by Nehemiah's faithful service to Artaxerxes. Nehemiah's expressed desire for the welfare of the king may be causing the king to be more open to listen to Nehemiah's concerns for the welfare of Jerusalem. How believers conduct themselves before unbelievers will go a long way in gaining the ear of unbelievers when speaking about things concerning the kingdom of God. Nehemiah applies the words of the prophet Jeremiah to his own life. Years earlier, the Lord spoke through Jeremiah, who wrote those words in exile, saying, "Seek the welfare of the city where I have sent you into exile, and pray to the LORD on its behalf; for in its welfare you will have welfare" (Jer 29:7). In the throes of fear, Nehemiah continues to trust God and obey his word.

B. Nehemiah's Courage Comes from a Dependence on God (2:4)

Nehemiah is not only genuine in his concern for the king, but he is also candid about his concern for Jerusalem, even though he avoids mentioning it by name. Instead, he speaks of "the city, the place of my fathers' tombs," and he states how it lays "desolate and its gates have been consumed." All the people of the ancient Near East, especially people of nobility and royalty, had the highest respect for ancestral tombs.[8] The Achaemenid kings took the burial of their ancestors quite seriously.[9] For instance, the monument of Darius the Great was an elaborate cross shaped tomb cut into the cliff at Naqsh-e Rustam. At the top of the monument, Darius is depicted in front of an altar praying to a god. At the left and right are the depictions of important royal servants to the king. The outside of the tomb depicts twenty-eight people, who represent the nations Darius had brought into subjugation. Moreover, the four-columned façade of the tomb is a replica of one of the entrances to his palace. The inside of the tomb contains rock-cut sarcophaguses for the king and his family. Three other tombs at this site following the same pattern are believed to be the tombs of Xerxes I, Artaxerxes I, and Darius II. The kings were embalmed, covered in wax, and deposited in the tombs along with extravagant clothing and furniture. Officials from the nobility, along with a large number of servants, were charged with the responsibility of keeping the tombs and ensuring sacrifices were offered at the tombs to their god for the benefit of the king's soul. The remains of the kings were well protected from the elements, from looters, and from the ill will of their gods.[10] Nehemiah's demeanor already has the attention of the king, but when Nehemiah expresses that the reason for

---

8. Williamson, *Ezra, Nehemiah*, 179.

9. Achaemenid is the name of the Persian dynasty of kings that ruled from about 550 to 331 BC.

10. Matthew P. Canepa, "Achaemenid and Seleucid Royal Funerary Practices and Middle Iranian Kingship," in *Commutatio et Contentio: Studies in the Late Roman, Sasanian, and Early Islamic Near East*, ed. Henning Börm and Josef Wiesehöfer (Düsseldorf: Wellem Verlag, 2010), 3–5. The following website is also informative: http://www.livius.org/articles/place/naqs-e-rustam/naqs-e-rustam-photos/naqs-e-rustam-achaemenid-tomb-iii/ (accessed February 16, 2017).

his sadness is the condition of the tombs of his fathers, the king is most attentive and sympathetic. Nehemiah's words reflect his time spent in prayer, fasting, and reflection about what he would say to the king when given the opportunity. Though he is afraid, he had prepared himself for this moment. Therefore, it is no surprise the king asks, "What would you request?"

The next statement reveals how completely Nehemiah depends on God: "So I prayed to the God of heaven." There is no greater indicator of how much one depends on God than one's propensity to pray. When one prays, one acknowledges the inadequacy of oneself and the total sufficiency of God to meet every need. When serving the Lord one needs wisdom, strength, deliverance, help, encouragement, healing, both physical and spiritual provision, mercy, grace, and physical, emotional, and spiritual protection. Nehemiah understands the truth of Psalm 46:1, which says, "God is our refuge and strength, a very present help in trouble," and the promise of Psalm 72:12, which states, "For he will deliver the needy when he cries for help, the afflicted also, and him who has no helper."

Charles Spurgeon writes,

> A help that is not present when we need it is of small value. The anchor which is left at home is of no use to the seaman in the hour of storm; the money which he used to have is of no worth to the debtor when a writ is out against him. Very few earthly helps could be called "very present": they are usually far in the seeking, far in the using, and farther still when once used. But as for the Lord our God, He is present when we seek Him, present when we need Him, and present when we have already enjoyed His aid. He is more than "present," He is very present. More present than the nearest friend can be, for He is in us in our trouble; more present than we are to ourselves, for sometimes we lack presence of mind. He is always present, effectually present, sympathetically present, altogether present. He is present now if this is a gloomy season. Let us rest ourselves upon Him. He is our refuge, let us hide in Him; He is our strength, let us array ourselves with Him; He is our help, let us lean upon Him; He is our very present help, let us repose in Him now. We need not have a moment's care, or an instant's fear. "The Lord of hosts is with us; the God of Jacob is our refuge."[11]

---

11. Charles Spurgeon, "December 22 Immediately Present," in *Faith's Checkbook* (1888), available online at http://www.gbfc-tx.org/Books/Public%20Domain/FAITH'S%20CHECKBOOK.PDF.

In that moment, Nehemiah trusts the Lord to be a very present help. Nehemiah's short prayer before answering the king is a continuation of his ongoing prayer that began when he received the devastating news concerning Jerusalem four months earlier. He was willing to wait on the Lord. It was this waiting that allowed him to renew his strength, to mount up with wings as eagles, to run and not be weary, to walk and not faint. His constant dependence on the Lord enables him to stand and speak to the king even in the midst of his fear. Courage is not the absence of fear but it is acting in the face of fear. Marvin Breneman aptly observes, "Quick prayers are possible and valid if one has prayed sufficiently beforehand."[12] Prayer helps with one's perspective. When a person who is afraid looks to God for help, the mere looking to God changes his perspective. David learns this when surrounded by his enemies. In Psalm 56:3–4 he writes, "When I am afraid, I will put my trust in You. In God, whose word I praise, In God I have put my trust; I shall not be afraid. What can *mere* man do to me?" Nehemiah's prayer not only revealed his dependence on the Lord, but it also emboldens him to speak for the Lord and his people. Why? Because as great as Artaxerxes' empire is, Nehemiah prays to the God of heaven. Every kingdom of humanity pales in comparison to the kingdom of God, which stretches high above and beyond the kingdoms of this earth. What is more, as great as Artaxerxes and others think he is, he does not compare to the God and King of all creation.

C. Nehemiah's Courage Enables Him to Communicate His Desire (2:5)

Nehemiah's tone toward the king is noteworthy. He continues to be respectful and deferential to Artaxerxes. There is no demanding involved, even though what he wants is for God's glory. Furthermore, he was delicate in how he makes his request. Instead of mentioning Jerusalem, he asks whether he can return "to Judah, to the city of my fathers' tombs" so that he can rebuild it. Since it was Artaxerxes who had put an end to the rebuilding of Jerusalem (Ezra 4:17b–22), Nehemiah allows the king to save face and still permit Nehemiah to go back home for a noble cause—respect for the city of the tombs of his fathers.[13] It is likely the king

---

12. Mervin Breneman, *Ezra, Nehemiah, Esther*, NAC 10 (Nashville: Broadman & Holman, 1993), 176.

13. Steinmann, *Ezra and Nehemiah*, 401.

is fully aware of what city Nehemiah is speaking of, but Nehemiah's discretion and discernment allow the king to respond in a way that is noble.

D. Nehemiah's Courage Results in Pleasing the King (2:6)

Nehemiah is prepared to give an answer when the king asks him how long it will take for Nehemiah to do what he needs to do in Judah. It appears Artaxerxes wants to be sure Nehemiah will return. All the text indicates is that Nehemiah gives the king a set time without indicating what that time is. Later Nehemiah indicates he served as governor in Jerusalem for twelve years before he returned to Artaxerxes (5:14; 13:6). A number of scholars believe the initial request here was for a shorter period but that Artaxerxes extended it when he received positive reports of Nehemiah's progress in Judah.[14]

It is difficult to know why the presence of the queen is mentioned in the text. Some believe it implies she was fond of Nehemiah and influenced the king to grant Nehemiah's request.[15] Others argue it means the setting was a private meal between just the king and queen.[16] Daniel 5:2 indicates King Belshazzar's wives were present at his banquet. The same Aramaic word šēgāl, meaning "queen" or possibly "concubine" or "harem favorite," is present in Daniel 5:2 and Nehemiah 2:6. The legitimate queen of Artaxerxes I was Damaspia.[17] Since it appears as a plural in Daniel 5:2, it is unlikely that it means "harem favorite," unless of course the king had "favorites."[18] Regardless, it is possible that mention of the queen indicates this encounter in Nehemiah 2 happened during a banquet. If so, it fits with the plausibility of its being a New Year's celebration, as already mentioned. A mediating proposal is that verses 1–5 describe the scene of the banquet, and the discussion in verse 6 happens after the party when Nehemiah is serving the

---

14. Breneman, *Ezra, Nehemiah, Esther*, 177; Kidner, *Ezra and Nehemiah*, 81; Steinmann, *Ezra and Nehemiah*, 401; Williamson, *Ezra, Nehemiah*, 180.

15. W. W. Tarn, "Xerxes and His Successors: Artaxerxes I and Darius II," in *The Cambridge Ancient History*, vol. 7, *Macedon 401–301 BC*, ed. J. B. Bury. S. A. Cook, and F. E. Adcock (Cambridge: Cambridge University Press, 1927), 2–3; Geo Widengren, "The Persian Period," in *Israelite and Judean History*, ed. J. H. Hayes and J. M. Miller (London: SCM Press, 1977), 528.

16. Breneman, *Ezra, Nehemiah, Esther*, 176; Kidner, *Ezra and Nehemiah*, 81; Jacob M. Myers, *Ezra, Nehemiah*, Anchor Bible 14 (New York: Doubleday, 1965), 98; Williamson, *Ezra, Nehemiah*, 180.

17. Williamson, *Ezra, Nehemiah*, 180.

18. Williamson, *Ezra, Nehemiah*, 180; see Ps 45:9–10.

king and queen privately.[19] However, the text does not seem to indicate a change of venue between verses 1–5 and verse 6.

Apparently, the king and queen are fond of Nehemiah, but there may be another motive for Artaxerxes' willingness to send Nehemiah to Judah. As mentioned earlier, Artaxerxes had dealt with major uprisings from both the Egyptians and the Greeks. It may be the king thinks it prudent to have a loyal servant such as Nehemiah in Judah, a province much closer to the locations of the rebels, to keep an eye on the region.[20] Who better to do this than his trustworthy cupbearer? Nevertheless, no matter how shrewd Artaxerxes may think himself to be, one must remember Proverbs 21:1, which states, "The king's heart is *like* channels of water in the hand of the LORD; He turns it wherever He wishes." The Lord can use even the shrewdly selfish schemes of a pagan king to accomplish his purposes.

E. Nehemiah's Courage Enables Him to Communicate His Needs (2:7–8a)

Nehemiah basically makes two requests. The first request is for letters ensuring his safe passage to Judah. As noted in the books of Ezra and Nehemiah, Judeans faced stiff resistance and oppression from their enemies (see Ezra 4–6; Neh 4). Obviously, Nehemiah knows of the dangers and asks the king for help. It may be of interest to know that about thirteen years earlier Ezra refused to ask the king for an escort to travel from Persia to Judah because he had told the king, "The hand of our God is favorably disposed to all those who seek Him, but His power and His anger are against all those who forsake Him" (Ezra 8:22b). Brown's comments are helpful for thinking about the differences between Ezra and Nehemiah:

> Everybody is different and there is nothing monochrome about God's servants. Thirteen years earlier Ezra had refused the offer of Persian soldiers to accompany his people on their way back to Judah, believing the "gracious hand of our God is on everyone who looks to him." But Nehemiah maintained that *because the gracious hand* of God was upon him, the king granted his request for protection. One man's commitment to God precluded the escort; the other welcomed it. Ezra regarded soldiers as a lack of confidence in God's power; Nehemiah viewed them as

---

19. F. Charles Fensham, *The Books of Ezra and Nehemiah*, New International Commentary on the Old Testament (Grand Rapids: Eerdmans, 1982), 162.

20. J. G. McConville, *Ezra, Nehemiah, and Esther* (Louisville: Westminster John Knox, 1985), 80.

evidence of God's superlative goodness. ... We must not rigidly stereotype believers into identical patterns of spirituality.[21]

Both Ezra and Nehemiah sought to honor God in what they did, and God blessed both of them for it. Depending on the Lord and acting in a way that brings him glory must be the preeminent goal. God will bless the efforts of such individuals regardless of the various paths they take to accomplish it.

Nehemiah's second request is for timber from "the king's forest," the necessary materials to complete his tasks. It is unclear where "the king's forest" was located. It is possible it was located in Lebanon, since the cedars of Lebanon were renowned and worthy of being called "the king's forest." Also, the timber for the temple came from Lebanon with the permission of Cyrus the Great, the Persian king at that time (Ezra 3:7). It is possible the forest was located nearer to Judah, especially since there were a number of forests in that region and the name of the keeper, Asaph, is a Hebrew name. However, Judeans served all over the empire, so in the end no one can know for sure where it was located.

Nehemiah has three projects in mind when he requests the timber. First, he needs lumber to repair "the gates of the fortress which is by the temple." This probably refers to the forerunner of what became the fortress of Antonia, which Herod the Great built north of the temple.[22] The northern approach to the temple was a very vulnerable location for attack. King Jehoash of the northern kingdom tore down part of the northern wall of Jerusalem when he attacked about 350 years earlier (2 Kgs 14:13; 2 Chr 25:23). The Letter of Aristeas, from the early to mid-third century BC, mentions a fortress in Jerusalem north of the temple.[23] Also, 1 Maccabees 13:52 states that Simon, the Hasmonean ruler, fortified the fortress sometime in his reign (141–135 BC). The second project is the wall of Jerusalem itself. Up to this point, Nehemiah left this need out of the conversation, but the previous tension is gone. The wood is needed mostly for the gates and towers, given the walls themselves were mostly of stone. However, wood appears to have

---

21. Raymond Brown, *The Message of Nehemiah*, The Bible Speaks Today (Downers Grove, IL: InterVarsity Press, 1998), 50.

22. Williamson, *Ezra, Nehemiah*, 181.

23. Verses 100–104 in "The Letter of Aristeas," available at http://www.ccel.org/c/charles/otpseudepig/aristeas.htm (accessed February 18, 2017).

been used in the walls themselves.²⁴ The third project is for Nehemiah's own residence. After all, much of Jerusalem is in disrepair. Nehemiah demonstrates that spirituality is not necessarily the same as impracticality. In fact, his practicality is another indication of his faith in God to provide all he needs.

III. The Favor Nehemiah Receives (2:8b–9)

⁸ And the king granted *them* to me because the good hand of my God *was* on me. ⁹ Then I came to the governors *of the provinces* beyond the River and gave them the king's letters. Now the king had sent with me officers of the army and horsemen.

People of faith recognize the hand of God on them. Even though Nehemiah apparently gave forethought to what he needed in order to go back to Jerusalem, he realizes that all that happened is providentially by the hand of God. Just like with Esther, it was the Lord who brought Nehemiah before a king for "such a time as this." It was the Lord who led Nehemiah to his important position as cupbearer. It was the Lord who orchestrated that Nehemiah would receive the report he did from his brother concerning Jerusalem. It was the Lord who heard Nehemiah's prayers. It was the Lord who gave Nehemiah the opportunity and courage to reveal his concerns and needs to the king. It was the Lord who moved in the king's heart and directed his course of action. It was the Lord who provided for all of Nehemiah's protection and provision to carry out the mission. And it was the Lord who led Nehemiah hundreds of miles from Susa back to his home and people in Jerusalem. Nehemiah gives credit where credit was due. Moreover, just in case there is any question, Nehemiah clearly states that all he requests comes to pass. Nehemiah's grand entrance with the king's escort into Jerusalem makes a strong statement both to his enemies and to his people. He comes in strength, not weakness, all by the hand of God.

IV. The Enemy Nehemiah Awakens (2:10)

¹⁰ When Sanballat the Horonite and Tobiah the Ammonite official heard *about it*, it was very displeasing to them that someone had come to seek the welfare of the sons of Israel.

---

24. Rudolf Naumann, *Architektur Kleinasiens von ihren Anfangen bis zum Ende der hethitischen Zeit* (Tübingen: Verlag Ernst Wasmuth, 1955), 51–52.

Ever since the first exiles returned to Judah in about 537 BC, there was opposition to them and their efforts to rebuild Jerusalem. At that time, the enemy's
efforts were successful in convincing Artaxerxes that the returned exiles were
rebuilding the city in order to begin an insurrection against the king, so he put
an end to the work (Ezra 4:11–23). Nevertheless, more exiles continued to return
to Judah. Ezra led about three thousand people back to Jerusalem in 458/57 BC.[25]
More importantly, Ezra came with the backing and authority of the Persian king.
Note Artaxerxes' decree:

> You, Ezra, according to the wisdom of your God which is in your hand,
> appoint magistrates and judges that they may judge all the people who
> are in *the province* beyond the River, *even* all those who know the laws of
> your God; and you may teach anyone who is ignorant *of them.* Whoever
> will not observe the law of your God and the law of the king, let judgment
> be executed upon him strictly, whether for death or for banishment or for
> confiscation of goods or for imprisonment. (Ezra 7:25–26)

Doubtless, Judah's enemies saw this development as a major setback. Now, about
thirteen years later, Nehemiah the Judean shows up in Jerusalem as the newly
appointed governor with the authority and supplies to rebuild and reinforce the
walls of Jerusalem.

Sanballat the Horonite was probably the governor of Samaria, north of Judah,
and probably from Beth-Horon, also north of Judah. Sanballat is a Babylonian name
meaning "Sin (the moon god) gives life." According to the Elephantine Papyri, two
of his sons had names that contained an abbreviated form of the name Yahweh in
them. It is possible he had assumed some responsibility of overseeing Judah between
the time Nehemiah's predecessor stopped governing and Nehemiah's arrival. It
would account for what appears to be jealousy at Nehemiah's arrival.[26] Tobiah the
Ammonite servant was probably an official serving Artaxerxes in Ammon. His
name is Hebrew and means "Yahweh is good." It is probable Tobiah was of mixed
descent—Judean and some other people group—and that he mixed pagan ideas
with the worship of Yahweh.[27] The names of Sanballat's sons lend to the possibility
that he too mixed pagan ideas with the worship of Israel's God. If so, this situation

---

25. Steinmann, *Ezra and Nehemiah*, 305.

26. Williamson, *Ezra, Nehemiah*, 182. Williamson discusses the debate about Sanballat's origins,
but no suggestion is conclusive.

27. Steinmann, *Ezra and Nehemiah*, 403.

corresponds well with the offer the enemies of Judah and Benjamin made to help Zerubbabel build the temple. It also fits well with Zerubbabel's, Jeshua's, and the rest of heads of the houses' response to them, saying, "You have nothing in common with us in building a house to our God" (Ezra 4:3). They would have no association with those involved in such abominable worship. Nevertheless, when the people of God rise up to do the work of God, it will infuriate the enemies of God. Nehemiah knows this truth, and it is for this reason he acquires the king's help. As Jesus says, "Behold, I send you out as sheep in the midst of wolves; so be shrewd as serpents and innocent as doves" (Matt 10:16).

CONCLUSION

Nehemiah wants nothing other than the revival of God's people and the rebuilding of the holy city, Jerusalem. His heart's desire is for God to receive glory. He patiently and actively waits on the Lord to give him the opportunity to take action. He demonstrates patience by waiting four months; he demonstrates active waiting by his fasting, praying, and obvious contemplating about what needed doing during those four months. Everything he does is bathed in prayer. He is totally dependent on God and therefore attributes all that occurs to the hand of God on him. Nehemiah experiences the protection and provision of God. The Lord once again demonstrates his support for those whose hearts are fully his by changing the mind of one of the most powerful kings on the planet at that time. Nehemiah acts both spiritually and practically. His dependence on God gives him courage and enables him to press ahead in spite of the obstacles that are before him. He trusts that the Lord is with him and believes God is willing to use an ordinary man such as himself to accomplish an extraordinary feat for God's glory. If only we all had such trust and belief in God!

FINAL THOUGHTS

1. How important is the revival of the church today to you?
2. What fears are keeping you from stepping out in faith and accomplishing God's will for you?
3. What does your prayer life indicate about your dependence on God?
4. How might you conduct yourself so that unbelievers are more willing to listen to you?
5. How does your spirituality reveal itself in practicality?

PREPARING TO REBUILD

Nehemiah 2:11–20

INTRODUCTION

MotoGP is basically racing motorcycles. On one fan site it states, "In MotoGP, a start can change the rest of a rider's race. Starting well means hitting the first turn at the head of the pack and not wasting energy trying to move up in the first laps, with the risk of falling that it implies."[1] Whenever beginning something new, such as a race in MotoGP or a building project the magnitude of what Nehemiah was planning to do in Jerusalem, it is important to get off to a good start if you wish to succeed. Nehemiah 2:11–20 recounts Nehemiah's first days after he arrives in Jerusalem. His first actions upon his arrival in Jerusalem demonstrate how significant the project is to Nehemiah and how determined he is to complete it. He too recognizes the importance of a good start.

STRUCTURE

The passage is made up of three sections. The first section (2:11–16) relates Nehemiah's first steps in his preparation for rebuilding the walls of Jerusalem by personally and privately inspecting the walls and assessing what needs to be done. The second section (2:17–18) recounts how Nehemiah enlists the help of the people of Jerusalem to join in the work of rebuilding the walls. And the third section (2:19–20) describes how enemies of the returnees begin opposing the rebuilding of Jerusalem and how Nehemiah's faith and commitment do not waver.

---

1. "The Importance of a Good Start," Box Repsol, http://www.boxrepsol.com/en/motogp-en/la-importancia-de-una-buena-salida/ (accessed April 2, 2017).

SUMMARY OF THE PASSAGE

The passage demonstrates how thoughtful and methodical Nehemiah is in preparing for the work ahead of him. His careful approach is apparent by his assessment of the walls, his enlistment of workers, and even by his response to opposition.

OUTLINE OF THE PASSAGE

I. Preparation for Rebuilding Requires an Assessment (2:11–16)

    A. Nehemiah's preparation begins with proper relaxation (2:11)

    B. Nehemiah's preparation begins with a private examination (2:12, 16)

    C. Nehemiah's preparation begins with a thorough investigation (2:13–15)

II. Preparation for Rebuilding Requires Enlistment (2:17–18)

    A. Nehemiah gives those he recruits an honest evaluation (2:17a)

    B. Nehemiah gives those he recruits a direct exhortation (2:17b)

    C. Nehemiah gives those he recruits the proper motivation (2:17c)

    D. Nehemiah gives those he recruits a divine verification (2:18a)

    E. Nehemiah gives those he recruits the necessary authorization (2:18b)

    F. Nehemiah receives from those he recruits a firm affirmation (2:18c)

III. Preparation for Rebuilding Reveals the Resistant (2:19)

IV. Preparation for Rebuilding Reveals the Persistent (2:20)

DEVELOPMENT OF THE EXPOSITION

I. Preparation for Rebuilding Requires an Assessment (2:11–16)

[11] So I came to Jerusalem and was there three days. [12] And I arose in the night, I and a few men with me. I did not tell anyone what my God was putting into my mind to do for Jerusalem and there was no animal with me except the animal on which I was riding. [13] So I went out at night by the Valley Gate in the direction of the Dragon's Well and on to the Refuse Gate, inspecting the walls of Jerusalem which were broken down and its gates which were consumed by fire. [14] Then I passed on to the Fountain Gate and the King's Pool, but there was no place for my mount to pass. [15] So I went up at night by the ravine and inspected the wall. Then I entered the Valley Gate again and returned. [16] The officials did not know where I had gone or what I had done; nor had I as yet told the Jews, the priests, the nobles, the officials or the rest who did the work.

A. Nehemiah's Preparation Begins with Proper Relaxation (2:11)

Verse 11 states Nehemiah waits three days before he gives full attention to inspecting the walls of Jerusalem. He has just traveled a distance of at least 850 miles by land. It was probably more like a thousand miles given the normal routes in the Fertile Crescent at that time. At any rate, it was a very long trip that probably took at least a month to complete.[2] Therefore, it is reasonable that, like Ezra (Ezra 8:32), Nehemiah most likely takes a few days to rest, secure accommodations, and familiarize himself with his new surroundings and its people.

It is interesting to note how important rest is in the Scriptures. For instance, the law stipulates the necessity to rest. The fourth commandment states the people of God are to work six days and to rest on the seventh, just as the Lord did in creation (Exod 20:8–11). While many people today may think of the Sabbath as a day of worship, in the Old Testament the emphasis is on its being a day of rest. The command to keep a day of rest was unique to Israel in the ancient Near East.[3] The Sabbath serves to remind Israel how God saved them from bondage and called them into the rest of his covenant (Deut 5:15). Certainly, there are theological reasons for the importance of keeping the Sabbath by remembering God as the Creator, as Israel's Deliverer, and the rest that is found in him. However, there has to be a practical aspect to it as well. Just because something is theologically significant does not preclude it from being practical also. Jesus says, "The Sabbath was made for man, and not man for the Sabbath" (Mark 2:27). Rest is both a blessing and a necessity for every person. Modern research indicates how a proper balance of work and rest increases one's productivity.[4] When we are fatigued, our judgment suffers, and our efficiency and effectiveness wane. Nehemiah knows he is about to commence on a major project. It will be demanding, and he needs to be at full strength. Rather than rushing ahead, it appears he prepares himself physically and personally before commencing the task before him. Some believers today confuse activity with spirituality, but the two are not necessarily the same. When one gives proper deliberation concerning the Lord's work, one will recognize the importance of strategic relaxation to carry it out.

---

2. This guess is based on the research of the Cartographer's Guild, https://www.cartographers-guild.com/showthread.php?t=19730 (accessed March 1, 2017).

3. Duane A. Garrett, *A Commentary on Exodus*, Kregel Exegetical Library (Grand Rapids: Kregel Academic, 2013), 477.

4. Tony Schwartz, "Relax! You'll Be More Productive," *New York Times*, February 9, 2013.

B. Nehemiah's Preparation Begins with a
Private Examination (2:12, 16)

Wisdom is knowing the right thing, doing the right thing, and doing it at the right time, in the right way, to the right extent. In all the Scriptures, Nehemiah is one of the best examples of a man who is wise. Proverbs 18:15 states, "The mind of the prudent acquires knowledge, and the ear of the wise seeks knowledge," and Proverbs 24:27 instructs, "Prepare your work outside and make it ready for yourself in the field; afterwards, then, build your house." Nehemiah already has demonstrated his wisdom by securing the needed lumber for the project ahead of time (2:8). Now, three days after he arrived in Jerusalem, he sets out on a reconnaissance mission to appraise what needs to be done. He goes out at night with only his mount, probably a donkey or mule, since they tend to be less skittish than a horse, and a few other men. It is possible there is only one mount in order to keep from drawing attention to the group.[5] It is also possible the reason is that it would be easier for the small group to identify Nehemiah in the dark if he is the only one on a mount. It would make it easier for him to see above everyone else as he makes his inspection. Also, it is possible it was in keeping with ancient Near Eastern practice for the leader to ride while the others walked. Knowing Nehemiah, he does it for practical reasons. Speaking of Nehemiah, Derek Thomas says, "Knowing that God is sovereign did not cripple him into inertia but motivated him to act prudently and wisely."[6]

The apparent reason for such a small company and its being at night is so they will keep from bringing attention to themselves. Nehemiah even keeps secret the purpose of this excursion from the men who go with him. There are evidently moles in the city that are ready to inform Jerusalem's enemies of what is going on. After catching his breath for three days, he needs to act privately and quickly so the enemy cannot shut down the project before it even gets off the ground. The private nature of this nocturnal venture gives him one last opportunity to think in peace about what needs to be done. Given the success of the enemy in the past in intimidating the returnees and shutting down the rebuilding of Jerusalem, it is important for Nehemiah to be very clear about what needs to be done and how it can be done once he addresses the city's leaders along with the people. There

---

5. Mervin Breneman, *Ezra, Nehemiah, Esther*, NAC 10 (Nashville: Broadman & Holman, 1993), 180.

6. Derek W. H. Thomas., *Ezra & Nehemiah*, Reformed Expository Commentary (Phillipsburg, NJ: P&R, 2016), 231.

is a time for silent, prayerful, thoughtful contemplation, and a time to speak. Nehemiah is able to discern between the two.

What made this mission especially important is that Nehemiah recognizes it is his God who is placing this burden for Jerusalem and desire to rebuild it on his heart. Therefore, it demands thoughtful planning so that everything he does glorifies the Lord. Some say that believers should serve the Lord and take care of the things pertaining to God the same way we take care of ourselves. However, one might be willing to settle for less than the best for oneself, but we must realize that in the Lord's service he deserves our very best efforts and resources. It requires careful planning. Removing the reproach that is on Jerusalem and honoring Yahweh with the completion of the rebuilding of the walls necessitates making sure everything is done in a way that will honor him.

C. Nehemiah's Preparation Begins with a Thorough Investigation (2:13–15)

Some of the places Nehemiah mentions from his expedition are impossible to recognize with certainty. Nothing is left of the walls and gates he inspected to the north, and later structures have covered up other places that appear to be where Nehemiah ventured.[7] Kathleen Kenyon asserts the King's Pool was probably the Pool of Siloam or possibly Birket el-Hamra.[8] The "ravine/valley" he mentions in verse 15 appears to have been the Kidron Valley.[9] It is understandable that Nehemiah had difficulty traversing around the Kidron Valley. The buildings in this area had been terraced down into the valley. When the Chaldeans destroyed the wall that supported the buildings, they were destroyed, and they collapsed down into the valley. There must have been heaps of debris. Archaeological evidence suggests it was so bad that Nehemiah decided to rebuild the wall on the crest of the hill rather than try to rebuild on the slope where it had been, making the boundaries of Nehemiah's completed Jerusalem smaller than what it had been before.[10] Nehemiah's thorough inspection of the area allows him to prepare

---

7. F. Charles Fensham, *The Books of Ezra and Nehemiah*, New International Commentary on the Old Testament (Grand Rapids: Eerdmans, 1982), 166.

8. Kathleen Kenyon, *Jerusalem: Excavating 3000 Years of History* (New York: McGraw-Hill, 1967), 107.

9. H. G. M. Williamson, *Ezra, Nehemiah*, Word Biblical Commentary (Nashville: Thomas Nelson, 1985), 190.

10. Kenyon, *Jerusalem: Excavating 3000 Years of History*, 108.

for the task the Lord has laid on his heart. If Nehemiah is to lead the people in rebuilding the walls, he needs to be thoroughly prepared himself. It is hazardous because of both his enemies and the physical conditions. It is obviously tedious and time consuming. Nevertheless, he courageously and patiently does what needs to be done because he is committed to doing what Yahweh has put into his mind. Nehemiah has a mind to do what the Lord has put into it.

II. Preparation for Rebuilding Requires Enlistment (2:17–18)

> ¹⁷ Then I said to them, "You see the bad situation we are in, that Jerusalem is desolate and its gates burned by fire. Come, let us rebuild the wall of Jerusalem so that we will no longer be a reproach." ¹⁸ I told them how the hand of my God had been favorable to me and also about the king's words which he had spoken to me. Then they said, "Let us arise and build." So they put their hands to the good *work*.

A. Nehemiah Gives Those He Recruits an Honest Evaluation (2:17a)

Nehemiah is a man of integrity. He tells the truth even when the reality of the truth is difficult for him. He faces it, and he wants those he recruits to help with the work to face it as well. Nehemiah would have no credibility if he acted as if the situation were not dire and there were no challenge before them. These people have been in the land for a number of years. They know, in some ways, better than Nehemiah that the walls are in ruins. Nevertheless, it is human nature to get used to poor conditions such that we barely notice them after a while. We learn to live with them, and what may have once been glaringly unacceptable can become completely ignored. I have experienced this in my travels, where I have visited communities covered with garbage just about everywhere, but the people in those communities seemed oblivious to it. Perhaps the people in Jerusalem need someone like Nehemiah to remind them that the condition of the walls is intolerable. God often uses his messengers and his word to shine a light on matters in our lives that are unacceptable to God and yet have become accepted by us. Jerusalem is "desolate." Perhaps they have grown accustomed to the disgrace. The first step in changing a situation is to honestly assess the situation. Only then will one recognize the need for change.

This concept is basic to the Scriptures. For instance, one must confess one's sin in order to be forgiven of sin. Inherently, this involves an honest evaluation. Consequently, it is no surprise that fundamental to the message of many of the prophets of Israel is, "You have sinned against God; turn back to God and be restored to him. Otherwise, suffer the consequences of your sin." The book of Romans, a treatise on the gospel, begins with the message that all have sinned. After providing an honest evaluation of the human condition, Paul explains how one may experience justification by faith and the forgiveness of sin. The message of the prophets and the gospel itself begin with an honest assessment of conditions before there is any hope for change of those conditions. If the circumstances in Jerusalem are going to change, the people first need to have an honest evaluation of the situation.

B. Nehemiah Gives Those He Recruits a Direct Exhortation (2:17b)

While having an honest evaluation of the situation is essential to the process, it alone will not get the work done. It is one thing for everyone to know what the situation is, but the real question is, "Now that you know what the situation is, what are you going to do about it?" It is like recognizing you have high blood pressure. It is good to know, but are you going to exercise and change your diet to help lower it? Nehemiah's honest evaluation of the condition of the walls is not enough. The people's agreement with Nehemiah's assessment is not enough. In order for the situation to change, it requires work—their work.

Also, it is noteworthy that Nehemiah continues to identify himself with the people of God: "You see the bad situation *we* are in. ... Come, let *us* rebuild." There are a lot of people who can easily point out bad situations, but it is a special person who not only sees a problem but also takes on that problem as her own and becomes a part of the solution. Nehemiah recognizes the importance of the community of faith. He is not an isolationist. He is not only committed to God and Jerusalem, the city where God manifested his presence with his people, but he is just as committed to the people of God themselves. Moreover, he loves them so much he is willing to exhort them to take action together as the people of God to do the work of rebuilding the walls of Jerusalem. One of the noblest things one can do is to encourage others to do what they should do and join them in doing it. It is a defining characteristic of one who genuinely desires to have an impact on others for God's glory.

C. Nehemiah Gives Those He Recruits
the Proper Motivation (2:17c)

So what is the motivation for doing this work? An article in *Psychology Today* titled "What Motivates People at Work" provides three key factors that are the building blocks for why people work.[11] The first key factor is security. The concern for security has been a matter for people of all ages and backgrounds throughout all of history. In the case of the people of Jerusalem, they certainly have reason to be concerned about security because of local threats and enemies, even if they are under the "protection" of the Persians. The primary reason ancient cities had walls was that the walls provided security to the inhabitants of the city. However, Nehemiah does not appeal to this concern. A second key factor is stimulation. People need to be challenged, and that is exactly what Nehemiah does when he calls the people to join him in this project. He challenges them to do what needs to be done. Yet Nehemiah does not mention this as the primary reason for doing the work. It is more than just a new challenge or new project.

While the first two factors are significant, Nehemiah appeals to the third key factor of motivation: identity. When the Lord made a covenant with Israel, he identified himself with them, and they were identified with him. Note the following passages:

> Say, therefore, to the sons of Israel, "I am the Lord, and I will bring you out from under the burdens of the Egyptians, and I will deliver you from their bondage. I will also redeem you with an outstretched arm and with great judgments. Then I will take you for My people, and I will be your God; and you shall know that I am the Lord your God, who brought you out from under the burdens of the Egyptians." (Exod 6:6–7)

> So I will turn toward you and make you fruitful and multiply you, and I will confirm My covenant with you. You will eat the old supply and clear out the old because of the new. Moreover, I will make My dwelling among you, and My soul will not reject you. I will also walk among you and be your God, and you shall be My people. (Lev 26:9–12)

---

11. Thuy Sindell and Milo Sindell, "What Motivates People at Work: The 3 Factors and 6 Sub-Factors That Motivate People," *Psychology Today*, https://www.psychologytoday.com/blog/the-end-work-you-know-it/201207/what-motivates-people-work (accessed March 30, 2017).

> But You, O LORD, abide forever,
> And Your name to all generations.
> You will arise *and* have compassion on Zion;
> For it is time to be gracious to her,
> For the appointed time has come.
> Surely Your servants find pleasure in her stones
> And feel pity for her dust.
> So the nations will fear the name of the LORD
> And all the kings of the earth Your glory.
> For the LORD has built up Zion;
> He has appeared in His glory.
> He has regarded the prayer of the destitute
> And has not despised their prayer. (Ps 102:12–17)

Therefore, Yahweh's reputation is connected to the reputation of his people, Israel, and their reputation is connected to his reputation among the nations. The Lord clearly reminds the people in the exile of this truth through his prophet Ezekiel (Ezek 36). Consequently, when Nehemiah calls the people to rebuild in order that "we will no longer be a reproach," the concern is as much about God's reputation as it is for that of the people of Jerusalem, because the reputations are connected to each other. Their shame puts God to shame. When God's reputation is foremost in the minds of his people, the people of God are concerned about how they represent him to the world. For believers today, it means every day is a commitment to be an ambassador for Christ (2 Cor 5:20). They are to be neither ashamed of him nor willing to act in a way that will bring shame on him.

D. Nehemiah Gives Those He Recruits a Divine Verification (2:18a)

Knowing what needs to be done and having the right reasons to do it is well and good, but the next looming question the people need answered is, "How can we do it?" Nehemiah understands their concerns and "told them how the hand of my God had been favorable to me." While it is a mistake to be stuck in the past, it is important to recall what God has done in the past so that one can trust him in the present and for the future. Believers must remember that the Lord is "the same yesterday, and today, and forever" (Heb 13:8). The psalmist writes, "You are the same, and Your years will not come to an end. The children of Your servants will continue, and their descendants will be established before You" (Ps 102:27–28). This kind of faith comes from someone who trusts in the Lord because he has witnessed his favor in the past.

Often believers underestimate the power of sharing a testimony of what God has done in their lives. Not only does it honor the Lord, but it also encourages and strengthens other believers—another important reason to be part of an authentic community of faith. Telling others of God's favor in our lives indicates just how much we acknowledge and appreciate all God has done for us. Moreover, Nehemiah's recounting of all that his God has done once again demonstrates how he gives God the credit for what he is doing. Nehemiah often refers to the Lord as "my God," and his words and actions give evidence that Yahweh certainly is his God. His words are reminiscent of the psalmist's words: "Come and see the works of God, Who is awesome in His deeds toward the sons of men. He turned the sea into dry land; They passed through the river on foot; There let us rejoice in Him!" (Ps 66:5–6). Because Nehemiah has already witnessed awesome deeds from his God, he expects to see more to come. Nehemiah recognizes both the transcendence and immanence of God at the same time.[12]

E. Nehemiah Gives Those He Recruits the Necessary Authorization (2:18b)

With all that Nehemiah tells the people, there is one more issue that needs clarifying—the authorization of Artaxerxes. After all, it was Artaxerxes who put a stop to the initial rebuilding of Jerusalem. So it is important the people know how Artaxerxes showed kindness to him and officially authorized Nehemiah to do what he deemed necessary for the welfare of Jerusalem. That is no small feat, given that Persian kings did not rescind their decrees. What appeared to be an impossibility became more than a possibility. It became a reality. What is more, the king provided Nehemiah with the means to procure whatever materials he needed to complete the work. It is worthwhile to note how Nehemiah first points to God before mentioning what the king did.

---

12. Raymond Brown, *The Message of Nehemiah*, The Bible Speaks Today (Downers Grove, IL: InterVarsity Press, 1998), 58.

F. Nehemiah Receives from Those He
Recruits a Firm Affirmation (2:18c)

The people's positive response is twofold: they speak, and then they take action. They say, "Let us arise and build," and then they "put their hands to the good work." What better response can the people of God have when the Lord calls them to service? Nehemiah's commitment to what the Lord has put on his heart is infectious. My father used to say he believed revival among the people of God is more caught than taught. Certainly the information Nehemiah communicates was essential, but the people are beginning to experience the same thing Nehemiah experienced. What God was putting into Nehemiah's heart God is putting into their hearts too.

III. Preparation for Rebuilding
Reveals the Resistant (2:19)

> [19] But when Sanballat the Horonite and Tobiah the Ammonite official, and Geshem the Arab heard *it*, they mocked us and despised us and said, "What is this thing you are doing? Are you rebelling against the king?"

Shortly after Nehemiah reveals his intentions to the people, the enemies of the people of God appear to receive news of Nehemiah's proposal as well. Their response indicates that Nehemiah had good reason to be cautious as he surveyed the walls. Their initial disgruntlement at Nehemiah's return turns into open ridicule, accompanied by an accusation that Nehemiah and the people are acting in rebellion to the king. A new enemy, Geshem the Arab, is introduced. It is difficult to know what his reasons for opposing the Judeans are. Perhaps he sees their welfare as some kind of threat to him, or it could be just a racial hatred for them. In truth, opposition to God and the people of God has no rational reason. Concerning the addition of Geshem to Nehemiah's list of enemies Kidner states, "With already a hostile Samaria and Ammon to the north and east, Judah was now virtually encircled, and the war of nerves had begun."[13]

Whenever the people of God do the work of God, it will always stir up the enemies of God. One thing they will do is try to belittle the people of God with mockery and ridicule, asking, "Who do you think you are?" When believers take their eyes off the Lord and look at themselves, it is a powerful tool against them.

---

13. Kidner, *Ezra and Nehemiah*, 91.

More often than not, the Lord calls his people to do great deeds that are impossible apart from him. Whenever believers think they are inadequate to do the Lord's work, they are correct. The key is to remember that God is more than adequate and able to carry out his work through his people when "they put their hands to the good work." A second thing enemies will do is try to scare believers. When these enemies imply the people are rebelling against the king, they are basically saying, "You are in big trouble now! You know what Artaxerxes does to those who rebel against him." They are attempting to intimidate them and at the same time get them to question what Nehemiah said. After all, they are basically acting on what Nehemiah told them. Third, it is a way of misrepresenting the motives of the people. The enemies of the people of God find it difficult to recognize any noble reasons for serving the Lord because they have such a dark, worldly perspective. They are blinded by their own warped minds and perspectives. Since everything they do is to feed their own fleshly desires, "the lust of the flesh and the lust of the eyes and the boastful pride of life" (1 John 2:16), it is impossible for them to conceive of godly motives in the life of a believer for serving the Lord. Unless the Lord himself opens their eyes, enemies will never understand.

IV. Preparation for Rebuilding
Reveals the Persistent (2:20)

> [20] So I answered them and said to them, "The God of heaven will give us success; therefore we His servants will arise and build, but you have no portion, right or memorial in Jerusalem."

Nehemiah's response is quite revealing. Since the opposition accuses him of rebelling against the king, it would make sense to pull out his papers from Artaxerxes and silence his enemies without a word. But Nehemiah does something else. Instead, he appealed to the greatest authority, the "God of heaven." Nehemiah's mission is not about political positioning. It is about the reputation of God and the people of God. It is about theological positioning. Jerusalem is the place where the Lord made his name and manifest presence known among his people. Therefore, it is work that needs to be accomplished by God's servants because Jerusalem is their "portion, right," and "memorial," and no one else's.

Additionally, Nehemiah has complete confidence that the Lord will give them success. His faith in God gives Nehemiah poise in the face of his enemies. He is not intimidated in the least. Nothing is going to keep him from doing what

God has put into his heart. There is such a thing as a "holy stubbornness." It is a resolve to obey God and seek his glory regardless of the cost and regardless of the difficulties that may come. Being a faithful follower of Christ is a call to have a stiff backbone in the face of opposition. The church needs to be full of believers with the same kind of dogged determination Nehemiah has. Whenever the opposition puts up stiff resistance, it is time for the people of God to overcome it with a strong-willed persistence.

CONCLUSION

After several months of prayer and fasting, after speaking to the king and securing his authority and provisions, after a very long and arduous trip across the Persian Empire, Nehemiah finally reaches Jerusalem. The importance and magnitude of what God has put into his heart causes him to do every action he does with great consideration, from a time of rejuvenation, to his secret inspection of the walls, to his revelation to the people in Jerusalem, to his rebuke of the opposition. Nehemiah has an unwavering trust in God and is committed to doing what God has put into his heart.

FINAL THOUGHTS

1. What part does rest play in your serving the Lord? Do you use it as a means to be more productive in Christ's service?
2. What does the way you begin a work or project to serve the Lord say about how significant that service is to you?
3. How regularly do you examine what needs to be done around you in the name of Christ?
4. What evidence in your life demonstrates your commitment to joining together with other believers to do his work?
5. What has God put into your heart to do?
6. What evidence is there in your life of a dogged determination to accomplish what God has put into your heart to do?

NEHEMIAH'S TEAM

Nehemiah 3:1–32

INTRODUCTION

Every believer comes to Christ by faith. However, many believers fail to realize that the call to Christ is also a call to become an essential member of the community of faith, the body of Christ, the church. Believers become a part of the people of God for the purpose of glorifying him by doing the work of God. Christopher Wright states, "It is not so much the case that God has a mission for His church in the world, as that God has a church for His mission in the world. Mission was not made for the church; the church was made for mission—God's mission."[1] Nehemiah 3 describes how Nehemiah and the people of God carry out the mission to which they have been called—the removal of the reproach of God's people by rebuilding the walls of Jerusalem. The chapter is like the beginning of every televised team sporting event. Just before the action commences, the commentators introduce the lineups of each of the competing teams. Nehemiah 3 introduces the reader to Nehemiah's lineup. It records his team of workers, the various groups who participate in the reconstruction project.

STRUCTURE

The structure of the passage unfolds around the counterclockwise locations of the workers with regard to their nearness to a city gate. Given that the passage appears to be a mundane listing of the groups of workers and their locations, it can pose a problem for expositors to know how to approach the text or even to decide whether it is really meaningful to do so in the context of preaching. Some commentators give little to no ink toward this passage. However, since all Scripture is profitable to New Testament believers for teaching, for reproof,

---

1. Christopher J. H. Wright, *The Mission of God: Unlocking the Bible's Grand Narrative* (Downers Grove, IL: IVP Academic, 2006), 62.

for correction, and for training in righteousness so that we might be adequate, equipped for every good work, then it is imperative we study it, apply it, and proclaim it so that we may receive its profit (2 Tim 3:16–17). Therefore, the following comments will first address the text as it is presented, gate by gate. However, after that there is a list of words accompanied by observations that will hopefully assist in grasping the message and significance of this chapter.

SUMMARY OF THE PASSAGE

Accomplishing God's work requires all of God's people to cooperatively and sacrificially give their time, abilities, resources, and best efforts to carry it out.

OUTLINE OF THE PASSAGE

I. Work Near the Sheep Gate (3:1–2)
II. Work Near the Fish Gate (3:3–5)
III. Work Near the Old Gate (3:6–12)
IV. Work Near the Valley Gate (3:13)
V. Work Near the Refuse Gate (3:14)
VI. Work Near the Fountain Gate (3:15–25)
VII. Work Near the Water Gate (3:26–27)
VIII. Work Near the Horse Gate (3:28–30)
IX. Work Near the Inspection Gate (3:31–32)

DEVELOPMENT OF THE EXPOSITION

I. WORK NEAR THE SHEEP GATE (1:1–2)

¹ Then Eliashib the high priest arose with his brothers the priests and built the Sheep Gate; they consecrated it and hung its doors. They consecrated the wall to the Tower of the Hundred *and* the Tower of Hananel. ² Next to him the men of Jericho built, and next to them Zaccur the son of Imri built.

Eliashib was the high priest and the grandson of Joshua the high priest who ministered with Haggai and Zechariah during the rebuilding of the temple. Joshua was the high priest who returned to Judah with the first returnees in about 536 BC, and Haggai and Zechariah were prophets who ministered to the people in Jerusalem during the time of the rebuilding of the temple in 515 BC. Their prophetic messages are in the biblical books named after them. That the description of the work begins with the high priests, the remainder of the priests, and the Sheep Gate is significant. As they are spiritual leaders of the community, it is essential the priests take the lead in the project, for it is more than a reconstruction project. It is a God-ordained work, turning the reproach of Jerusalem into glory to God. They are on a spiritual mission, and they understand that spiritual leadership requires being an example to everyone else.

The Sheep Gate was in the northeast corner of the wall. It was where the sheep that were to be sacrificed were brought into the city, given the gate's nearness to the temple. Their consecration of the wall is not only for what the spiritual leaders have done, but being at the beginning of this discourse, it is a dedication of the entire undertaking. One could think of it as sort of a firstfruits offering, with the understanding that all the work moving forward will be done unto the Lord. They dedicate their work to God, recognizing its divine purpose. Through his prophet Jeremiah, the Lord promised to restore Jerusalem, and this project is essential to the fulfillment of God's word of restoration (Jer 29:14). It is also essential to the fulfillment of God's promise through the prophet Ezekiel, who emphatically promised that the returnees would be blessed with security in the land. "They will live in it securely; and they will build houses, plant vineyards and live securely when I execute judgments upon all who scorn them round about them. Then they will know that I am the LORD their God" (Ezek 28:25–26). Up to this point, the people in Jerusalem have yet to experience any security with the walls in shambles, so this work is a holy endeavor, the fulfillment of God's promise to his people. It is important for everyone to remember these truths as the work moves forward.

Apparently, the northern wall was the only one to have had two towers that were not directly attached to a gate, the Tower of the Hundred and the Tower of Hananel. Though their exact locations are unknown, the reason is probably that the approach to Jerusalem from the north is the only one that has reasonably flat ground to travel. It was the easiest approach, and therefore the easiest to attack. One need only recall Jehoash's assault on Jerusalem and his destruction of the northern wall (2 Kgs 14:13). Steep inclines buttressed the defenses of the other walls around the city.[2] Of the two towers, the Tower of Hananel is the only one mentioned elsewhere in the Old Testament, in Jeremiah 31:38 and Zechariah

---

2. Mervin Breneman, *Ezra, Nehemiah, Esther*, NAC 10 (Nashville: Broadman & Holman, 1993).

14:10. Both of these eschatological passages point to the restoration of Jerusalem with the coming of the new covenant and the rule of the Messiah, highlighting once again the spiritual significance of the work. This tower was probably situated at the northernmost point of Jerusalem and connected to the temple fortress.[3]

II. Work Near the Fish Gate (3:3–5)

> [3] Now the sons of Hassenaah built the Fish Gate; they laid its beams and hung its doors with its bolts and bars. [4] Next to them Meremoth the son of Uriah the son of Hakkoz made repairs. And next to him Meshullam the son of Berechiah the son of Meshezabel made repairs. And next to him Zadok the son of Baana *also* made repairs. [5] Moreover, next to him the Tekoites made repairs, but their nobles did not support the work of their masters.

The Fish gate is where the traders and merchants brought their fish, which probably came from the Sea of Galilee and the Mediterranean Sea, to market. It was located somewhere near the northwest corner of the city or just to the south of it.[4] It was also possibly called the Ephraim Gate, mentioned when Jehoash destroys the northern wall (2 Kgs 14:13; see Neh 8:16; 12:39).

Verse 5 indicates that men from Tekoa participate in the project, but the nobles of Tekoa do not. Tekoa was located about 11.5 miles south of Jerusalem, not far from Bethlehem. It was the home of the prophet Amos. Tekoa was located near the region governed by Geshem the Arab, a staunch opponent of Nehemiah and the rebuilding of Jerusalem's walls. Perhaps these nobles were intimidated by Geshem and afraid of reprisals against them if they were to lend their involvement to the work and therefore declined to participate in the project.[5] Regardless of the courageous commitment of the other men from Tekoa and that of other nobles from other locales in Judah, these men refuse to submit to their leaders and join the project.[6] The Hebrew text indicates the nobles are unwilling to "bend their neck" to the work. The phrase is reminiscent of the expression "stiff-necked"

---

3. H. G. M. Williamson, *Ezra, Nehemiah*, Word Biblical Commentary (Nashville: Thomas Nelson, 1985), 204.

4. Williamson, *Ezra, Nehemiah*, 204.

5. Breneman, *Ezra, Nehemiah, Esther*, 186.

6. Derek Kidner, *Ezra and Nehemiah*, Tyndale Old Testament Commentaries 12 (Downers Grove, IL: IVP Academic, 1979), 94–95.

(literally "hard of neck"), found elsewhere in the Scriptures (see Exod 32:9; 33:3; Deut 9:6; 2 Chr 36:13; Jer 17:23; Acts 7:51). The expression is an agricultural one used to describe an ox that was uncontrollable or stubborn. The biblical writers use it to describe the willful spirit of people who refuse to submit to God.[7] It is possible these nobles think the kind of manual labor to which Nehemiah called them is beneath them. Jesus, on the other hand, calls his followers to take his yoke on them as a metaphor for serving God through faith in Christ (Matt 11:29–30).[8]

III. Work Near the Old Gate (3:6–12)

> [6] Joiada the son of Paseah and Meshullam the son of Besodeiah repaired the Old Gate; they laid its beams and hung its doors with its bolts and its bars. [7] Next to them Melatiah the Gibeonite and Jadon the Meronothite, the men of Gibeon and of Mizpah, also made repairs for the official seat of the governor *of the province* beyond the River. [8] Next to him Uzziel the son of Harhaiah of the goldsmiths made repairs. And next to him Hananiah, one of the perfumers, made repairs, and they restored Jerusalem as far as the Broad Wall. [9] Next to them Rephaiah the son of Hur, the official of half the district of Jerusalem, made repairs. [10] Next to them Jedaiah the son of Harumaph made repairs opposite his house. And next to him Hattush the son of Hashabneiah made repairs. [11] Malchijah the son of Harim and Hasshub the son of Pahath-moab repaired another section and the Tower of Furnaces. [12] Next to him Shallum the son of Hallohesh, the official of half the district of Jerusalem, made repairs, he and his daughters.

The exact location of the Old Gate is unknown. It is possible it is what is sometimes called the Corner Gate, since it appears to have been near the northwest corner of Jerusalem, west of the Fish Gate. It opened up into a new quarter that is often called the Mishneh, meaning "second." This quarter was located on the western hill of Jerusalem.[9]

It is noteworthy to recognize the workers on the Old Gate includes goldsmiths and perfumers. Obviously, these people have a vested interest in the

---

7. Walwyn Evans, "Stiff-Necked," Biblestudy.com, www.biblestudytools.com/dictionary/stiff-necked/ (accessed August 16, 2017).

8. Andrew E. Steinmann, *Ezra and Nehemiah*, Concordia Commentary (St. Louis: Concordia, 2010), 420.

9. Williamson, *Ezra, Nehemiah*, 204–5.

security of the city in order for their businesses to flourish. Nevertheless, these tradesmen step out of their comfort zones to make a contribution to the work at hand. Given that the list of workers in Nehemiah 3 appears to provide a broad description of those who participate in the project, it is safe to surmise there are many other trades represented by the workmen who make repairs on the gates and walls of the city. Also, the families of the governors of Jerusalem pitch in to help. Unlike the nobles of Tekoa, these noble families commit themselves to the work. The text mentions that Shallum, the son of one of these governors, brings his daughters to work alongside him, either because he has no sons or because it is unusual for women to do this kind of work alongside the men in what is a very male-dominated society. Whatever the reason, mention of them points to something out of the ordinary.

IV. WORK NEAR THE VALLEY GATE (3:13)

> [13] Hanun and the inhabitants of Zanoah repaired the Valley Gate. They built it and hung its doors with its bolts and its bars, and a thousand cubits of the wall to the Refuse Gate.

The Valley Gate faced the Tyropoeon Valley, thus its name. It was centrally located on the western wall of the city and was therefore its most important gate on that wall. Also, the Valley Gate appears to have been part of a longer stretch of wall than usual, which explains the inclusion of its distance to the Refuse Gate. This distance was approximately five hundred yards. Given that the western side of Jerusalem was less susceptible to attack on account of the terrain, it is possible this section of wall was in better condition than the other sections of wall around the city.[10] Furthermore, the Valley Gate was the gate where Nehemiah began his initial inspection of the walls when he first arrived in Jerusalem (2:13, 15).

V. WORK NEAR THE REFUSE GATE (3:14)

> [14] Malchijah the son of Rechab, the official of the district of Beth-haccherem repaired the Refuse Gate. He built it and hung its doors with its bolts and its bars.

The Refuse or Dung Gate was located at the southern end of the city facing south-west, where the Tyropoeon Valley and the Hinnom Valley meet. It exited out to

---

10. Breneman, *Ezra, Nehemiah, Esther*, 189; Williamson, *Ezra, Nehemiah*, 207.

the garbage dump of the city. It also is probably the place where the priests took the parts of animals that were unacceptable for sacrifices to be burned outside the camp (see Exod 29:14; Lev 4:11–12; Num 19:5). If so, it was on the complete opposite side of the city from the location of the temple and the Sheep Gate, where the priests took the remaining parts of the animals to be consumed by fire. The priests' taking the refuse of the sacrificial animals to the farthest point away from the temple but still in proximity to the city demonstrates their desire to remove it as far away as practicable from the sacred place.

Furthermore, the verse states that another official's family participated in the work of rebuilding the gates and walls of Jerusalem. It is a mark of true leadership for the people of God.

VI. Work Near the Fountain Gate (3:15–25)

¹⁵ Shallum the son of Col-hozeh, the official of the district of Mizpah, repaired the Fountain Gate. He built it, covered it and hung its doors with its bolts and its bars, and the wall of the Pool of Shelah at the king's garden as far as the steps that descend from the city of David. ¹⁶ After him Nehemiah the son of Azbuk, official of half the district of Beth-zur, made repairs as far as *a point* opposite the tombs of David, and as far as the artificial pool and the house of the mighty men. ¹⁷ After him the Levites carried out repairs *under* Rehum the son of Bani. Next to him Hashabiah, the official of half the district of Keilah, carried out repairs for his district. ¹⁸ After him their brothers carried out repairs *under* Bavvai the son of Henadad, official of *the other* half of the district of Keilah. ¹⁹ Next to him Ezer the son of Jeshua, the official of Mizpah, repaired another section in front of the ascent of the armory at the Angle. ²⁰ After him Baruch the son of Zabbai zealously repaired another section, from the Angle to the doorway of the house of Eliashib the high priest. ²¹ After him Meremoth the son of Uriah the son of Hakkoz repaired another section, from the doorway of Eliashib's house even as far as the end of his house. ²² After him the priests, the men of the valley, carried out repairs. ²³ After them Benjamin and Hasshub carried out repairs in front of their house. After them Azariah the son of Maaseiah, son of Ananiah, carried out repairs beside his house. ²⁴ After him Binnui the son of Henadad repaired another section, from the house of Azariah as far as the Angle and as far as the corner. ²⁵ Palal the son of Uzai *made repairs* in front of the Angle and the

tower projecting from the upper house of the king, which is by the court of the guard. After him Pedaiah the son of Parosh *made repairs*.

The Fountain Gate faced east and was located in the southeastern portion of the wall of the city. Its name probably comes from its association with the Pool of Shelah, which is known as the Pool of Siloam in the Gospel of John, where Jesus gives sight to a blind man (John 9:7–11), or with the Gihon Spring, which feeds it. Another possibility is its association with the spring En-Rogel, which was also in the vicinity.[11] From this point forward, it appears the building project diverts from the location of the preexilic wall, which was located farther down the steep slope.[12] The walls had toppled to the bottom of the slope and would have needed to be reterraced, adding a great deal more difficulty to an already major project. Given the threats of their enemies, time appears to be of an essence. It is hardly believable they could have accomplished the work in the fifty-two days it took them had they have tried to follow the original path of the wall in this area. What's more, it was unnecessary given the city's reduced population. It was much easier to rebuild the wall at the top of the eastern slope of the city of David than farther down it. The location of the "artificial pool" is difficult to locate, but most likely it was a man-made retention pool.[13]

Here again, one witnesses how people from various walks of life cooperate with one another to work on the wall. There are the priests and their associates, the Levites; there are members of families of civil administrators from various places outside Jerusalem; and there are those who work just outside their homes. All work together to accomplish the task at hand, and some, such as Baruch the son of Zabbai, do so zealously.

VII. Work Near the Water Gate (3:26–27)

[26] The temple servants living in Ophel *made repairs* as far as the front of the Water Gate toward the east and the projecting tower. [27] After them the Tekoites repaired another section in front of the great projecting tower and as far as the wall of Ophel.

11. Williamson, *Ezra, Nehemiah*, 189.

12. Kathleen Kenyon, *Digging Up Jerusalem* (London: Ernest Benn, 1974), 183–84.

13. Steinmann, *Ezra and Nehemiah*, 422.

The Water Gate faced east and was associated with the palace-temple complex and its access to the Gihon Spring.[14] The wall of Ophel refers to a hill just south of the temple. Therefore, it makes sense that the temple servants are working here. These temple servants may be associates of the Levites, who in turn are associates to the priests.[15] Given the new path of the eastern wall at the top of the slope, this section circumvents the Water Gate from the preexilic era. Also of note is the work of the Tekoites. The men of Tekoa work on two sections of the wall, here and near the Fish Gate (3:5), more than making up for the shameful stubbornness of their nobles. It will be near the Water Gate where Ezra reads the law to the people (8:1).

VIII. Work Near the Horse Gate (3:28–30)

> [28] Above the Horse Gate the priests carried out repairs, each in front of his house. [29] After them Zadok the son of Immer carried out repairs in front of his house. And after him Shemaiah the son of Shecaniah, the keeper of the East Gate, carried out repairs. [30] After him Hananiah the son of Shelemiah, and Hanun the sixth son of Zalaph, repaired another section. After him Meshullam the son of Berechiah carried out repairs in front of his own quarters.

There has been some debate about the Horse Gate. Was it the gate where Athaliah was executed going within the palace precincts (2 Kgs 11:16; 2 Chr 23:15), or was it a gate in the city wall, as Jeremiah appears to indicate (Jer 31:40)? There certainly appears to have been a specific entrance into the royal grounds where horses were brought in, but this particular gate appears to be the one to which Jeremiah refers that was a gate into the city. It would have been the gate the horses used to enter into the city as they headed to the grounds of the palace just south of the East Gate, a gate into the temple and not part of the city wall (see Ezek 10:19).[16] Therefore, it makes sense that the priests work on this section of the wall, since it is near their homes.

---

14. Breneman, *Ezra, Nehemiah, Esther*, 191; Williamson, *Ezra, Nehemiah*, 209.

15. Williamson, *Ezra, Nehemiah*, 35.

16. Breneman, *Ezra, Nehemiah, Esther*, 433.

IX. Work Near the Inspection Gate (3:31–32)

> [31] After him Malchijah, one of the goldsmiths, carried out repairs as far
> as the house of the temple servants and of the merchants, in front of the
> Inspection Gate and as far as the upper room of the corner. [32] Between
> the upper room of the corner and the Sheep Gate the goldsmiths and the
> merchants carried out repairs.

The exact place of the Inspection Gate, located between the East Gate and the
northeast corner of the wall, is uncertain. It was a place of gathering and inspection, but whether it was the priests, the temple guard, or others who gathered
there for inspection is also uncertain.[17] It possibly is the same as the Benjamin
Gate mentioned in Jeremiah 20:2.

HIGHLIGHTS OF NEHEMIAH 3

The following words should help highlight and summarize various aspects of
Nehemiah 3.

The People Respond *Quickly*

Nehemiah 2:18 indicates that when the people of Judah hear Nehemiah's exhor-
tation and challenge to rebuild the walls, they verbally affirm they will join
Nehemiah, and then they "put their hands to the good work." They do not drag
their feet. Instead, Nehemiah 3 describes how they quickly organize and get to
work. Their verbal response is quickly followed up with action. Too often we
say we will serve the Lord in some capacity, but then we procrastinate. We can
be sure that, just as the enemies of God were active in Nehemiah's time, as we
have already witnessed in the book and will see even more of in the following
chapter, the enemy is actively working in the present. If the people of God are
going to do the work of God, then they must quickly get to it. There is no time
for the dragging of feet. Too much is at stake, and the window of opportunity is
small. As Jesus said in John 9:4, "We must work the works of Him who sent Me
as long as it is day; night is coming when no one can work."

---

17. Steinmann, *Ezra and Nehemiah*, 423.

THE PEOPLE RESPOND *VOLUNTARILY*

No one forces the people to join the rebuilding project. Everyone working on the walls is doing so because they volunteered. With Nehemiah's help, they recognize the need, and they recognize Nehemiah's call to work is from the Lord. When people are zealous for the glory of God and the removal of any reproach that is associated with the people of God, it is natural for them to volunteer to serve him. No coercion is necessary. They are more than mere hirelings. What they do is out of conviction. Moreover, if they had not volunteered to do the work, then the work would not have been done. Similarly, if believers today fail to answer God's call to serve, it is a sign that they lack passion in their love for Christ and the display of his glory in and through the church. Also, volunteer work should not mean shabby work. We should give our best to God's work, not our leftovers. Too often we give our best to our employers because they pay us, but when it comes to voluntarily serving God we become slackers. Too many local churches are in disrepair, both physically and spiritually, because believers fail to voluntarily give to Christ their best.

THE PEOPLE RESPOND *SACRIFICIALLY*

Many of these volunteers leave their families and jobs so that they can work on the walls in Jerusalem. Many leave their fields and responsibilities to their spouses and children and travel miles away from home to do the work. They come from Jericho, Tekoa, Gibeon, Mizpah, Zanoah, Beth Hakkerem, Beth Zur, and Keilah. Nehemiah 4:22 indicates these workers are not able to leave Jerusalem on account of the enemies' threats against them, so many of the workers are away from their families for quite some time. Nehemiah 5 reveals the hardship many of the workers' families face as a result of their sacrifice. Not only is there the threat of the enemies to the builders, but there is the threat of starvation of their families. The sacrifices they make to do the Lord's work are no small thing.

THE PEOPLE RESPOND WITH *ANONYMITY*

This statement may seem odd, since there are so many names of people mentioned in this passage. However, a closer reading of Nehemiah 3 indicates there are many more people doing the work whose names are unknown to us: "the priests," "the men of Jericho," "the sons of Hassenaah," "the Tekoites," "the men of Gibeon and of Mizpah," Shallum's "daughters," "the inhabitants of Zanoah," "the Levites," "brothers," "the temple servants," and "the goldsmiths and the merchants." They undertake this great project not to make a name for themselves but to remove the reproach of the people and to glorify the name of the Lord.

THE PEOPLE'S RESPONSE IS MARKED BY *DIVERSITY*

People from all walks of life come together to rebuild the walls of Jerusalem. They come from various places. They come from various occupations. They represent a wide age range. They represent a wide socioeconomic spectrum. Some are governors and nobility, while others are barely able to make ends meet. Some are single, and some are married. Some are men, and some are women. Some have dedicated their lives to service in the temple, and others have dedicated their lives to learning a skill or to tending their fields or flocks. Nevertheless, all of them come together to answer God's call through his servant Nehemiah.

THE PEOPLE'S RESPONSE IS MARKED BY *SOLIDARITY*

All of the workers have one purpose—to rebuild the walls of Jerusalem so that they will no longer be a reproach (2:17–18). No matter where they work on the wall and no matter what particular task each person undertakes, they all have the singular purpose of rebuilding the wall. They have the big picture in mind as they work in their particular places. It is essential that God's servants keep the overall mission in mind and remember they are not the only ones working as they give full attention to the task before them on their assigned portion of the "wall."

THE PEOPLE'S RESPONSE IS MARKED BY *RESPONSIBILITY*

There were forty to forty-one areas where repairs need to be done, and everyone who works has a particular area of responsibility. Each person knows what is expected of her. Not everyone is expected to do everything, but everyone is expected to do something. What was true then is true for the church today. Not everyone in the church can do everything, nor are we expected to do everything, but every one of us is called to do something in the Lord's service. What would have happened if the men of Jerusalem were negligent with their area of responsibility? It would have left a breach in the wall, leaving everyone in danger. What's more, the reproach on the people would have remained. One of the greatest reasons the church suffers today is that there are those refusing to take responsibility for what God has called them to do. As a result, the church fails in its mission of making disciples and brings reproach on itself. It too is then vulnerable to attack. A church's greatness is not measured by its size. It is measured by the percentage of people taking responsibility for what Christ has called them to do in his service. Greatness in the kingdom is marked by service.

THE PEOPLE RESPOND *DEVOTEDLY*

Once the people commence working, they persist all day and night for fifty-two days until the wall is complete (4:21–23; 6:15). Though they work often under duress and without much rest, no one quits until they finish the job. In order for God's work to be done unto God's glory, the people of God must be characterized by devotion and dependability. Whether Shallum's zeal or the men of Tekoa's doubled efforts, their work is marked by enthusiastic devotion.

THE PEOPLE RESPOND *COOPERATIVELY*

It would be naïve to assume that with such a large number of people working on this project that everyone will get along with everyone else all the time. Nevertheless, they are willing to lay aside any differences they may have in order to cooperate with each other in doing the work to which they have been called. Think about how much is accomplished when people lay aside their differences in order to accomplish something, and then think about how little gets accomplished when people fail to cooperate with one another. How many believers stunt the work of the church and the cause of Christ because of an unwillingness to cooperate with other believers?

THE PEOPLE WORK WITHIN *PROXIMITY* TO OTHERS

Several times the text states "next to him" or "after him." The survey of the work on one section of the wall, and then the next section, and then the next, and so on, shows they not only work in cooperation with one another, but they work on each section of the wall side by side. In the American Civil War, soldiers marched into battle shoulder to shoulder. It served at least two purposes. First, when they fired their rifles, it concentrated their fire for the greatest effect on the enemy. Second, marching shoulder to shoulder into the withering fire helped instill courage because they realized they were not alone. Similarly, when the people of God work side by side, what we do has the greatest effect on the enemy. Also, when we face the task with others beside us, it keeps us from being overwhelmed. The Lord has made us part of the body of Christ in order to function together as one in him.

The People Respond *Simultaneously*

Everyone works together at the same time. It is the only way the work can get done in a timely manner. When the people of God work together simultaneously, it has an exponential effect. We see this in the book of Acts as the apostles simultaneously blanket the world with the proclamation of the gospel.

The People Respond *Comprehensively*

Nehemiah's report provides a complete counterclockwise description of every part of the wall. The people leave no stone unturned in ensuring the work is completed. The work is organized, efficient, and effective. Any endeavor done in obedience to God's call should be marked by these characteristics.

CONCLUSION

It is a wonderful thing to witness the wholehearted devotion of the people of God to his call on their lives. Nehemiah 3 provides a picture of what can happen when believers join together and harmoniously work side by side for the cause of Christ, carrying out the Great Commission. Nehemiah and the people who joined him in rebuilding the walls could have said what Jesus said when he told his disciples, "My food is to do the will of him who sent me and to accomplish his work" (John 4:34). This should be the motto of every believer today. Instead of passing over Nehemiah 3 as a list of ancient names from a distant time, let us profit from the example of these godly people who sacrificially and enthusiastically fulfill God's calling on their lives.

FINAL THOUGHTS

1. What are you doing to serve Christ within the community of faith?
2. What sacrifices are you willing to make in order to serve Christ?
3. How committed are you to working together with other believers in fulfilling the Great Commission?
4. Is your life marked by a dogged devotion to complete the work God has called you to do with excellence?
5. How important is it to you to receive credit or recognition for what you do in Christ's service? How willing are you to gladly serve Christ in anonymity to others?

FACING OPPOSITION
TO GOD'S WORK

Nehemiah 4:1–23

INTRODUCTION

Whenever believers get serious about obeying God's call on their lives, they can count on opposition. Such opposition is depicted about a half-century earlier than Nehemiah's arrival in Jerusalem when the temple was rebuilt in 515 BC. At that time, the prophet Zechariah saw a vision where he witnessed Satan standing ready to accuse the high priest, Joshua. Zechariah witnessed,

> The LORD said to Satan, "The LORD rebuke you, Satan! Indeed, the LORD who has chosen Jerusalem rebuke you! Is this not a brand plucked from the fire?" Now Joshua was clothed with filthy garments and standing before the angel. He spoke and said to those who were standing before him, saying, "Remove the filthy garments from him." Again he said to him, "See, I have taken your iniquity away from you and will clothe you with festal robes." Then I said, "Let them put a clean turban on his head." So they put a clean turban on his head and clothed him with garments, while the angel of the LORD was standing by. (Zech 3:2–4)[1]

Furthermore, in 1 Chronicles 21:1, the writer of Chronicles, often called "the Chronicler," records, "Then Satan stood up against Israel and moved David to

---

1. Yahweh addresses Satan as *haśśāṭān*, literally "the satan." As in Job 1:6, some scholars insist this term is to be understood as "the accuser" and not the proper name for Satan because of the definite article. However, here in Zech 3:2 *haśśāṭān* is a vocative, meaning he is the one being directly addressed. In this instance, it may be understood as a proper name. This happens with the word for God, *ʾĕlōhîm*. Sometimes it is written as *hāʾĕlōhîm* and could literally mean "the gods" or "the God." Yet when it is a vocative or the recipient of direct address, such as in Judg 16:28, for example, where Samson prays, "Strengthen me only this once, O God," it is clearly a direct address to God, with his proper name in view. Russell Fuller explains this as the "article of dominance," as he calls *haśśāṭān* a proper name in Job 1:6 in *Invitation to Biblical Hebrew Syntax: An Intermediate Grammar* (Grand Rapids: Kregel, 2017), 163.

number Israel."[2] Of interest is the fact that many scholars date the writing of Chronicles in near proximity to the time of Nehemiah, ranging from possibly 515 BC, the time of the completion of the temple, to the actual time of Ezra and Nehemiah. Jewish tradition posits Ezra as the author of Chronicles, at least the portion that records events up until his time.[3] In this instance, Satan "moved/allured/incited" David to take the census, and the text recognizes that Satan was "against Israel," God's covenant people. It demonstrates how the Chronicler understood Satan as an enemy of the people of God and as one who incited sin against God.

While the people of Zechariah and Nehemiah's day may have had less revelation from God's word concerning the enemies of God and the people of God than New Testament believers have, it would be careless to ignore such revelation as we who are New Testament believers today look at this passage. In Ephesians 2:2–3, the apostle Paul identifies those who are in opposition to the Lord: those who walk "according to the course of this world, according to the prince and power of the air, of the spirit that is now working in the sons of disobedience." The powers of darkness will not sit idly while the people of God rise up to build, whether they are building a wall, as in Nehemiah's day, or building Christ's kingdom, as we are called to do today. J. I. Packer writes the following:

> The real theme of Nehemiah 4–6 is spiritual warfare, and Nehemiah's real opponent, lurking behind the human opponents, critics, and grumblers who occupied his attention directly, was Satan, whose name means "adversary" and who operates as the permanent enemy of God, God's people, God's work, and God's praise. Nehemiah does not mention him (few Old Testament books do), but that does not mean that he was not there. Direct opposition on the human level to those who are obeying God, and the use of "flaming arrows" of discouragement (Eph. 6:16) to

---

2. This is the only instance where *śāṭān* is found without the definite article attached to it in the OT. Its previous usage as a proper noun with the definite article transitioned to a proper noun without the definite article, as it appears in Second Temple Jewish and NT literature. It may be likened to the expression "the Christ," which referred to one individual, transitioning to Jesus later being called "Christ" without the definite article. See Eugene H. Merrill, *A Commentary on 1 & 2 Chronicles*, Kregel Exegetical Library (Grand Rapids: Kregel Academic, 2015), 245; Sydney H. Page, *Powers of Evil: A Biblical Study of Satan and Demons* (Grand Rapids: Baker, 1995) 33–35.

3. See the following for discussions on the dating of Chronicles and this passage in particular: Martin J. Selman, *1 Chronicles*, Tyndale Old Testament Commentaries (Nottingham, UK: IVP Academic, 1994), 67–78; Merrill, *Commentary on 1 & 2 Chronicles*, 43–46; Roddy Braun, *1 Chronicles*, Word Biblical Commentary 14 (Nashville: Thomas Nelson, 1986), xxix.

destroy hope, induce fear, and so paralyze their endeavors, are two of his regular tactics, and both are in evidence in these chapters. When you see Satan's fingerprints on events, it is a safe bet that Satan himself is actively present, even if he carefully keeps himself out of sight.[4]

Nehemiah 4 shows how people who are in rebellion to God will often be in conflict with the people of God. A biblical understanding of opposition to God's work through his people lays responsibility for this opposition on people who are set against God, on this world system, and on "the ruler of this world," the devil (John 12:31; 14:30; 16:11). This chapter not only teaches believers to expect opposition when doing God's work, but it also gives instruction on how to face it and overcome it.

STRUCTURE

Like the Visigoth barbarians who invaded Italy and stormed Rome, the attacks on Jerusalem's builders come in three waves.[5] Therefore, the structure of Nehemiah 4 is constructed around these three waves of assaults on Jerusalem's builders, which threaten the people's resolve to continue the work, followed by a description of the measures Nehemiah and the people take in order to safely complete the work they began. The first section depicts the threat that comes from a verbal assault, and Nehemiah and the people's response (4:1–6). The second describes the threat that comes from a physical assault, and again Nehemiah and the people's response (4:7–9). The third section recounts the threat of an internal assault that arises among the workers and Nehemiah's response to them (4:10–14). The three attempts at stopping the work are followed by a description of the actions the workers take to defend against the threats and ensure completion of the project (4:15–23).

SUMMARY OF THE PASSAGE

Nehemiah 4 describes both the attempts of the enemies of the people of God to thwart the rebuilding of the wall of Jerusalem and the measures the people take to persevere and complete what they began.

---

4. J. I. Packer, *A Passion for Faithfulness: Wisdom from the Book of Nehemiah* (Wheaton, IL: Crossway, 1995), 93.

5. The Visigoths were a coalition of Germanic tribes who brought about what historians call the sack of Rome in AD 410. They were the first enemy to conquer the city in over 800 years.

OUTLINE OF THE PASSAGE

I. The First Wave: A Verbal Assault (4:1–6)

    A. The enemy's ridicule (4:1–3)

    B. The people of God's response (4:4–6)

        1. A defiant prayer (4:4–5)

        2. A determined mind-set (4:6)

II. The Second Wave: A Physical Assault (4:7–9)

    A. The enemy's conspiring (4:7–8)

        1. The escalation of the enemies of God

        2. The isolation of the people of God

    B. The people of God's response (4:9)

III. The Third Wave: An Internal Assault (4:10–14)

    A. The enemy's influence (4:10–12)

    B. The people of God's response (4:13–14)

        1. Actions

        2. Exhortations

IV. The Enemy's Frustration (4:15)

V. Countermeasures to Future Assaults (4:16–23)

    A. They take up arms

    B. They establish an alarm system

    C. They remain vigilant

DEVELOPMENT OF THE EXPOSITION

I. The First Wave: A Verbal Assault (4:1–6)

[1] Now it came about that when Sanballat heard that we were rebuilding the wall, he became furious and very angry and mocked the Jews. [2] He spoke in the presence of his brothers and the wealthy *men* of Samaria and said, "What are these feeble Jews doing? Are they going to restore *it* for themselves? Can they offer sacrifices? Can they finish in a day? Can they revive the stones from the dusty rubble even the burned ones?" [3] Now Tobiah the Ammonite *was* near him and he said, "Even what they are building—if a fox should jump on *it*, he would break their stone wall down!" [4] Hear, O our God, how we are despised! Return their reproach on their own heads and give them up for plunder in a land of captivity. [5] Do not forgive

their iniquity and let not their sin be blotted out before You, for they have demoralized the builders. ⁶ So we built the wall and the whole wall was joined together to half its *height*, for the people had a mind to work.

A. The Enemy's Ridicule (4:1–3)

News of the progress of the building project reaches one of the Jews' archenemies, Sanballat the Horonite. Verse 4 describes him as emphatically angry. It appears he cannot control his tongue from expressing his contempt for the Jews. A strong Jerusalem would threaten his place of prominence in the region, especially economically. Therefore, the first wave of assault begins with verbal ridicule in an attempt to bring down the morale of the builders in Jerusalem. It is the easiest way to try to undermine the work for at least two reasons. First, verbal ridicule requires very little of the person doing it, especially when that person is twelve miles away from the people he ridicules. Sanballat was most likely the governor of Horon, a town about twelve miles northwest of Jerusalem. Horon was connected to one of the main thoroughfares going to Jerusalem. Sanballat has to know he is under no threat from the Judeans in his own home, especially as he addresses an army of people, many of whom serve in his military. It is much like liquid or internet courage today, which is defined as "bravery leading to a form of brazen expression, often offensive, enacted over the world wide web."⁶ Sanballat's mocking takes little effort.

Sanballat asks five questions, all in an attempt to demoralize the workers, saying they are weak, incapable, hopeless, overly ambitious, and without sufficient resources. It is the same ploy Satan uses to discourage believers today. Then Tobiah the Ammonite, Sanballat's apparent sidekick, taunts them by saying their work will be for naught. A wall around a city was expected to stand up against the assaults and sieges of its enemies. Tobiah says their work on the wall is so poorly done that a fox's paw could bring it down. Their effort to protect the city will be wasted. With all their labors, in the end they will still be defenseless. Ultimately, their derision is aimed as much at God as it is toward his people. The enemies of the people of God fail to see what God is capable of doing in and through his people. Sanballat and Tobiah are either ignorant of or ignoring the words of the prophet Zechariah, who spoke of the day when "Jerusalem will rise and remain

---

6. Hayley Rose Horzepa, "Internet Courage," Huffington Post, http://www.huffingtonpost.com/hayley-rose-horzepa/online-dating_b_2507216.html (accessed August 24, 2017).

on its site from Benjamin's Gate as far as the place of the First Gate to the Corner Gate, and from the Tower of Hananel to the king's wine presses. People will live in it, and there will no longer be a curse, for Jerusalem will dwell in security" (Zech 14:10b–11). Sanballat and Tobiah can no more conceive of God's blessing on Jerusalem and the quick completion of its reconstruction than can the high priest and Jesus' accusers believe Jesus can rise again from the grave after his execution (Matt 26:60–63).[7]

The second reason Sanballat's ridicule is the easiest approach to try to undermine the work is the Persian king's support of Nehemiah and the rebuilding project of Jerusalem. Gene Getz writes, "Threat usually creates one of two basic reactions—fear and retreat, or anger and aggression—and in most instances there is a mixture of both. There is no question as to which was Sanballat's *primary* response. He became intensely angry and aggressive. But it was also anger mixed with fear, for he did not initially attack the children of Israel with military force."[8] Any overt action beyond words would probably be perceived by the Persians as insubordination, and Sanballat certainly does not want that. His courage can go only so far. Not only is Sanballat threatened by a strengthened Jerusalem, but he also is threatened by its benefactor, King Artaxerxes, who just happened to have sent Nehemiah to Jerusalem with a contingent of Persian guards.

It is unclear as to how news of what Sanballat says reaches Nehemiah. Perhaps there are traders who heard it and pass it along to Nehemiah when they come to Jerusalem, or maybe Sanballat sent "messengers" to Jerusalem to ensure Nehemiah hears what he said. Undoubtedly, he wants the builders to hear of it.[9] It is a typical cheap bullying tactic.

B. The People of God's Response (4:4–6)

The response to the verbal threat of the enemy is twofold: prayer and continued, committed work on the wall.

---

7. Matthew Levering, *Ezra & Nehemiah*, Brazos Theological Commentary on the Bible (Grand Rapids: Brazos, 2007), 69.

8. Gene Getz, *When Your Goals Seem Out of Reach: Take a Lesson from Nehemiah*, Biblical Renewal Series (Ventura, CA: Regal Books, 1981), 69.

9. Derek W. Thomas, *Ezra & Nehemiah*, Reformed Expository Commentary (Phillipsburg, NJ: P&R, 2016), 249–50.

1. A Defiant Prayer

Charles Swindoll writes, "Nehemiah fought his battles through prayer. We have seen it numerous times in his life. Through the therapeutic process of time on his knees, he laid out his concerns before God."[10] However, this prayer is different from our normal prayers today. Our Western way of thinking causes many to wince when reading imprecatory prayers such as Nehemiah's prayer. Many believe it contradicts the teaching of Christ in his Sermon on the Mount concerning loving one's enemy (Matt 5:44).[11] The problem is that the Sermon on the Mount is mainly about us and our personal relationships with others, but the imprecatory psalms and prayers of the Bible are mainly about God, his glory, and his justice, laying down one's anger at God's feet and trusting his vindication just as the imprecatory psalms often do (see Pss 5; 17; 79; 83 for examples). Packer writes,

> Difficulty is felt today with biblical prayers that God will take vengeance, partly because of the oriental exuberance of expression, which to us sounds like bloodthirstiness and gloating (imaginative detail about anyone's evil prospects is culturally unacceptable to Westerners), but mainly because the pure zeal for God's glory that these prayers express is foreign to our spiritually sluggish hearts. The key principle here is stated in Psalm 139:21–22: "Do I not hate those who hate you, O Lord … ? I have nothing but hatred for them; I count them my enemies." The nearer we come to this state of mind, which is a spinoff from the desire that God's will be done, his kingdom come, and his name be hallowed and glorified, the less problem shall we have with vengeance prayers.[12]

In sermons and Bible studies, we are often exhorted to love more, but we are rarely encouraged to hate more. Yet there are things believers should hate. We should hate sin and its consequences, which ultimately are loss of blessing and loss of life. Sin always results in loss. Believers should hate anything that opposes God, his glory, and his character. The problem for many believers is we equate ambivalence toward and acceptance of evil with being Christlike. Nothing could be further from the truth. Nehemiah and the psalmists' concern in their imprecatory prayers is not for personal vengeance. It is a zeal for the furtherance of

---

10. Charles R. Swindoll, *Hand Me Another Brick* (Nashville: Thomas Nelson, 1978), 79.

11. Thomas, *Ezra & Nehemiah*, 252.

12. Packer, *Passion for Faithfulness*, 101–2.

the kingdom of God and the removal of anything that opposes it. Moreover, to oppose the people of God who are enthusiastically doing the will of God is to be in opposition to God himself. This is an eternal truth. Of course believers should be loving, but we will never love God and others as we should if we do not have a Christlike hatred toward evil. The psalmist states, "God ... has indignation every day" (Ps 7:11). If God is indignant toward wickedness, perhaps we should be as well. Let us pray for the day when the Lord will put an end to sin and death.

2. A Determined Mind-Set

Nehemiah's initial response of prayer once again demonstrates his complete dependence on God in this project. Nevertheless, the legitimacy of Nehemiah's faith in God is not just his propensity to pray but also his determination to act. As James writes, "Even so faith, if it has no works, is dead, being alone" (Jas 2:17). Prayer followed by action appears to be a pattern in Nehemiah's life. It is the way of life for people of faith. Nehemiah and the builders are determined to work and not allow this verbal assault to distract them or prevent them from doing what God called them to do.

Also, in most significant projects the halfway point is the time when it is easiest to become discouraged. For the builders, the work is getting more diffi-cult. The higher up they get with the wall, the more effort it requires. The initial zeal can begin to wane as the reality of time and difficulty begins to take its toll. Coupled with the verbal assault of Sanballat, it is a vulnerable time in the proj-ect. For this reason, the resolve of the builders at this point is crucial. Why are there so many articles online about how to finish what you have started? It is because many of us fail to finish most of the projects we begin. For this reason, the writer of Ecclesiastes writes, "The end of a matter is better than its beginning; Patience of spirit is better than haughtiness of spirit" (Eccl 7:8). The New Living Translation states it this way: "Finishing is better than starting. Patience is better than pride." It is significant that the people rally around Nehemiah to begin build-ing the wall of Jerusalem. However, it was even more significant that as the work becomes more difficult and the enemy becomes more persistent, the builders have a dogged determination to persevere, true evidence of their faith in God.

II. The Second Wave: A Physical Assault (4:7–9)

⁷ Now when Sanballat, Tobiah, the Arabs, the Ammonites and the Ashdodites heard that the repair of the walls of Jerusalem went on, *and* that the breaches began to be closed, they were very angry. ⁸ All of them conspired together to come *and* fight against Jerusalem and to cause a disturbance in it. ⁹ But we prayed to our God, and because of them we set up a guard against them day and night.

A. The Enemy's Conspiring (4:7–8)

Two expressions describe the circumstances that develop: the escalation of the enemies of God and the isolation of the people of God.

1. The Escalation of the Enemies of God

One might surmise that if one prays and continues to faithfully and obediently serve the Lord, then circumstances in life will improve. But Nehemiah 4:7–8 indicates there are times when believers do the right things in the face of opposition and that opposition grows and intensifies. Instead of cooling down, the hostilities heat up. In Nehemiah's case, the numbers of the adversaries grow. Instead of the threat coming from an isolated group to their north, now there are a number of groups ready to thwart the efforts of the builders. Furthermore, not only is there an escalation in the number of enemies, but there is also an escalation in what they are willing to do to stop the work. Most of us are familiar with the children's saying "Sticks and stones may break my bones, but words will never harm me." The saying basically means "Your insults have no effect on me."[13] However, the saying also recognizes physical attack can hurt someone and have quite an effect. Since Sanballat and Tobiah's words appear to have no effect on the builders, it is time to intensify their efforts with physical harm.

If we are knowledgeable of the Scriptures, believers should know that when we continue to faithfully serve Christ in the midst of opposition, sometimes matters get much more difficult before they get better. For example, the burden of the children of Israel in Egypt got worse for them before they actually exited Egypt when the Pharaoh began requiring them to gather their own straw to make their

---

13. "Sticks and Stones May Break My Bones," phrases.org.uk, http://www.phrases.org.uk/meanings/sticks-and-stones-may-break-my-bones.html (accessed August 26, 2017).

bricks (Exod 5:6–9). Another example is when Saul, the national leader, used all his resources to pursue David to kill him before David eventually became king over all of Israel (1 Sam 23:7–24:22). Furthermore, growing opposition to Christ culminated in his arrest, trial, and crucifixion and was an awful time for the disciples before Jesus rose again from the tomb on the third day. The enemies' escalation in number and physical threat is no small thing.

2. *The Isolation of the People of God*

To make matters worse, the builders in Jerusalem are now surrounded by their enemies. Sanballat and the Samaritans were on their northern border. The Arabs were located in the southern Transjordan and the Negev. So they were on Judah's southern border. Ammon is east of Judah, so the Ammonites were on Judah's eastern border. And Ashdod was part of the Philistine plain on Judah's western border. So Jerusalem is surrounded and isolated by its enemies. Each of the four Persian provinces surrounding Judah are plotting to stage a four-pronged attack on Jerusalem. Jerusalem's supply lines are cut off, and the enemy is closing in from all directions, a grave situation indeed.[14]

B. The People of God's Response (4:9)

At this point, Nehemiah's reaction is typical. He leads the people to pray to God for help, and then they take action by setting up an around-the-clock guard against their enemies—prayer and action. Being practical can be as spiritual an act as anything else a believer may do. It is like the story "The Drowning Man," which goes like this:

> A fellow was stuck on his rooftop in a flood. He was praying to God for help.
>
> Soon a man in a rowboat came by and the fellow shouted to the man on the roof, "Jump in, I can save you."
>
> The stranded fellow shouted back, "No, it's OK, I'm praying to God and he is going to save me."
>
> So the rowboat went on.
>
> Then a motorboat came by. The fellow in the motorboat shouted, "Jump in, I can save you."

---

14. F. Charles Fensham, *The Books of Ezra and Nehemiah*, New International Commentary on the Old Testament (Grand Rapids: Eerdmans, 1982), 184.

To this the stranded man said, "No thanks, I'm praying to God and he is going to save me. I have faith."

So the motorboat went on.

Then a helicopter came by and the pilot shouted down, "Grab this rope and I will lift you to safety."

To this the stranded man again replied, "No thanks, I'm praying to God and he is going to save me. I have faith."

So the helicopter reluctantly flew away.

Soon the water rose above the rooftop and the man drowned. He went to Heaven. He finally got his chance to discuss this whole situation with God, at which point he exclaimed, "I had faith in you but you didn't save me, you let me drown. I don't understand why!"

To this God replied, "I sent you a rowboat and a motorboat and a helicopter, what more did you expect?"[15]

Nehemiah prays to God to do for them what they cannot do themselves, and he uses what God has already given him—his mind and the community of faith. Nehemiah uses all the available resources from God.

III. The Third Wave: An Internal Assault (4:10–14)

[10] Thus in Judah it was said, "The strength of the burden bearers is failing, Yet there is much rubbish; And we ourselves are unable to rebuild the wall." [11] Our enemies said, "They will not know or see until we come among them, kill them and put a stop to the work." [12] When the Judeans who lived near them came and told us ten times, "They will come up against us from every place where you may turn," [13] then I stationed *men* in the lowest parts of the space behind the wall, the exposed places, and I stationed the people in families with their swords, spears and bows. [14] When I saw *their fear*, I rose and spoke to the nobles, the officials and the rest of the people: "Do not be afraid of them; remember the Lord who is great and awesome, and fight for your brothers, your sons, your daughters, your wives and your houses."

---

15. "The Drowning Man," Truthbook, http://truthbook.com/stories/funny-god/the-drowning-man (accessed August 26, 2017).

A. The Enemy's Influence (4:10–12)

The continued threats of Jerusalem's enemies on top of the challenge of such an enormous rebuilding project begin having an effect on the people of Judah. The people of God begin believing what the enemy is saying about them. Perhaps they are too weak and are incapable of finishing the task. Maybe it is a hopeless endeavor and they have been overly ambitious. And, possibly, there really is insufficient reusable materials out of all the rubble to rebuild the wall. Sanballat just might be correct in his assessment of them after all.

Moreover, the enemy's threat of attack has become palpable. The people who live near the borders of their enemies are overwhelmed with constant reports of the enemy's impending attack. The threats are so real that the people who live near the enemy report what they are hearing ten times to the builders in Jerusalem. It is impossible for the people living near the borders constantly to listen to the claims of the enemy without being influenced by them. Surely, many of these reports come from the wives and families of those who left their homes to go to Jerusalem to work on the wall.[16] It has to be unsettling for just about everyone throughout Judah.

The same principle is true today for believers. We cannot expect to constantly listen to the enemy without being influenced by them. Paul writes, "Do not be deceived; 'Bad company corrupts good morals'" (1 Cor 15:33). The constant bombardment of the world will take its toll on the strongest of believers unless they spend time listening to and reading the truth of God's word and drawing encouragement from experiencing fellowship with other believers. When believers are outnumbered and assaulted from every direction from the enemy, when they begin to feel isolated, it is then they most need the word of God and the people of God, the church. The tragedy is that when we experience the intense pressure from the enemy, many of us withdraw from God's word and the community of faith, the very things God has given every believer to encourage us when the enemy appears to have the upper hand. It is good that the people go to Nehemiah with their reports, because they need to see and hear Nehemiah's response.

B. The People of God's Response (4:13–14)

The people's response involves actions and exhortations.

---

16. Raymond Brown, *The Message of Nehemiah*, The Bible Speaks Today (Downers Grove, IL: InterVarsity Press, 1998), 79.

1. Actions

Nehemiah's first response is to station the people in the exposed places. It shows the people of Judah and any potential attackers there are no easy places to slip in and attack, as the enemy threatened to do. Also, while it is a morale boost to the builders and their families, it is a significant deterrent to the enemy. Second, Nehemiah stations the people with their families, providing them with even greater incentive to fight. It is one thing to fight for strangers and mere associates; it is another to fight for one's family. Third, Nehemiah makes sure they have what they need to defend themselves—swords, spears, and bows. They can defend themselves at a distance, and they are prepared to fight in close quarters if need be.

Nehemiah's actions provide an example of how believers today should face the enemy. We must be especially vigilant in the areas of our lives where we are most vulnerable to temptation. That means we must first be aware of those vulnerabilities. Second, we must prioritize the Lordship of Christ in our homes. It means looking out for the spiritual welfare of one another even when it is ill-received and unpopular. Third, we must be well equipped for spiritual warfare. Ephesians 6:10–20 provides believers with a list of everything we need to be victorious against the waves of assaults of the enemy.

2. Exhortations

While taking the necessary actions to defend themselves against the enemy is essential, the builders need to hear Nehemiah's exhortations. Nehemiah gives the people three. First, "Do not be afraid." Throughout the Scriptures, the Lord and his messengers tell his people "Do not be afraid" (see Deut 3:22; 7:21; 31:6; Josh 1:9; Pss 23:4; 27:1; 34:7; 55:22; 91:1–16; 118:6–7; Prov 29:25; Isa 35:4; 41:10, 13–14; 43:1; 46:1; Zeph 3:17; Matt 6:34; Mark 4:39–49; 5:36; 6:50; Luke 12:22–26; John 14:27; Phil 4:6–7; 2 Tim 1:7; 1 Pet 5:6–7; Rev 1:17). Second, "Remember the Lord who is great and awesome." When the people of God remember God is great and awesome, they realize they are unbeatable when doing his will. Just like Peter when he takes his eyes off the Lord and begins sinking in the sea (Matt 14:29–31), it is when we take our eyes off the Lord and begin looking at ourselves and the circumstances around us that we begin to falter. And third, "Fight for your brothers, your sons, your daughters, your wives and your houses." Nehemiah already grouped the people with their families as they took their defensive positions. The people need to be reminded that the lives of their loved ones are at stake. Either they fight or they watch people they love perish and all that God blessed them with be destroyed. The same is true for believers today. Peter writes, "Be of sober spirit, be on the alert. Your adversary, the devil, prowls around like a roaring lion, seeking someone to devour" (1 Pet 5:8). And Paul writes, "Put on the full armor of God, so that you will be able to stand firm against the schemes of the devil" (Eph 6:11). Thomas states, "The world, the flesh, and the devil will seek every opportunity to oppose all forms of spiritual vitality and attempts to demonstrate it."[17] Believers must not be intimidated by the enemy. Instead, we must be of sober spirit, on the alert, and equipped with the full armor of God because lives that matter to God and to us are at stake in this spiritual war.

IV. The Enemy's Frustration (4:15)

> [15] When our enemies heard that it was known to us, and that God had frustrated their plan, then all of us returned to the wall, each one to his work.

It is important to note when they all return to their work. It is when the enemies realize the builders are aware of their schemes and God has frustrated their plan. The key to victory in spiritual warfare is for the believer to realize that it is God who fights for her. If we all truly recognized this truth, that the battle truly belongs to the Lord, then all of us would be courageous warriors for Christ and be able to go on with the work to which he has called us.

V. Countermeasures to Future Assaults (4:16–23)

> [16] From that day on, half of my servants carried on the work while half of them held the spears, the shields, the bows and the breastplates; and the captains *were* behind the whole house of Judah. [17] Those who were rebuilding the wall and those who carried burdens took *their* load with one hand doing the work and the other holding a weapon. [18] As for the builders, each *wore* his sword girded at his side as he built, while the trumpeter *stood* near me. [19] I said to the nobles, the officials and the rest of the people, "The work is great and extensive, and we are separated on the wall far from one another. [20] At whatever place you hear the sound of the trumpet, rally to us there. Our God will fight for us."

---

17. Thomas, *Ezra & Nehemiah*, 261.

²¹ So we carried on the work with half of them holding spears from dawn until the stars appeared. ²² At that time I also said to the people, "Let each man with his servant spend the night within Jerusalem so that they may be a guard for us by night and a laborer by day." ²³ So neither I, my brothers, my servants, nor the men of the guard who followed me, none of us removed our clothes, each *took* his weapon *even to* the water.

Verses 15–23 summarize the countermeasures Nehemiah and the people take against the enemy's threats and their result.

A. *They Take Up Arms*

The first precaution they take is to carry a weapon with them at all times. Nehemiah's own personal entourage splits up, with half of them working while the other half carry weapons and armor. Furthermore, the military commanders are on high alert. As for the rest of the workers, those who are moving loads do so with only one hand so that they can carry a weapon in the other. And as for those who are actually on the wall building, one might say they have a trowel in one hand and a sword in the other. They wear a sword at all times.

B. *They Establish an Alarm System*

Second, Nehemiah gathers the people and announces the establishment of an alarm system in order to rally the people should danger arise. Note how Nehemiah reminds them that their God will fight for them. Nehemiah echoes what God's word communicates many times in regard to his people (see Exod 14:14; Deut 1:30; 3:22; 20:4; Josh 10:14, 42; 23:10; 2 Chr 32:8; Ps 127:1). They may be surrounded by their enemies and isolated from the world, but their God is with them, ready to fight for them.

C. *They Remain Vigilant*

Verse 22 indicates the builders have to make a tremendous sacrifice by staying in Jerusalem. Many have families several miles away and probably take whatever opportunity they can to go see their families and lend them some support. But with the threat of the enemy looming over them, it is necessary to stay in Jerusalem so that the builder's servant could stand guard at night and awaken his master if there was an attack. Nehemiah sets the example, showing the people that he and his entourage will be as vigilant as he is asking everyone else to be.

CONCLUSION

Brown states, "The story of adversity becomes a testimony to the abundant sufficiency of God."[18] Often we tend to focus on ourselves and see the book of Nehemiah *only* as a how-to book on leadership and Christian living. However, if we do, we fail to acknowledge its greatest gift to believers—the revelation of God himself. Brown points out important truths God reveals of himself in Nehemiah 4:

1. God is unique.
2. God is attentive.
3. God is righteous.
4. God is powerful.
5. God is holy.
6. God is sovereign.
7. God is unfailing.
8. God will fight for us.[19]

Let us always remember God's word is first and foremost his revelation of himself. It is about him. In light of this truth, we can begin to deduce what it means for the people of God.

FINAL THOUGHTS

1. How seriously do you take spiritual warfare in your life?
2. What can we learn from Nehemiah about spiritual warfare?
3. How do prayer and action work together in the Christian life?
4. What does Nehemiah 4 reveal about the enemies of God and his people?
5. What does Nehemiah 4 reveal about God, and what difference does it make?

---

18. Brown, *Message of Nehemiah*, 83.
19. Brown, *Message of Nehemiah*, 83.

A GODLY LEADER'S CONCERN

Nehemiah 5:1–19

INTRODUCTION

To divide and conquer means to gain and then maintain power by breaking up existing power structures into groups smaller than the one implementing the strategy so that the one implementing the strategy can dominate or defeat the smaller groupings one at a time. It is often used politically by causing strife between the smaller groups so that they will weaken one another and become easier to defeat.[1] Throughout history national and military leaders have used the divide-and-conquer strategy of conquest with great effectiveness. For instance, Hammurabi used this strategy in ancient Mesopotamia to become one of the most powerful leaders in all of history. He often instigated wars between two of his rival city-states so they would weaken each other before swooping in himself with his army to conquer both of them.

It is a strategy as old as humanity itself. Satan used it in the garden of Eden to bring about a separation between God and Adam and Eve. He succeeded in bringing about dissension between the man and the woman. And what's more, in all of this Satan successfully employed this strategy to become "ruler of this world" (John 12:31). It has been an effective tactic for the devil. Ultimately he will be cast out, but until the time he is, he will continue to exploit it, just as he attempted to do so during the time of Nehemiah. With the external threat contained, Nehemiah has to face an unexpected internal threat of dissension, division, and exploitation within his own ranks. It is a threat that could bring the work on the wall to a screeching halt.

---

1. Illa Xypolia, "Divide et Impera: Vertical and Horizontal Dimensions of British Imperialism," *Critique* 44 (July 2016): 221.

STRUCTURE

Nehemiah 5 is divided into three sections. The first section, verses 1–5, recounts the allegations of people about their countrymen because of the desperate situation brought about by famine, taxes, and the greed of these wealthy Judean brothers. The next section, verses 6–13, describes how Nehemiah deals with the situation in order to bring relief to the people. The final section, verses 14–19, relates how Nehemiah personally shows compassion to the host of needy people who are part of the community of faith.

SUMMARY OF THE PASSAGE

With the external threat to the workers contained and the continued work on the wall, Nehemiah needs to contend with a new difficulty that threatens the completion of the project: internal dissension among the people of God.

OUTLINE OF THE PASSAGE

I. A Godly Leader Shows Concern by Hearing Petitions (5:1–5)
  A. The first cry for help (5:1–2)
  B. The second cry for help (5:3)
  C. The third cry for help (5:4–5)
II. A Godly Leader Shows Concern by Giving Protection (5:6–13)
  A. Giving protection to the community of faith sometimes springs from righteous anger (5:6)
  B. Giving protection to the community of faith always requires careful contemplation (5:7)
  C. Giving protection to the community of faith occasionally demands a difficult confrontation (5:7–12)
  D. Giving protection to the community of faith at times necessitates a public demonstration (5:13)
III. A Godly Leader Shows Concern by Expressing Compassion (5:14–19)
  A. Compassion because of a fear of God
  B. Compassion because of an affection for the people of God

DEVELOPMENT OF THE EXPOSITION

I. A Godly Leader Shows Concern by Hearing Petitions (5:1–5)

¹ Now there was a great outcry of the people and of their wives against their Jewish brothers. ² For there were those who said, "We, our sons and our daughters are many; therefore let us get grain that we may eat and live." ³ There were others who said, "We are mortgaging our fields, our vineyards and our houses that we might get grain because of the famine." ⁴ Also there were those who said, "We have borrowed money for the king's tax *on* our fields and our vineyards.

⁵ Now our flesh is like the flesh of our brothers, our children like their children. Yet behold, we are forcing our sons and our daughters to be slaves, and some of our daughters are forced into bondage *already*, and we are helpless because our fields and vineyards belong to others."

A. The First Cry for Help (5:1–2)

The team of laborers who came from all over Judah to do the work in restoring the walls surrounding Jerusalem are now facing a crisis. These workers left their normal professions to do the necessary work for the project. Many are nonlandowners who live at subsistence levels, depending on daily earnings just to live before they left their jobs to build the wall. The sacrifices these volunteers made are now beginning to have a detrimental effect on their families. The larger families, in particular, are becoming destitute with so many to feed. Furthermore, one should recall how in Nehemiah 4:22, Nehemiah requires the workers to stay in Jerusalem in order to "stand guard by night and work by day." Therefore, verse 1 mentions the workers' wives' involvement in making the complaint, probably because they are the ones having to contend with the harsh conditions and responsibilities with the continued absence of their husbands from home. Their complaint is against other Judeans who apparently are unwilling to share food with them and help them in their time of need. These neighbors fail to realize that if they are not going to go to Jerusalem to participate in the work, it is their responsibility to support the families of those who did. It is like our responsibility today to support those who go to do the work of missions. Some go, while the rest need to support those who go. These families desperately need the support of their Judean countrymen. They need food.

B. The Second Cry for Help (5:3)

The second group who complains to Nehemiah are the landowners who are now having to mortgage their properties to buy food. Exacerbating the situation is a famine that apparently has been going on for some time. No doubt, those merchants who had grain to sell jacked up the prices to squeeze the people for every shekel they had, not unlike the time when there was a shortage of food in Samaria in Elisha's day, when "a donkey's head sold for thirty-four ounces of silver, and a cup of dove's dung sold for two ounces of silver" (2 Kgs 6:22). Even though the text does not specify when these problems happened, it is likely they occurred shortly before the completion of the wall. It would have been just before the end of harvest, and those farmers who had borrowed money for seed and the paying of hirelings to work the harvest would have been required to pay off creditors with interest. However, the work on the wall most likely caused a shortage in the workforce during the critical time of ingathering, putting a strain on the entire agriculturally dependent economy on top of the already difficult conditions of famine.[2] All of these issues contributed to a lack of food. Like those in the first group, these people also need food.

C. The Third Cry for Help (5:4–5)

The third group are in similar straits but for a different reason: the Persian king's taxes. Most likely, they had to be paid in silver. If so, this would have resulted in making the situation worse, since only the wealthy would have had silver on hand. Most people would have gotten their silver after harvest.[3] The taxes are so excessive that these landowners have borrowed money to pay their taxes, but now they are finding it impossible to pay off their loans. Many resorted to subjecting their children to slavery to help pay off the loans, loans that had interest rates of anywhere between 20 and 50 percent. They are not able to redeem their children from the slavery because they have no more assets. Even worse, it is

---

2. H. G. M. Williamson, *Ezra, Nehemiah*, Word Biblical Commentary (Nashville: Thomas Nelson, 1985), 235–36.

3. Peter Altmann, *Economics in Persian-Period Biblical Texts* (Tübingen: Mohr Siebeck, 2016), 267.

possible their daughters who were taken by creditors were being prostituted as payment for the loans.[4]

The Persian monarchs were shrewd. They were different from their predecessors, the Assyrians and the Chaldeans. The Assyrians and Chaldeans displaced entire people groups into exile and forced them to embrace their culture and religious practices, such as in Daniel's younger years. The Persians, on the other hand, allowed conquered peoples to live in their own countries and encouraged them to worship their gods. Although they drafted people for military service and building projects, the Persians' greatest oppression of its conquered peoples was financial or socioeconomic oppression. The taxes they required were severe. Artaxerxes ruled over twenty-six great satrapies or provinces. The satrap of Persia was exempt from paying taxes, so the other twenty-five satraps paid for the splendor of the heart of the empire.[5] The amount of gold and silver they acquired from the satraps is enormous. One scholar of ancient Persia writes,

> Little of this vast sum was ever returned to the satrapies. It was the custom to melt down the gold and silver and to pour it into jars which were broken and the bullion stored. Only a small portion was ever coined, and then usually for the purchase of foreign soldiers or of foreign statesmen. … For a time, credit made possible a continuance of business, but the insensate demand for actual silver in the payment of taxes drove the landlords in increasing numbers to the loan sharks, who gave money in exchange for the pledge—the actual use of the field or the slave, whose services were thus lost until the improbable redemption. As coined money became a rarity, hoarded by the loan sharks, credit increased the inflation, and rapidly rising prices made the situation still more intolerable.[6]

When Alexander the Great conquered Susa, one of four Persian capitals, he discovered some 270 tons of gold and 1,200 tons of silver there.[7]

Therefore, one may conclude there were a number of issues that contributed to the difficulties the people were facing during the rebuilding of the walls of Jerusalem: the lack of concern and support for the families of those working on

---

4. Williamson, *Ezra, Nehemiah*, 238.

5. A. T. Olmstead, *History of the Persian Empire* (Chicago: University of Chicago Press, 1948), 291.

6. Olmstead, *History of the Persian Empire*, 298.

7. Mervin Breneman, *Ezra, Nehemiah, Esther*, NAC 10 (Nashville: Broadman & Holman, 1993), 201.

the walls by their Judean neighbors, a famine, the probable overpricing of food by greedy merchants, the exorbitant amount of taxes the Persian king collected, and astronomical interest rates by greedy loan sharks who were taking advantage of their own countrymen.

II. A GODLY LEADER SHOWS CONCERN
BY GIVING PROTECTION (5:6–13)

> [6] Then I was very angry when I had heard their outcry and these words. [7] I consulted with myself and contended with the nobles and the rulers and said to them, "You are exacting usury, each from his brother!" Therefore, I held a great assembly against them. [8] I said to them, "We according to our ability have redeemed our Jewish brothers who were sold to the nations; now would you even sell your brothers that they may be sold to us?" Then they were silent and could not find a word *to say*. [9] Again I said, "The thing which you are doing is not good; should you not walk in the fear of our God because of the reproach of the nations, our enemies? [10] And likewise I, my brothers and my servants are lending them money and grain. Please, let us leave off this usury. [11] Please, give back to them this very day their fields, their vineyards, their olive groves and their houses, also the hundredth *part* of the money and of the grain, the new wine and the oil that you are exacting from them." [12] Then they said, "We will give *it* back and will require nothing from them; we will do exactly as you say." So I called the priests and took an oath from them that they would do according to this promise. [13] I also shook out the front of my garment and said, "Thus may God shake out every man from his house and from his possessions who does not fulfill this promise; even thus may he be shaken out and emptied." And all the assembly said, "Amen!" And they praised the LORD. Then the people did according to this promise.

Nehemiah responds with anger, but he does not allow his anger to cloud his judgment. After seriously considering the matters, he confronts the nobles concerning their breaking God's law by charging interest on loans to their own countrymen (see Exod 22:24–26; Lev 25:35–37; Deut 23:20–21). Next, he calls an assembly. While they were purchasing their enslaved countrymen from foreigners, they themselves were putting their brothers back into slavery and selling them to others. Nehemiah challenges them to give back the properties and interest they have acquired by the loans they made, and they agree to do so. Next, he makes them publicly take an oath to do what they promised. Nehemiah follows this with a pronounced curse on them should they fail to keep their oath. All of this results in the people's praising the Lord and doing what they promised to do. Two things stand out about Nehemiah's confrontation with the moneylenders. First, he includes himself in the rebuke. Second, Nehemiah is concerned about the reputation of God's people. Why? Because the reputation of the people of God is closely tied to the Lord's reputation. The people of God bringing reproach on themselves means bringing reproach on God.

A. Giving Protection to the Community of Faith Sometimes Springs from Righteous Anger (5:6)

Nehemiah states, "Then I was very angry when I had heard their outcry and these words." Was Nehemiah's anger a sin? Possibly. The Bible records what the people of God did, but that does not mean what they did was always right. Is it ever right for a believer to get angry? And if the answer is "yes," then when is it right for a believer to get angry? The idea of righteous anger is difficult for many to comprehend. After all, overall the Scriptures appear to frown on the emotion of anger. For instance, James writes, "for the anger of man does not achieve the righteousness of God" (Jas 1:20). And the apostle Paul writes, "Let all bitterness and wrath and anger and clamor and slander be put away from you, along with malice. Be kind to one another, tender-hearted, forgiving each other, just as God in Christ also has forgiven you" (Eph 4:31–32). Taken at face value, James' and Paul's words appear to be very clear. However, just four verses earlier Paul writes, "Be angry, and yet do not sin; do not let the sun go down on your anger, and do not give the devil an opportunity."

Therefore, according to Paul, there are times a believer may be angry. So, when are those times? Bob Deffinbaugh's study "Righteous Anger" is helpful. In it he outlines the characteristics of righteous indignation, which are distinct from the anger of humankind that fails to achieve the righteousness of God.[8] Here are the characteristics:

1. "Godly people are angry when God is angry. It is anger which is consistent with the holy and righteous character of God."

---

8. Bob Deffinbaugh, "Righteous Anger (Ephesians 4:26–27)," Bible.org, https://Bible.org/seriespage/14-righteous-anger-ephesians-426-27 (accessed August 30, 2017).

2. "Godly anger is legal anger. It is wrath based upon men's violation
    of God's law, and it is anger which is lawfully expressed. ... Godly
    anger is not vigilante justice, it is legal justice. Those who hate
    abortion but express their anger in the burning of abortion clin-
    ics (and thereby endangering other lives) are not expressing their
    anger legally" (see 2 Pet 2:8).

3. "Godly anger is not explosive, but is only slowly provoked" (see
    Exod. 34:6).

4. "God does not take pleasure in expressing His anger in the judg-
    ment of men" (2 Pet 3:9).

5. "Godly anger is always under control. ... Godly anger is always
    under the control of the one expressing it, rather than anger taking
    control of them" (Ps 78:38).

This fifth characteristic is apparent when Jesus cleanses the temple (John 2:13–17).
Verse 15 states Jesus "made a scourge of cords." He demonstrates a cool head
as he meticulously takes the time to make the whip. Jesus' actions are deliber-
ate and measured. He is in full control of his emotions. Verse 17 in this passage
reveals another characteristic of righteous indignation or anger. When Jesus is
done clearing out the moneychangers from the temple, the disciples remember
that it is written in Psalm 69:9, "For zeal for Your house has consumed me, and
the reproaches of those who reproach you have fallen on me." And even though
the first characteristic on Deffinbaugh's list covers this, a sixth characteristic
should be added to the list for emphasis. The sixth characteristic is "Godly anger
is zealous for that which pertains to God and for the glory of God." Jesus' anger
when he cleared out the temple arose out of a zeal for the house of God and the
glory of God. Also, there is a seventh characteristic of righteous anger that Jesus
demonstrates. "Righteous anger seeks to put an end to wrongdoing and injustice." It will be done in a godly or "legal" way, as Deffinbaugh states, but action
will be taken nonetheless.

So, given these seven characteristics, is Nehemiah's anger a righteous anger?
The prophet Amos makes it clear that God is angered when the people of God
take advantage of their brothers and sisters in the community of faith, especially when these brothers and sisters are in desperate straits. Nehemiah is angry
because some of the Judeans are taking advantage of their brothers and sisters
during a difficult time. So Nehemiah's anger has the first characteristic.

What about the second characteristic? As noted above, the moneylenders are breaking the law by charging other Judeans interest on loans. It is within the law to make a loan to a fellow Judean. They just are not allowed to charge interest on those loans (see Exod 22:24–26; Lev 25:35–37; Deut 23:20–21). Also, it is lawful to make loans and charge interest on loans to foreigners. The other issue is that on the one hand, as much as possible, the Judeans paid off the debts of fellow Judeans who had entered into servitude to foreigners because of their inability to pay off their loans. This is commendable and an application of what the law teaches in Leviticus 25:47–49. However, the Judean moneylenders are doing what the gentiles did. They are taking and keeping what little the poor have in their possession from them. This is a clear violation of the law (see Exod 22:25; Deut 24:10–11). As if that were not bad enough, they are selling them into slavery to gentiles—a repugnant act indeed and certainly contrary to God's will (see Ezek 27:13; Joel 3:3–8; Amos 1:9).[9] They are definitely in violation of God's law.

What about the third characteristic? Is Nehemiah's anger slowly provoked? Nehemiah's response comes after taking time to listen to all of the people's allegations. His anger is slowly provoked. What about the fourth characteristic? Nehemiah demonstrates no joy in confronting the nobles, as the following verses indicate. The only joy in the passage is the joy of everyone when the moneylenders repent of what they did (5:13). What about the fifth characteristic? Is Nehemiah in control of his anger? That he takes some time to think before he confronts the nobles and rulers affirms Nehemiah is indeed in control of his anger. And the sixth characteristic—Is Nehemiah zealous for that which pertains to God and the glory of God? Nehemiah's question in verse 9, "Should you not walk in the fear of our God because of the reproach of the nations, our enemies?" points not only to God's glory but Nehemiah's concern for the people of God. Nehemiah is zealous for the reputation of God's people and its reflection on the glory of God. Finally, Nehemiah's anger bears the seventh characteristic of righteous anger as he seeks a way to put an end to the injustice, and he does so in a godly manner. Nehemiah not only provides believers with an example of what is righteous anger, but he also shows us the kind of things that should make us angry and why. We should note that righteous anger is concerned about others and God—not about us.

---

9. Joseph Blenkinsopp, *Ezra-Nehemiah: A Commentary*, Old Testament Library (Philadelphia: Westminster, 1988), 259.

B. Giving Protection to the Community of Faith
Always Requires Careful Contemplation (5:7)

Proverbs 13:16 states, "Every prudent man acts with knowledge, but a fool displays folly." And Proverbs 17:27 states, "He who restrains his words has knowledge, and he who has a cool spirit is a man of understanding." In her article "Think before You React: Do You Think It Through or Automatically React?" Marci Fox writes the following concerning reacting to a situation:

> Take your emotional temperature and if it's high give yourself a timed "time out" to calm down the intensity of whatever you are feeling. That will give you the time you need to chill so that you can then think about your thoughts. Sometimes you realize that you were thinking about the situation incorrectly or may have overreacted all together. Other times you realize that your thinking was right on track but that you may need to figure out your next steps.[10]

In this potentially explosive situation, Nehemiah exercises wisdom by giving himself time to cool off and think about what needs to be done. The stakes are too high for him to react rashly. If he said or did the wrong thing, it would have jeopardized the entire project and brought greater reproach on him and the people. As Brown aptly states, "Anger is an appropriate but not a sufficient response. Emotional distress was followed by intellectual reflection which in turn led to practical action."[11]

C. Giving Protection to the Community of Faith Occasionally
Demands a Difficult Confrontation (5:7–12)

Nehemiah practices the same procedure as Ezra did in confronting those who were breaking God's law. He calls an assembly of everyone, winning the popular support. Then he isolates the lawbreakers who were exploiting the situation and the people and publicly confronts them. He calls them out for their exacting interest on loans to their brothers, for the confiscation of their properties, and for their repulsive practice of human trafficking, selling their countrymen into

---

10. Marci G. Fox, "Think before You React: Do You Think It Through or Automatically React?," Psychology Today, https://www.psychologytoday.com/blog/think-confident-be-confident/201106/think-you-react (accessed August 31, 2017).

11. Raymond Brown, The Message of Nehemiah, The Bible Speaks Today (Downers Grove, IL: InterVarsity Press, 1998), 89.

slavery. As a result, he forces them immediately to cease their damaging practices and make things right.[12]

D. *Giving Protection to the Community of Faith at Times Necessitates a Public Demonstration (5:13)*

Effective communication involves more than just words. Nehemiah understood this truth and employed the power of a public demonstration to communicate symbolically how important it was for the lenders to keep their word and the severity of God's judgment on them should they fail to do so. Concrete symbols are an effective way of solidifying the meaning of a message.[13] As Nehemiah shook out the front of his clothing he conveyed how God would "shake out every man from his house and his possessions" should he fail to keep his oath in the matter. Everyone not only heard the message but also vividly witnessed it in Nehemiah's emphatic, symbolic act.

III. A GODLY LEADER SHOWS CONCERN BY EXPRESSING COMPASSION (5:14–19)

[14] Moreover, from the day that I was appointed to be their governor in the land of Judah, from the twentieth year to the thirty-second year of King Artaxerxes, *for* twelve years, neither I nor my kinsmen have eaten the governor's food *allowance*. [15] But the former governors who were before me laid burdens on the people and took from them bread and wine besides forty shekels of silver; even their servants domineered the people. But I did not do so because of the fear of God. [16] I also applied myself to the work on this wall; we did not buy any land, and all my servants were gathered there for the work. [17] Moreover, *there were* at my table one hundred and fifty Jews and officials, besides those who came to us from the nations that were around us. [18] Now that which was prepared for each day was one ox *and* six choice sheep, also birds were prepared for me; and once in ten days all sorts of wine *were furnished* in abundance. Yet for all this I did not demand the governor's food *allowance*, because the

---

12. Blenkinsopp, *Ezra-Nehemiah*, 259.

13. Jim Durkel, "Nov-Verbal Communication: Cues, Signals and Symbols," Texas School for the Blind and Visually Impaired, https://www.tsbvi.edu/preschool/1725-non-verbal-communication-cues-signals-and-symbols (accessed November 11, 2019).

servitude was heavy on this people. [19] Remember me, O my God, for good, *according to* all that I have done for this people.

It is only now that Nehemiah mentions the king's appointment of him as governor over Judah. While Nehemiah's conversation with Artaxerxes in chapter 2 does not suggest either one of them thought Nehemiah would be in Jerusalem as long as he was, it is most probable the appointment came after Nehemiah arrived and they realized his work would require a longer commitment of time. Nehemiah reports he was governor over Judah for twelve years (445–433 BC).[14] Given Judah's reputation for being a rebellious region, the king was likely pleased to have someone he could trust overseeing and administrating the province. Given his ability to deal with issues that arose in the region, Nehemiah's tenure as governor must have brought more stability to the region—a benefit Persian kings certainly appreciated.

It is clear from the text that Nehemiah is quite wealthy. It is also apparent that as governor he collects the taxes for the king and is due a sizable income from the people as his salary. The per diem of provisions of various kinds of meats and wine the former governors required from the people amounted to a value of forty shekels. The idea that it was a heavy burden should probably be understood both figuratively and literally. It was a difficult burden for the people to pay, and it was literally heavy for them to carry.[15] It is possible the governors just took shekels for the taxes. If so, then it would explain the lending and borrowing that was happening and the people's inability to pay back the lenders. However the daily provisions for the governors was paid, the amount was a heavy burden to the people. The exploitation of the poor had been systemic in Judah for what appears to have been quite some time since their return from exile.

However, Nehemiah is committed to putting an end to the exploitation and instead shows compassion to the people of God. Every day he feeds 150 people in his home. Is Nehemiah's table actually able to fit 150 people around it at one time? Today the longest dining table in the world is in India, and it can accommodate one hundred people at a time.[16] The Persians were known for their opu-

---

14. Breneman, *Ezra, Nehemiah, Esther*, 207.

15. Altmann, *Economics in Persian-Period Biblical Texts*, 276.

16. "A Scorpion Shaped Building Holds the World's Largest Dinner Table! And It's in India!," MSN, https://www.msn.com/en-in/travel/tripideas/a-scorpion-shaped-building-holds-the-worlds-largest-dinner-table-and-its-in-india/ar-BBsQyhV (accessed September 6, 2017).

lence in many ways surpassing what even exists today, so it is possible a Persian governor might have such a table. However, it is more likely it should be understood metaphorically, given one Persian text indicates the Persian king's horses ate from the royal table.[17] But whether it should be understood literally or metaphorically, the point is the wealth Nehemiah has is vast, yet he uses it to be a blessing to the people of Judah.

A. Compassion Because of a Fear of God

About fifty to sixty years earlier, the prophet Zechariah preached these words to the people of Jerusalem,

> Thus has the LORD of hosts said, "Dispense true justice and practice kindness and compassion each to his brother; and do not oppress the widow or the orphan, the stranger or the poor; and do not devise evil in your hearts against one another. But they refused to pay attention and turned a stubborn shoulder and stopped their ears from hearing. They made their hearts *like* flint so that they could not hear the law and the words which the LORD of hosts had sent by His Spirit through the former prophets; therefore great wrath came from the LORD of hosts. And just as He called and they would not listen, so they called and I would not listen," says the LORD of hosts; "but I scattered them with a storm wind among all the nations whom they have not known. Thus the land is desolated behind them so that no one went back and forth, for they made the pleasant land desolate." (Zech 7:9–14)

Zechariah's words echo the law and the prophets who came before him, but for the most part, Israel ignored them. Nevertheless, while many of the people of Israel failed to listen to the warnings of God's prophets concerning their treatment of one another, especially their treatment of the weak and poor, Nehemiah gets the message loud and clear. He is not about to make the same mistakes others before him made and many of his contemporaries are making. To fear God involves being in awe of him. It also includes obeying God. It means identifying with God.

---

17. Wouter F. M. Henkelman, "'Consumed before the King': The Table of Darius, That of Irdabama and Irtaštuna, and That of His Satrap, Karkiš," in *Der Achämenidenhof: Akten des 2. Internationalen Kolloquiums zum Thema "Vorderasien im Spannungsfeld klassischer und altorientalischer Überlieferungen," Landgut Castelen Bei Basel, 23.–25. Mai 2007*, ed. B. Jacobs and R. Rollinger (Wiesbaden: Harrassowitz, 2010), 684.

Whatever God values, the one who fears him values too. Furthermore, it means having a healthy fear of God's discipline when one is disobedient to God. God's discipline of his children may be for our good, but it still often hurts. Nehemiah is a man who fears God and is not about to make the mistake others made and are making by being a burden to the people of God. For believers today, this takes on greater meaning as we realize the church is the bride of Christ. Our Lord will not overlook the mistreatment of his bride, and we should beware of being guilty of doing so.

B. Compassion Because of an Affection for the People of God

Therefore, it is natural to speak of having compassion for the community of faith because of a fear of God and having compassion for it because of affection for it. People who love God will identify themselves with his people and have an affection for his people. Peter Altmann states it well when he writes, "the passage emphasizes (1.) Nehemiah's solidarity with 'the people' in his economic decisions as provincial authority and (2.) his attempt to firm up his authority by causing others to become receivers from his table. Nehemiah conducts himself in a manner that puts community thriving above his financial opulence."[18] Every day Nehemiah generously feeds people out of his own pocket. Nehemiah is an example to the nobles of how a godly man of means should be sensitive to the needs of the less fortunate. We need to remember the words of James: "What use is it, my brethren, if someone says he has faith but he has no works? Can that faith save him? If a brother or sister is without clothing and in need of daily food, and one of you says to them, 'Go in peace, be warmed and be filled,' and yet you do not give them what is necessary for *their* body, what use is that? Even so faith, if it has no works, is dead, *being* by itself" (Jas 2:14–17).

Nehemiah has wealth, but his wealth does not have him. What "has" Nehemiah is a burning desire for removing the reproach from the people of God and a fervent commitment to bring glory to God. That is what Nehemiah wants God to see in him and what he wants to be remembered for.

---

18. Altmann, *Economics in Persian-Period Biblical Texts*, 278.

CONCLUSION

Believers can learn a number of lessons from Nehemiah in this passage. First, Christians who care about the needs of others see the needs, listen to concerns, and do not ignore them. True concern for others may begin with an emotion, but it is always accompanied with action. Too often Christian leaders get so embroiled in administration they fail to communicate sincere concern to the very people to whom they desire to minister. They are so busy doing "the Lord's work" that they don't have time to see people's needs or listen to their concerns. They unintentionally ignore the very people to whom God has called them to minister. Busyness is often the enemy of godliness. Second, in the spirit of Christ believers should actively oppose the exploitation of others, especially the exploitation of fellow believers by other believers. It should be done with a desire for reconciliation and restoration for the glory of Christ. Third, to be effective in serving others, believers must be people of integrity. They must practice what they preach. If we are to have an impact for the kingdom of Christ, people must not only hear our message but they must also see it genuinely lived out in our lives daily. There is no place for a "do as I say, not as I do" mentality among the people of God. Finally, when believers serve others, they can rest assured God will not forget what they have done. Jesus taught that when we serve others, we serve him, and there is no way he will be indebted to us and "owe us one." He will remember our compassion for others (Matt 25:31–46).

FINAL THOUGHTS

1. What needs do you see in people's lives around you, and what are you doing to help them?
2. In what ways might you be guilty of taking advantage of others?
3. When you get angry, is it more often righteous anger or self-centered anger?
4. How does a fear of God impact your decisions and how you live?
5. In what ways are you an example to others of a believer whose desire is to serve others for the glory of Christ?

OPPOSITION BY MANIPULATION AND INTIMIDATION

Nehemiah 6:1–19

INTRODUCTION

Thirty years ago I was pastoring my first church. It had been a very strong church in that community, but because of infighting it had dwindled to but a handful of people when I became its pastor at twenty-three years of age. Things were relatively calm at first, but as we began to grow I began to witness just what had happened to nearly kill the church: manipulation by intimidation. In the church's business meetings, it was the loudest and most intimidating people who began bullying and cowing others to get their way. There were good people in the church, but they had been worn down by the years of browbeating. Godly people do not enjoy fighting, but ungodly people thrive on it. However, the manipulators and intimidators were unable to stop the work. By the grace of God the church survived, and God blessed its ministry as it continued to grow. One of the enemy's strategies to destroy the work of the people of God is manipulation and intimidation. It is what Nehemiah deals with as the building project is coming to completion.

STRUCTURE

The passage has two sections. The first section (6:1–14) recounts how the enemies of God attempt to manipulate and intimidate Nehemiah. The second section (6:15–19) announces the completion of the wall and the reactions of the enemy to the wall's completion.[1]

---

1. H. G. M. Williamson divides the chapter into three sections: vv. 1–9, 10–14, and 15–19. Literally, this is accurate, as it forms kind of a simple chiastic structure, but topically, the actions of 1–14 are all connected, with various attempts by Nehemiah's enemies to stop him before the completion of the wall. Williamson admits vv. 1–9 and 10–14 are closely connected, while vv. 15–19 appear to be "somewhat more isolated" in the chapter. See Williamson, *Ezra, Nehemiah*, Word Biblical Commentary

SUMMARY OF THE PASSAGE

The passage demonstrates what the enemies of God are willing to do to try to destroy God's work, and it depicts what happens when they realize they cannot succeed in opposing him.

OUTLINE OF THE PASSAGE

I. The Opposition to the Completion of the Wall: Manipulation and Intimidation (6:1–14)

    A. Phase One: False friendship (6:1–4)

    B. Phase Two: Subversive slander (6:5–9)

    C. Phase Three: Compromised commitment (6:10–14)

II. The Declaration of the Completion of the Wall: Affirmation and Attestation (6:15)

III. The Reaction to the Completion of the Wall: Deflation and Aspiration (6:16–19)

    A. The reaction at large (6:16)

    B. The reaction of a few (6:17–19)

DEVELOPMENT OF THE EXPOSITION

I. The Opposition to the Completion of the Wall: Manipulation and Intimidation (6:1–14)

¹ Now when it was reported to Sanballat, Tobiah, to Geshem the Arab and to the rest of our enemies that I had rebuilt the wall, and *that* no breach remained in it, although at that time I had not set up the doors in the gates, ² then Sanballat and Geshem sent *a message* to me, saying, "Come, let us meet together at Chephirim in the plain of Ono." But they were planning to harm me. ³ So I sent messengers to them, saying, "I am doing a great work and I cannot come down. Why should the work stop while I leave it and come down to you?" ⁴ They sent *messages* to me four times in this manner, and I answered them in the same way .⁵ Then Sanballat sent his servant to me in the same manner a fifth time with an open letter in his hand. ⁶ In it was written, "It is reported among the nations, and

---

(Nashville: Thomas Nelson, 1985), 251. Semitic chiastic structures can pose a challenge to Western preachers and teachers because they are different from usual Western structures of logic or argument.

Gashmu says, that you and the Jews are planning to rebel; therefore you are rebuilding the wall. And you are to be their king, according to these reports. ⁷ You have also appointed prophets to proclaim in Jerusalem concerning you, 'A king is in Judah!' And now it will be reported to the king according to these reports. So come now, let us take counsel together." ⁸ Then I sent *a message* to him saying, "Such things as you are saying have not been done, but you are inventing them in your own mind." ⁹ For all of them were *trying* to frighten us, thinking, "They will become discouraged with the work and it will not be done." But now, *O God*, strengthen my hands. ¹⁰ When I entered the house of Shemaiah the son of Delaiah, son of Mehetabel, who was confined at home, he said, "Let us meet together in the house of God, within the temple, and let us close the doors of the temple, for they are coming to kill you, and they are coming to kill you at night." ¹¹ But I said, "Should a man like me flee? And could one such as I go into the temple to save his life? I will not go in." ¹² Then I perceived that surely God had not sent him, but he uttered *his* prophecy against me because Tobiah and Sanballat had hired him. ¹³ He was hired for this reason, that I might become frightened and act accordingly and sin, so that they might have an evil report in order that they could reproach me. ¹⁴ Remember, O my God, Tobiah and Sanballat according to these works of theirs, and also Noadiah the prophetess and the rest of the prophets who were *trying* to frighten me.

A. Phase One: False Friendship (6:1–4)

Recognizing the wall is near completion and that their strategies so far to stop the work have failed, Nehemiah's enemies make last-ditch efforts to eliminate Nehemiah himself. If they could eliminate the leader, perhaps they could completely derail the efforts to revitalize Jerusalem. Brown states it well when he writes,

> The opponents saw that there was little hope of destroying Nehemiah's work but there was still time to bring him down personally. By now they realized that he had not just come to Jerusalem to tackle an important building assignment. He was determined to establish the community as well as secure the city. He was not simply a works manager. God had raised up an influential spiritual leader. So his enemies set their hearts on

destroying him, and the only way to get at such a well-protected citizen was to lure him from his colleagues and on to enemy territory. Once kidnapped, they could easily dispose of him. In order to satisfy the Persian king, a plausible story could be easily fabricated attributing his death to the sudden attack of robbers.[2]

The Plain of Ono was located near the border of the provinces of Judah, Samaria, and Ashdod and was most likely near a number of people who wanted Nehemiah dead.[3] It definitely was a great distance from Nehemiah's home and allies, twenty-seven miles northwest of Jerusalem. Sanballat, Tobiah, Geshem, and those who joined them try to appear more conciliatory toward Nehemiah in their message, as they literally come to meet him halfway, given the wall itself is completed but for the hanging of some doors in the gates. They try to appeal to Nehemiah's sense of accomplishment, his pride and sense of reason, which essentially can be pride.[4] Basically, their message is, "We recognize we have openly ridiculed you and the work you have been doing, but we are big enough to admit we were wrong. You accomplished a great feat, and we have the utmost respect for you and your ability to assert yourself to become such a powerful and influential man. As likeminded men of renown ourselves and fellow leaders of our peoples, let us come together for a summit where we can celebrate your success and converse about our mutual goals and advancement in the region." Yet all along, their intention is to harm him.

What they were attempting to do is similar to what Pope John XXIII (who was pope from 1410 to 1415 and not to be confused with the modern pope of the same name) did to one of Luther's heroes, John Huss. Huss came to realize that the Scriptures were the sole authority for believers. This conviction solidified when the pope authorized the selling of indulgences in order to finance a campaign against one of his rivals. Huss preached that Christ alone is the head of the church and that the pope can make mistakes, and that to refuse to submit to such a pope is the will of Christ. The Holy Roman Emperor Sigismund urged Huss to

---

2. Raymond Brown, *The Message of Nehemiah*, The Bible Speaks Today (Downers Grove, IL: InterVarsity Press, 1998), 100.

3. Joseph Blenkinsopp, *Ezra-Nehemiah: A Commentary*, Old Testament Library (Philadelphia: Westminster, 1988), 268.

4. J. I. Packer, *A Passion for Faithfulness: Wisdom from the Book of Nehemiah* (Wheaton, IL: Crossway, 1995), 128.

come to the Council of Constance in November 1414 to give an account of his doctrine. Sigismund promised Huss safe conduct, and because the council had the potential of bringing about substantial church reforms, Huss consented to go. When he arrived Huss was immediately arrested and harassed in an attempt to denounce his beliefs. When he realized he was being railroaded by the council he stated, "I appeal to Jesus Christ, the only judge who is almighty and completely just. In his hands I plead my cause, not on the basis of false witnesses and erring councils, but on truth and justice." In July 1415 John Huss was burned at the stake as a heretic as he recited from the Psalms.[5]

In more recent history, it was much like what the Nazis did in the German-Soviet Non-aggression Pact of 1939, in which leaders of Nazi Germany and the Soviet Union signed an agreement of peace with each other, paving the way for their mutual domination of Eastern Europe and Germany's attack on France. However, unknown to Stalin, as the pact was being signed, Hitler was already making plans to conquer the Soviet Union. Operation Barbarossa, the invasion of Soviet-held territories and the Soviet Union itself, began in the summer of 1941.[6] The guise of false friendship is a common ploy of the wicked.

Nonetheless, unlike Huss or Stalin, Nehemiah does not fall for the trap of his enemies. McConville observes Nehemiah's enemies must really be hoping this strategy will work, seeing as they will not take no for an answer and attempt it four times.[7] Acclaim and complimentary words accompanied by a recognition of accomplishment and power can all work together to become an intoxicating temptation to pride. Just as strong is the temptation to want others to see us as reasonable as opposed to hardheaded and intractable. The temptation is to "go along" with others so that we can "get along" with others. Most believers want to be seen by others as peaceable and reasonable, not antagonistic and close-minded. And, of course, as believers we should want to be peaceable and reasonable. However, when our desire to be peaceable and reasonable is so that we can somehow benefit from it ourselves and gain the respect of others, with little to no concern for what is right before God and his calling on our lives, it quickly turns into compromise and pride.

---

5.   "John Huss: Pre-Reformation Reformer," *Christianity Today*, http://www.christianitytoday.com/history/people/martyrs/john-huss.html (accessed September 13, 2017).

6.   Christopher Klein, "The Secret Hitler-Stalin Pact," history.com, http://www.history.com/news/the-secret-hitler-stalin-pact-75-years-ago (accessed September 12, 2017).

7.   J. G. McConville, *Ezra, Nehemiah, and Esther* (Louisville: Westminster John Knox, 1985), 104.

Nehemiah's response is telling in what he says and by what he does not say. What he says was, "I am doing a great work and I cannot come down. Why should the work stop while I leave it and come down to you?" Nehemiah is focused on what God put into his heart to do. If there is a word that can describe believers who make a profound impact for the kingdom of Christ it is the word "focused." Nehemiah's message is similar to that of the apostle Paul, who writes the Philippians, "Brethren, I do not regard myself as having laid hold of *it* yet; but one thing I *do*: forgetting what *lies* behind and reaching forward to what *lies* ahead, I press on toward the goal for the prize of the upward call of God in Christ Jesus" (Phil 3:13–14). Nehemiah's words also reveal the attitude of the Lord Jesus Christ himself, who tells his disciples, "My food is to do the will of him who sent me and to accomplish his work" (John 4:34). Like Christ, Nehemiah states he is not about to be distracted from completing the will of his heavenly Father for his life.

However, not only is what Nehemiah says revealing, but what he does not say is revealing as well. He does not give in to the powerful temptation of pride. It is all too easy to become intoxicated by the praise of others. Nehemiah keeps himself away from such pride. His ability to do this is evidenced throughout the book, but in this chapter, verse 9 reveals it again when he prays, "But now, O God, strengthen my hands." Nehemiah's continued dependence on God protects him from the sin of pride and at the same time fills him with courage.

What's more, Nehemiah sees through their ruse. How could men who have all along opposed Nehemiah and threatened the lives of the workers now turn about-face and want to befriend Nehemiah? Nehemiah has had plenty of dealings with them to know the truth about them. If these men had truly repented, then they would have demonstrated fruit of repentance in a manner at least equal to the measure of their assaults against Nehemiah and the workers. Nehemiah is unwilling to get attached to wicked men. Unlike King Joram of Judah, who attached himself to the wicked house of King Ahab in Israel by marrying his daughter Athaliah, bringing God's judgment on himself and Judah, Nehemiah stays away from dangerous attachments no matter how alluring they may present themselves to be (see 2 Kgs 8:16–29). Nehemiah is not misled. He realizes "bad company corrupts good character" (see 1 Cor 15:33).

B. Phase Two: Subversive Slander (6:5–9)

When he realizes the parley is a bust after four attempts at it, casting away any of his false pretenses, Sanballat dips into his hat to try a strategy similar to what proved successful in the past with King Artaxerxes. When the Judean exiles first returned to Jerusalem, they began rebuilding the temple in Jerusalem. The reaction of their enemies was to write a letter to Artaxerxes saying that the returnees were rebuilding Jerusalem in order to rebel against the king. The letter stated the king was about to lose the province and the revenues he took from it. As a result, Artaxerxes put a stop to the rebuilding of Jerusalem and stated they could not do any more reconstruction until he decreed they could resume the work (Ezra 4:6–24).

In this instance, Sanballat decides against sending Artaxerxes a letter. Instead, he sends an open letter to Nehemiah, accusing Nehemiah of insurrection against the king. The text does not indicate why Sanballat chooses not to send a letter directly to Artaxerxes, but it is probably because he realizes Nehemiah is liked by the king. If Sanballat were to send false accusations against Nehemiah to Artaxerxes, it is possible the king would believe them, but it is just as possible the accusations could anger the king and Artaxerxes might have Sanballat executed. It is safer for Sanballat to try to frighten Nehemiah without directly involving the king. And if word of such a rumor got back to Artaxerxes, Sanballat would be less likely to be implicated.

The accusations are serious because Judah actually does have a history of rebelling against its suzerains. They rebelled twice against Nebuchadnezzar, with the result that he ordered the complete destruction of Jerusalem because of their rebellions (2 Kgs 25:1–30). Also, the Persians were particularly sensitive to the threat of rebellion. Because of the vastness of their empire, it was difficult to keep control over everyone. Rebellions popped up quite often. So Sanballat's accusations are linked to irrefutable past actions of Judah. The best lies come as near to the truth as possible. Furthermore, it was no secret that the prophets were anticipating a Davidic Messiah who would restore Jerusalem to future and independent glory. One of the most messianic preaching prophets, Zechariah, prophesied to Jerusalem when the returnees rebuilt the temple. Was Nehemiah of Davidic descent? Probably not. *But* he could have been. Was King Artaxerxes' friend and confidant really seeking a throne for himself? No. *But* he could have been. After all, past confidants and even sons of the king had attempted to take the throne of past Persian kings, so why not Nehemiah?[8] Sanballat's craftiness knows no end. Given the past, these claims are at least plausible from a Persian perspective. Barber describes what Sanballat is hoping to accomplish quite well when he writes,

> This attack on Nehemiah takes advantage of an important psychologi-
> cal principle. People are always quick to believe the worst about others.
> Think, if you will, of how often scandal spreads through an office or a
> church. The faintest hint at indiscreet behavior and the person concerned
> is pronounced guilty. To malign Nehemiah's motives is, therefore, very
> easy. The libel may be totally false, yet it is impossible for the victim of
> such calumny ever to clear his name with everyone who gives ear to the
> reports. The implication of Nehemiah's supposed treasonous activities
> is nothing less than attempted blackmail. The strength of their scheme
> lies in man's innate fear of reprisal. To anyone less heroic, their diabolic
> threat would have been overwhelmingly powerful.[9]

Nehemiah's response to this wicked and absurd accusation is to the point: "Such things as you are saying have not been done, but you are inventing them in your own mind." Nehemiah understands the enemy's ploy to frighten him and the people of Jerusalem, but he is not intimidated. Instead, he prays to God to "strengthen" his hands. This is the response every believer should have when the devil tries to frighten us from obediently serving the Lord. If all of us had the same trust in God Nehemiah had, then we would all be equally courageous.

C. Phase Three: Compromised Commitment (6:10–14)

In verses 10–14, Nehemiah encounters two temptations to compromise his com-
mitment to Yahweh. The first temptation comes from the mouth of a prophet named Shemaiah. The text indicates Shemaiah was confined to his home, but it provides no explanation for the confinement.[10] It is possible he confined himself because he believed or was acting like he believed his life was in danger. It is possible he was confined to his home because of being in an unclean state, but if

---

8. F. Charles Fensham, *The Books of Ezra and Nehemiah*, New International Commentary on the Old Testament (Grand Rapids: Eerdmans, 1982), 201–2.

9. Cyril J. Barber, *Nehemiah: An Expositional Commentary* (Eugene, OR: Wipf & Stock, 1991), 112–13.

10. For an overview of these possibilities see Fensham, *Books of Ezra and Nehemiah*, 205.

this were the case, then it makes no sense he would suggest going to the temple because he would not have been permitted to go there. Another suggestion is that he confined himself to convey a symbolic message to Nehemiah, demonstrating that Nehemiah needed to protect himself by confining himself in the temple. Whatever the reason for Shemaiah's confinement, it was a convenient way of getting Nehemiah to come to him instead of his going to Nehemiah. By doing so, it could possibly make Nehemiah look weak, uncertain, and in need of counsel, for surely such a visit from the governor would have become public knowledge.[11] Shemaiah's prophecy is simple. He tells Nehemiah that his enemies are coming to kill him, they are coming to kill him that very night. But unlike many people who are bearers of bad news without any solution, Shemaiah also proposes a plan to save Nehemiah. He states that he and Nehemiah should go into the temple for asylum. So the first temptation is twofold: (1) hide and show yourself a coward, and (2) disregard God's law concerning your being forbidden to enter the temple since you are not a priest and save your life. It is possible Shemaiah was himself permitted to enter the temple since he was of Delaiah's family. In Ezra 2:60, there is a Delaiah who is part of the Levites, associates to the priests in the temple, and 1 Chronicles 24:18 mentions a Delaiah who is a priest. If Shemaiah was related to either of these Delaiahs, then he would have at least been well acquainted with the temple precincts, and if he were a priest, then he would have actually been permitted to enter the temple. Nevertheless, by God's law Nehemiah is not permitted to enter (see Num 18:2–7).[12] Had Nehemiah entered into the temple, he would have been guilty of committing a capital offense. Thus, Tobiah and Sanballat could have accomplished Nehemiah's execution without getting their own hands dirty.

Even though Nehemiah initially does not realize Shemaiah was paid by Tobiah and Sanballat to proclaim this false prophecy to Nehemiah in order to frighten him and cause him to sin, Nehemiah has enough discernment to reject Shemaiah's message. Why? Because he is unwilling to do anything that would bring further reproach to his people on top of what they have already suffered, and he is unwilling to disobey his God.

---

11. Derek Kidner, *Ezra and Nehemiah*, Tyndale Old Testament Commentaries 12 (Downers Grove, IL: IVP Academic, 1979), 108.

12. Delaiah appears to have been a common name, so it is just as possible the Delaiah in this passage has no Levitical or priestly connection.

So what is the second temptation Nehemiah dealt with in this incident? It is the temptation to lose faith in God because of losing faith in spiritual leaders. Apparently, Shemaiah is accompanied by Noadiah the prophetess and other prophets who also try to frighten Nehemiah. Shemaiah is not alone. Nevertheless, Nehemiah does not waver in his faith in God or his service to the people of God. In chapter 8, we can see how Nehemiah goes on to join with Ezra the priest and scribe and other spiritual leaders to minister God's word to the people. Multitudes have turned away from God and the people of God because of the misdeeds of so-called spiritual leaders. It is a strong temptation to become disillusioned and quit serving the Lord because of ungodly laypeople and leaders in the community of faith, whether in Old Testament Israel or in the church today. Like Nehemiah, using Jesus' analogy of wheat and tares, we must not allow the "tares" among us to keep us from faithfully serving Christ and his church (Matt 13:24–30). We must not be surprised, disheartened, or cynical about Christ's church or serving him on account of sinful people, even if they are brothers and sisters in Christ. Even our Lord had an imposter as one of his disciples. Years ago a friend of mine went to be the pastor of a church where the former pastor had several moral failures, to the chagrin of the church. Soon after my friend got to the church, a woman came up to him and said, "I will never trust another pastor ever again." She was a nurse, so my friend replied to her, "Well, I will never trust another nurse again." She got the message. Just because a person may have experienced poor medical care by a doctor or nurse, it does not mean they will never go to another one. It just means they will go to a different one. And just because there are ungodly laypeople and leaders in churches, it does not mean all of the laypeople and leaders in the church are ungodly. Nehemiah is able to make that distinction, and it will do us well to be able make the same distinction too.

Typically, after responding to Shemaiah, Nehemiah prays. One might be surprised by the tenor of Nehemiah's prayer, thinking it sounds vindictive. However, Nehemiah's prayer is God-centered, not Nehemiah-centered. The enemy's attempt to intimidate Nehemiah is an attempt to put an end to the work God put in Nehemiah's heart and ordained his people to do. It is impossible for Nehemiah to be committed to God's call on his life and at the same time not be in opposition to those who opposed God, the people of God, and the mission of God. Nehemiah prays in the spirit of David, who under the inspiration of the Holy Spirit in Psalm 68:1 writes, "Let God arise, let His enemies be scattered, And let those who hate Him flee before Him." Nehemiah's prayer also is in line with what Christ will do in the future when "He has abolished all rule and all authority and power. For He must reign until He has put all His enemies under His feet" (1 Cor 15:24–25). A legitimate question believers might ask today is, "Are our prayers in line with the prayers and purpose of Nehemiah, David, and the Lord Jesus Christ in these passages?"

II. THE DECLARATION OF THE COMPLETION OF THE WALL: AFFIRMATION AND ATTESTATION (6:15)

> [15] So the wall was completed on the twenty-fifth of *the month* Elul, in fifty-two days.

A concise, direct statement of truth carries much more weight than the bloviations of the masses. In the midst of the swirling gossip, intrigue, and instigating going on all around Nehemiah and the wall, he affirms what the peoples heard and attests to its validity by stating the actual date the work was completed and how long it took the workers of Jerusalem to do so. About six months after Nehemiah first heard of the condition of Jerusalem, while he was the cupbearer to the king in Susa, that which had been seemingly insurmountable was accomplished. The work had begun in the month of Ab, in early August. The completion of the project occurred in Elul, somewhere between mid-September and early October in 445 BC.[13]

Commentators provide several reasons why the workers completed their task in such a timely manner. For instance, restoration work had already been done on the wall previous to Nehemiah's arrival. Nehemiah was a great leader and administrator. The people were motivated by their fear of attack from their enemies. Jerusalem was small at the time. The work was of inferior quality, suggesting they did not take the time that would have been required to build a wall of high standard. And Nehemiah altered the location of the wall from its previous location in areas where the work would have been much more difficult to follow the same trek of the previous wall.[14] However, even though these statements are true, there are at least three overriding reasons the work was accomplished as it was. First, Nehemiah was committed to the glory of Yahweh and the removal of

---

13. The most popular date scholars believe the wall to have been completed on is Oct. 2. See Mervin Breneman, *Ezra, Nehemiah, Esther*, NAC 10 (Nashville: Broadman & Holman, 1993), 213.

14. See Fensham, *Books of Ezra and Nehemiah*, 206–7; Williamson, *Ezra, Nehemiah*, 260–61.

the reproach that had come on the people of God. Second, Nehemiah prayerfully and actively trusted in the Lord to give him and the people success in doing the work. And third, the people of God joined together cooperatively and enthusiastically to rebuild the wall. They had a mind to work. These three reasons provide a recipe for the successful execution and completion of God's purposes for his people. God will show himself strong and do amazing things on behalf of his people and through his people when the people of God follow this strategy.

III. The Reaction to the Completion of the Wall: Deflation and Aspiration (6:16–19)

> [16] When all our enemies heard *of it*, and all the nations surrounding us saw *it*, they lost their confidence; for they recognized that this work had been accomplished with the help of our God. [17] Also in those days many letters went from the nobles of Judah to Tobiah, and Tobiah's *letters* came to them. [18] For many in Judah were bound by oath to him because he was the son-in-law of Shecaniah the son of Arah, and his son Jehohanan had married the daughter of Meshullam the son of Berechiah. [19] Moreover, they were speaking about his good deeds in my presence and reported my words to him. Then Tobiah sent letters to frighten me.

A. The Reaction at Large (6:16)

In the Hebrew text, it literally states that "when all our enemies heard, and all the surrounding nations saw, they fell greatly in their own eyes." This indicates what one of their problems was all along: they were too great in their own eyes—so great they thought they could successfully oppose God and the people of God. At the heart of all sin is pride. These enemies of God overestimated their own strength and underestimated what the people of God could accomplish through God's strength.

Furthermore, anyone who tries to explain away the quickness and efficiency of Nehemiah and the workers through modern notions of effective leadership, administrative skill, and previous work on the wall without recognizing the hand of God in this project fails to recognize what not only Nehemiah and the workers recognized but also what their enemies recognized. Nehemiah literally states in Hebrew that the enemies surrounding Judah "knew that it was because of our God this work was accomplished." Everything and everyone that contributed to the accomplishment of the project was the result of God's divine hand. Both the people of God and the enemies of God know this truth. And as a result, the enemies are stunned, and their egos are deflated. Moreover, Sanballat's recruiting the nations surrounding Judah to join him in opposing the people of God only serves to display the magnificent work of Yahweh to a larger audience. Mervin Breneman summarizes it well, stating, "Judah's enemies tried to make Nehemiah and the Jews afraid; but in the end they were the ones who feared."[15]

These events foreshadow what happens on a grander scale between the nations of the earth and their kings in relationship to the Lord Jesus Christ. Psalm 2:1–9 declares the following:

> Why are the nations in an uproar
> And the peoples devising a vain thing?
> The kings of the earth take their stand
> And the rulers take counsel together
> Against the LORD and against His Anointed, saying,
> "Let us tear their fetters apart
> And cast away their cords from us!"
> He who sits in the heavens laughs,
> The Lord scoffs at them.
> Then He will speak to them in His anger
> And terrify them in His fury, saying,
> "But as for Me, I have installed My King
> Upon Zion, My holy mountain."
> "I will surely tell of the decree of the LORD:
> He said to Me, 'You are My Son,
> Today I have begotten You.
> 'Ask of Me, and I will surely give the nations as Your inheritance,
> And the *very* ends of the earth as Your possession.
> 'You shall break them with a rod of iron,
> You shall shatter them like earthenware.'"

Ultimately, the enemies of the Lord can never prevail, and the Lord Jesus Christ will terrify them and put an end to their foolish striving once and for all.

---

15. Breneman, *Ezra, Nehemiah, Esther*, 213–14.

B. The Reaction of a Few (6:17–19)

Nevertheless, even though they faced the reality of God's hand on Nehemiah and the people who worked to rebuild the wall, there are a few who are still determined to oppose Nehemiah. Throughout these events, opposition continues to be a reality with which Nehemiah contends. Tobiah, who is apparently a fellow Judean, persists to undermine Nehemiah. At first, Tobiah tries to appear noble in his efforts. After all, Tobiah's name means "Yahweh is good," and he named his son Jehohanan, meaning "Yahweh is gracious." Tobiah is very well connected and apparently wants to grasp a position of power in Judah. Tobiah married into two families of the Judean aristocracy. His son married the daughter of Meshullam, the son of Berachiah. He is most likely the same Meshullam who worked on the wall.[16] Also, Nehemiah 13:4 indicates he is related by marriage to Eliashib the priest. Tobiah's close association with Sanballat and his connections in Jerusalem no doubt explains how Nehemiah's enemies are so well-informed. All of this points to the possibility that there are those who are willing to help Nehemiah in rebuilding the wall who are less supportive of Nehemiah himself and the comprehensive reformation he envisions for the people of God.[17] Once the work is done, they are ready for Nehemiah to step aside. When Nehemiah does not fall for their letters commending Tobiah, Tobiah resorts to sending letters to Nehemiah in order to frighten him. Tobiah reveals his true intentions of opposing Nehemiah.

CONCLUSION

The enemy's attempt to get Nehemiah to compromise his calling is similar to what the tempter attempts to do to Jesus in the wilderness (see Matt 4:1–11; Mark 1:12–13; Luke 4:1–13). However, being a godly man, Nehemiah is not dissuaded from what he understands to be God's purpose for him. Similarly, the Lord Jesus Christ was not deterred from his mission of redemption. Success in the Christian life requires the believer have a clear understanding of God's word and will and a steadfast determination to fulfill it.

---

16. Andrew E. Steinmann, *Ezra and Nehemiah*, Concordia Commentary (St. Louis: Concordia, 2010), 470–71.

17. Williamson, *Ezra, Nehemiah*, 261.

FINAL THOUGHTS

1. Why should believers not be surprised by opposition to God's work? Why are we, then?
2. Given what happened to Nehemiah, from where might believers expect opposition?
3. What can believers learn from Nehemiah and his encounter with spiritual opposition?
4. How does prayer help believers in the midst of spiritual warfare? What should be the focus of such prayer?
5. What does Nehemiah 6 reveal about God?
6. How does Nehemiah 6 anticipate the person and work of the Lord Jesus Christ?

PRIORITIES IN MINISTRY

Nehemiah 7:1–73

INTRODUCTION

When I told a friend about my taking on this project of providing a resource for preachers and teachers to preach and teach through the book of Nehemiah, he asked me how I could possibly find anything useful to preach or teach from Nehemiah 7. I am sure my friend believes Nehemiah 7 has useful information for the person who wants to know what Nehemiah did immediately after the completion of the wall. However, I believe what he actually was asking was, "How is Nehemiah 7 'profitable for teaching, for reproof, for correction, for training in righteousness so that the man of God may be adequate, equipped for every good work' as stated in 2 Timothy 3:16–17?" Paul wrote this concerning "all Scripture." So, how do these seventy-three verses really benefit New Testament believers today? These are legitimate questions that should be asked of every passage of the Bible, especially because of what Paul wrote to Timothy in 2 Timothy 3.

Nehemiah 7 serves as a transition chapter for the book. The first half of the book of Nehemiah informs the reader of all the turn of events leading up to the beginning of the project of building the wall of Jerusalem and what happens all the way up to the point of its completion. The second half of the book reveals what steps Nehemiah takes to revitalize Jerusalem and be a catalyst for spiritual reformation and national revival for the people of God. Nehemiah 7 reports what Nehemiah does immediately after the wall is completed with an eye toward the future. It brings closure to the building project while introducing what Nehemiah is about to do to revitalize the city. Rebuilding the wall is only Nehemiah's first step in removing the reproach from those who returned from exile. The walls do not exist for their own sake. Their significance depends on what is supposed to be happening inside Jerusalem itself, the thriving of the community of God for the glory of God.

STRUCTURE

The passage is divided into two disproportionate sections. The first section (7:1–3) explains the steps and precautions Nehemiah takes to ensure the right kind of leadership and the safety of Jerusalem. The second section (7:4–73) shows how Nehemiah methodically sets out to strengthen Jerusalem's population by taking a census of the returnees.

SUMMARY OF THE PASSAGE

Now that the wall of the city of Jerusalem is completed, the text describes how Nehemiah takes steps to evaluate and strengthen the city's population and infrastructure so that it will flourish. It reveals the character traits of Nehemiah that allow him to successfully execute his priorities for Jerusalem and the returnees from exile.

OUTLINE OF THE PASSAGE

I. Qualities of Nehemiah's Character
- A. Prudent (1:1–3)
- B. Perceptive (7:4)
- C. Pliable (7:5)
- D. Predictable (7:5)
- E. Painstaking (7:6–73)

II. Priorities of Nehemiah's Calling
- A. The Praise of God (7:1)
- B. The Principles of God (7:2–3)
- C. The People of God (7:4–73)
- D. The Purpose of God (7:1–73)

DEVELOPMENT OF THE EXPOSITION

I. Qualities of Nehemiah's Character

A. Prudent (1:1–3)

> [1] Now when the wall was rebuilt and I had set up the doors, and the gatekeepers and the singers and the Levites were appointed, [2] then I put Hanani my brother, and Hananiah the commander of the fortress, in

charge of Jerusalem, for he was a faithful man and feared God more than many. [3] Then I said to them, "Do not let the gates of Jerusalem be opened until the sun is hot, and while they are standing *guard*, let them shut and bolt the doors. Also appoint guards from the inhabitants of Jerusalem, each at his post, and each in front of his own house."

According to Merriam-Webster, "prudence" is "the ability to govern and discipline oneself by the use of reason; sagacity or shrewdness in the management of affairs; skill and good judgment in the use of resources; and caution or circumspection as to danger or risk."[1] There is no person who has ever lived, besides the Lord Jesus Christ, who has exemplified every aspect of prudence better than Nehemiah did, and verses 1–3 provide an example of this truth.

Nehemiah realizes the enemies of the people of God have continuously tried to thwart the work of rebuilding the walls. Therefore, he has every reason to believe these antagonists will continue attempting to bring about his demise along with that of the people and the city proper. So establishing security for the safety of the city is a priority. As soon as the walls are completed and Nehemiah has set the doors in the gates of the city in place, he makes sure "the gatekeepers and the singers and the Levites were appointed." Some commentators believe the mention of "singers" and "Levites" here is a gloss, suggesting the gatekeepers had a "secular" responsibility while the singers and Levites had a more "sacred" or cultic role, or that the three groups were commonly linked but that it makes no sense for singers and Levites to be on guard duty (see Ezra 2:70; 10:24, 29, 40; Neh 7:72.). However, just as all three of these groups are associated with liturgical/spiritual responsibilities in the life of Israel, their appointment to watch over Jerusalem sends a powerful message.

Gatekeepers, in both the books of Ezra and Nehemiah, are associated with the singers and those serving at the temple.[2] In fact, in Nehemiah 12–13, they are numbered among the Levites and receive tithes. In 1 and 2 Chronicles, the gatekeepers are assumed to have Levitical status. They guard the entrances to the temple to protect its ritual purity and oversee the temple's furniture and

---

1. "Prudence," merriam-webster.com, https://www.merriam-webster.com/dictionary/prudence (accessed November 7, 2017).

2. Joseph Blenkinsopp, *Ezra-Nehemiah: A Commentary*, Old Testament Library (Philadelphia: Westminster, 1988), 276; see 1 Chr 9:2, 17–32; 15:18, 23–24; 16:38; 23:5; 26:1–19; 2 Chr 23:4; 31:14; 34:13.

supplies. So along with the Levites, who serve as associates to the priests and are involved in explaining God's instruction to the people, and along with the musicians and singers, who have a central role in leading the people in corporate worship, the gatekeepers are part of this new security force for Jerusalem. These spiritual leaders in the community are appointed to keep a watchful eye for enemies who threaten the safety of the people. Those who have been entrusted with the spiritual care of the people of God are also entrusted with looking out for their physical safety.

The Old Testament provides pictures in the material realm of spiritual truths, and such is the case in this passage. Speaking of spiritual leadership in the church, the author of Hebrews writes, "Obey your leaders, and submit to them; for they keep watch over your souls, as those who will give an account" (Heb 13:17). Just as the spiritual leaders in Jerusalem were appointed to guard the people, spiritual leaders in the church should be on constant alert for the attacks and even potential attacks of the enemy against the people of God. It is a responsibility leaders must take seriously. Spiritual leadership calls for prudence, "caution or circumspection as to danger or risk." Moreover, the believer's defense against the attacks of the enemy essentially includes knowing God's word, praising God with spiritual songs, keeping oneself pure, and giving oneself and one's resources for kingdom causes—all matters with which the gatekeepers, the singers, and the Levites are collectively connected. Such is their role as spiritual guardians for the people of God.

However, one must not be too quick to spiritualize these verses in Nehemiah. All too often, we may be guilty of setting that which we see as spiritual up against what we deem physical. This kind of thinking seems foreign to the teaching of Scripture. While we may recognize spiritual concerns are the priority, given they are eternal, here, as in other passages in Scripture, the text demonstrates a concern for both the spiritual and physical needs of people. The spiritual concern reveals itself by whom was chosen to guard the people, but the emphasis in the text is a concern for the physical safety of the people. Humans in general struggle with trying to have a balanced perspective in just about any matter, and believers, being human, often struggle with it too when it comes to understanding that God's concern for his people is holistic and all-inclusive. Therefore, we should also be diligent to care for people's spiritual and physical needs—lest we forget Jesus taught that when we care for others with physical needs we minister to him. Failure to do so has severe consequences. Our helping people with physical needs is evidence of spiritual priorities (Matt 25:31–46). One might meet the physical needs of others and be devoid of any spiritual life, but it is impossible to be spiritually motivated to serve Christ and at the same time neglect the physically needy around us. In other words, for the believer, caring for the physical needs of others is a spiritual endeavor. As James so aptly writes, it is evidence of our faith in Christ (Jas 2:15–17).

To ensure someone can give complete attention to Jerusalem's security, Nehemiah appoints specific leadership with the responsibility. There is debate among scholars on how one should read verse 2 in the Hebrew text. The original text can be translated with the understanding that Hanani and Hananiah are two separate individuals, or it could technically be translated as Steinmann translates it, "I placed my brother Hanani, that is Hananiah, the commander of the fortress, in charge of Jerusalem." Steinmann understands "Hanani" to be the familiar, shortened name Nehemiah called his brother, whose proper name before the people was "Hananiah." Those scholars who understand the verse to refer to two men look to verse 3, where Nehemiah states, "Then I said to them." They understand the third-person common plural "them" to refer to the two men in verse 2. However, Steinmann believes "them" refers to everyone in verses 1 and 2. He also finds it odd that Nehemiah says "he was a faithful man" instead of "they were faithful men," and he thinks Nehemiah said this about his brother to defend against any suggestion of nepotism. Steinmann also suggests it would have been a poor leadership strategy to have two individuals sharing one position of leadership should they have a disagreement.[3]

Nevertheless, every major English translation understands the verse to refer to two men.[4] If it refers to two men, it is possible Nehemiah's word of commendation about Hananiah and not his brother is a way of highlighting that what he is doing is not nepotism. I have seen fathers completely ignore sons who have done exceptional work for them and give all the commendation for a job to others for fear of showing nepotism. Also, there are those who argue shared leadership can be very workable and successful by maximizing more skills and talents.[5] Last, one should remember that both Hanani and Hananiah answered to Nehemiah, the governor. Though on a much smaller scale, it is similar to the military leaders

---

3. Andrew E. Steinmann, *Ezra and Nehemiah*, Concordia Commentary (St. Louis: Concordia, 2010), 481–82.

4. See NASB, ESV, CSV, NIV, MEV, KJV, NET, ISV, ASV, etc.

5. Marshall Goldsmith, "Sharing Leadership to Maximize Talent," *Harvard Business Review*, https://hbr.org/2010/05/sharing-leadership-to-maximize (accessed November 8, 2017).

in the Pentagon, who are responsible for national security, answering to their civilian commander in chief. More enlightened voices provide more issues and options to consider, yet in the end, one makes the final decision.

Nehemiah's description of Hananiah is noteworthy: "he was a faithful man and feared God more than many." Hananiah is the commander of the fortress, so one can safely assume he is knowledgeable about defenses, security, and leading armed forces. Nevertheless, what stands out to Nehemiah is Hananiah's faithfulness and fear of God. In an environment where it is difficult to know whom one can trust, Hananiah is trustworthy, and he is trustworthy because he "feared God more than most." Those who fear God stand in reverential awe of him, love him, worship him, obey him, and live for him.[6] "Fearing God" or "the fear of the Lord" are frequent expressions used throughout the Scriptures, yet they are nearly extinct in the conversations of believers today. However, in biblical vernacular, there is no greater description one could be given than to be described as one who "feared God." It was a person with this character who is needed to lead the gatekeepers, the singers, and Levites as they watch over the people of God in Jerusalem. Not only can Nehemiah and the people trust in Hananiah's abilities, but they can trust his character.

Nehemiah also demonstrates his prudence by the instruction he gives in verse 3. The phrase "Do not let the gates of Jerusalem be opened until the sun is hot, and while they are standing guard" could either mean they are to shut the gates at the time of the afternoon siesta (a vulnerable time of day) or that they are to shut the gates before sunset. Either understanding is possible, but the first makes more sense.[7] Furthermore, Nehemiah instructs the leaders to appoint guards from among the inhabitants of the Jerusalem to keep watch close to their homes, sort of a neighborhood watch group—the idea being, who could better spot suspicious activities than people in their own neighborhoods? So there is a plan to watch over the people as a whole, but they also initiate a strategy to provide for the safety of the people in their neighborhoods and for each family. It is a good model for the people of God to use in meeting the needs of the church today—corporate activities combined with small groups.

---

6. For an exceptional work concerning fearing God see Jerry Bridges, *The Joy of Fearing God* (Colorado Springs: WaterBrook, 1998).

7. Mervin Breneman, *Ezra, Nehemiah, Esther*, NAC 10 (Nashville: Broadman & Holman, 1993), 216. Williamson points out the vulnerability of attack in the mid-afternoon in ancient times: H. G. M. Williamson, *Ezra, Nehemiah*, Word Biblical Commentary (Nashville: Thomas Nelson, 1985), 270.

B. Perceptive (7:4)

> [4] Now the city was large and spacious, but the people in it were few and the houses were not built.

Nehemiah perceives Jerusalem will never become the strong city it once was or could be again until it has a thriving commerce and population. However, since its destruction at the hands of the Babylonian king Nebuchadnezzar in 587 BC, the city limped along at best. It nearly was in complete disrepair. Therefore, Jerusalem does not offer the opportunities the countryside offered to the returnees to make a living off the land. Furthermore, to see the holy city in such poor conditions and unprotected must have been emotionally disturbing to the exiles who had returned, just as it had been for Nehemiah when he received his brother's initial report concerning the city's condition.

Now that the renovations of the city and rebuilding of the wall are completed, the city is a "large and spacious" place ready to be inhabited and brought back to at least some semblance of its former glory. In many ways, this endeavor is probably more difficult than the rebuilding of the wall itself, since it requires the heads of households to move their families from their established homes and from their means of providing for the families in the countryside to a completely new urban environment. Nevertheless, Nehemiah has a God-given discernment, perceiving what needs to be done in order to completely restore Jerusalem to the glory of God. Our prayer should be that God would raise up more believers like Nehemiah with a God-given discernment to know and do God's will to God's glory.

C. Pliable (7:5)

> [5] Then my God put it into my heart to assemble the nobles, the officials and the people to be enrolled by genealogies. Then I found the book of the genealogy of those who came up first in which I found the following record:

According to Merriam-Webster.com, to be pliable means to be "yielding readily to others."[8] It is certainly an appropriate adjective to describe Nehemiah because

---

8. "Pliable," merriam-webster.com, https://www.merriam-webster.com/dictionary/pliable (accessed November 7, 2017).

he yields readily to whatever God "put into" his heart. As a result, Nehemiah has a heart for what is on God's heart, and Jerusalem is on God's heart. It always was and always will be. Note the following passages:

> Great is the LORD, and greatly to be praised,
> In the city of our God, His holy mountain.
> Beautiful in elevation, the joy of the whole earth,
> Is Mount Zion *in* the far north,
> The city of the great King.
> God, in her palaces,
> Has made Himself known as a stronghold.
> For, lo, the kings assembled themselves,
> They passed by together.
> They saw *it*, then they were amazed;
> They were terrified, they fled in alarm.
> Panic seized them there,
> Anguish, as of a woman in childbirth.
> With the east wind
> You break the ships of Tarshish.
> As we have heard, so have we seen
> In the city of the LORD of hosts, in the city of our God;
> God will establish her forever. *Selah.* (Ps 48:1–8)

> For the LORD has chosen Zion;
> He has desired it for His dwelling:
> "This is My resting place forever;
> here I will dwell, for I have chosen it.
> I will abundantly bless her provisions;
> I will satisfy her poor with bread.
> I will also clothe her priests with salvation,
> and her godly ones shall shout for joy." (Ps 132:12–16)

> So the angel who was speaking with me said to me, "Proclaim, saying, 'Thus says the LORD of hosts, "I am exceedingly jealous for Jerusalem and Zion."'" (Zech 1:14)

Because of his love and devotion to God, Nehemiah is easily influenced by him. Nehemiah acts on whatever God puts into his heart. What difference would it make in the church and world today if believers were as receptive and obedient to what God put into their hearts as Nehemiah was? Nehemiah is sensitive to the needs of the people in Jerusalem because he is receptive to God's will for his life. Moreover, Nehemiah is zealous for the revitalization of Jerusalem because God is. When we love God and are devoted to him, we love what he loves and are devoted to that to which he is devoted.

D. Predictable (7:5)

How is Nehemiah predictable in verse 5? It is predictable that once God puts something into Nehemiah's heart, he acts on it. Since the very beginning of his story, when Nehemiah heard about the reproach of Jerusalem and wept, fasted, prayed, and looked for an opportunity to do more by speaking to the king about it, Nehemiah has acted on what God put into his heart. In this instance, he finds the book of the genealogy of those who first returned to Jerusalem in order to begin formulating an equitable way to revitalize the city. Once again, Nehemiah's spiritual conviction is accompanied by practical action. The book of genealogy informs him of who returned and where they most likely settled on their return.

How many believers are satisfied with their inactivity when it comes to what God has called them to do? Perhaps we quickly come up with excuses for why we are unable to do it. Not so with Nehemiah—he does not allow time for doubt and excuses to creep in. Even if it means praying, fasting, and waiting for God to give him more direction, Nehemiah does what he knows he can do in response to God's call while he patiently waits for God to show him what more he needs to do. May we be so predictable that when God puts something into our hearts we always will enthusiastically respond to it with action.

E. Painstaking (7:6–73)

> [6] These are the people of the province who came up from the captivity of the exiles whom Nebuchadnezzar the king of Babylon had carried away, and who returned to Jerusalem and Judah, each to his city, [7] who came with Zerubbabel, Jeshua, Nehemiah, Azariah, Raamiah, Nahamani, Mordecai, Bilshan, Mispereth, Bigvai, Nehum, Baanah.
>
> The number of men of the people of Israel: [8] the sons of Parosh, 2,172; [9] the sons of Shephatiah, 372; [10] the sons of Arah, 652; [11] the sons of Pahath-moab of the sons of Jeshua and Joab, 2,818; [12] the sons of Elam, 1,254;

¹³ the sons of Zattu, 845;¹⁴ the sons of Zaccai, 760; ¹⁵ the sons of Binnui, 648; ¹⁶ the sons of Bebai, 628; ¹⁷ the sons of Azgad, 2,322; ¹⁸ the sons of Adonikam, 667; ¹⁹ the sons of Bigvai, 2,067; ²⁰ the sons of Adin, 655; ²¹ the sons of Ater, of Hezekiah, 98; ²² the sons of Hashum, 328; ²³ the sons of Bezai, 324; ²⁴ the sons of Hariph, 112; ²⁵ the sons of Gibeon, 95; ²⁶ the men of Bethlehem and Netophah, 188; ²⁷ the men of Anathoth, 128; ²⁸ the men of Beth-azmaveth, 42; ²⁹ the men of Kiriath-jearim, Chephirah and Beeroth, 743; ³⁰ the men of Ramah and Geba, 621; ³¹ the men of Michmas, 122; ³² the men of Bethel and Ai, 123; ³³ the men of the other Nebo, 52;³⁴ the sons of the other Elam, 1,254; ³⁵ the sons of Harim, 320; ³⁶ the men of Jericho, 345; ³⁷ the sons of Lod, Hadid and Ono, 721; ³⁸ the sons of Senaah, 3,930.

³⁹ The priests: the sons of Jedaiah of the house of Jeshua, 973; ⁴⁰ the sons of Immer, 1,052; ⁴¹ the sons of Pashhur, 1,247; ⁴² the sons of Harim, 1,017.

⁴³ The Levites: the sons of Jeshua, of Kadmiel, of the sons of Hodevah, 74. ⁴⁴ The singers: the sons of Asaph, 148. ⁴⁵ The gatekeepers: the sons of Shallum, the sons of Ater, the sons of Talmon, the sons of Akkub, the sons of Hatita, the sons of Shobai, 138.

⁴⁶ The temple servants: the sons of Ziha, the sons of Hasupha, the sons of Tabbaoth, ⁴⁷ the sons of Keros, the sons of Sia, the sons of Padon, ⁴⁸ the sons of Lebana, the sons of Hagaba, the sons of Shalmai, ⁴⁹ the sons of Hanan, the sons of Giddel, the sons of Gahar, ⁵⁰ the sons of Reaiah, the sons of Rezin, the sons of Nekoda, ⁵¹ the sons of Gazzam, the sons of Uzza, the sons of Paseah, ⁵² the sons of Besai, the sons of Meunim, the sons of Nephushesim, ⁵³ the sons of Bakbuk, the sons of Hakupha, the sons of Harhur, ⁵⁴ the sons of Bazlith, the sons of Mehida, the sons of Harsha,⁵⁵ the sons of Barkos, the sons of Sisera, the sons of Temah, ⁵⁶ the sons of Neziah, the sons of Hatipha.

⁵⁷ The sons of Solomon's servants: the sons of Sotai, the sons of Sophereth, the sons of Perida,⁵⁸ the sons of Jaala, the sons of Darkon, the sons of Giddel, ⁵⁹ the sons of Shephatiah, the sons of Hattil, the sons of Pochereth-hazzebaim, the sons of Amon.

⁶⁰ All the temple servants and the sons of Solomon's servants *were* 392.

⁶¹ These *were* they who came up from Tel-melah, Tel-harsha, Cherub, Addon and Immer; but they could not show their fathers' houses or their

descendants, whether they were of Israel: [62] the sons of Delaiah, the sons of Tobiah, the sons of Nekoda, 642. [63] Of the priests: the sons of Hobaiah, the sons of Hakkoz, the sons of Barzillai, who took a wife of the daughters of Barzillai, the Gileadite, and was named after them. [64] These searched *among* their ancestral registration, but it could not be located; therefore they were considered unclean *and excluded* from the priesthood. [65] The governor said to them that they should not eat from the most holy things until a priest arose with Urim and Thummim.

[66] The whole assembly together *was* 42,360, [67] besides their male and their female servants, of whom *there were* 7,337; and they had 245 male and female singers. [68] Their horses were 736; their mules, 245; [69] *their* camels, 435; *their* donkeys, 6,720.

[70] Some from among the heads of fathers' *households* gave to the work. The governor gave to the treasury 1,000 gold drachmas, 50 basins, 530 priests' garments. [71] Some of the heads of fathers' *households* gave into the treasury of the work 20,000 gold drachmas and 2,200 silver minas. [72] That which the rest of the people gave was 20,000 gold drachmas and 2,000 silver minas and 67 priests' garments.

[73] Now the priests, the Levites, the gatekeepers, the singers, some of the people, the temple servants and all Israel, lived in their cities.

And when the seventh month came, the sons of Israel *were* in their cities.

Basically, the list of names in this passage is the same as that in Ezra 2:1–70, with the exception of some small differences in a handful of numbers and names. It is possible that the book of the genealogy is a copy of Ezra's list or that Ezra and Nehemiah both recorded their lists from the book of genealogy. It is also possible someone in the process rounded the numbers and used the shortened forms or more familiar forms of people's names, while another used only precise numbers and formal names. Williamson argues that the list in Ezra 2 is dependent on Nehemiah 7.[9] Others argue Ezra's list came first. It is difficult to tell for sure.[10] In any case, the differences are negligible and have no bearing on one's understanding of what Nehemiah was doing.

---

9. Williamson, *Ezra, Nehemiah*, 28–32.

10. Fensham, *Books of Ezra and Nehemiah*, 49.

Nehemiah's list not only indicates that he learns who the first returnees were and where they probably settled, but it reveals what the people's standing or roles in the community are by how it is organized. Verse 7 most likely indicates who the leaders of the returnees are. Verses 8–25 reveal the number of people who belong to each clan that returned. Verses 26–38 indicate the villages and cities to which they belong. The largest number of people are from Senaah. The size of its number compared to the other numbers in this section and the fact that Senaah's location is unknown has caused a number of scholars to question whether it was a village or the name of a person or the designation of a particular type of people, such as commoners.[11] However, given its context in the list, it appears to have been a larger village or town. The next section of the list provides the names of the temple personnel in verses 39–60: the priests, the Levites, the temple singers, the gatekeepers, the temple servants, and the sons of Solomon's servants. The list concludes with the people's servants and livestock. Following the list of returnees, the text shows how they are a generous and sacrificially giving people (vv. 70–72). They give their material wealth and lives in order to glorify God. These godly people serve as a tremendous example of what the people of God are meant to be. Concerning this list, Warren Wiersbe rightly observes, "The important thing is not to count the people but to realize that these people counted. In leaving Babylon, they did much more than put their names on a list. They laid their lives on the altar and risked everything to obey the Lord and restore the Jewish nation. They were 'pioneers of faith' who trusted God to enable them to do the impossible."[12]

These are exactly the kind of people Nehemiah needed to move their families once again and revitalize God's holy city, Jerusalem. They are a sacrificially giving people (vv. 70–72). They give their material wealth and lives in order to glorify God. Yesterday's victories are foreshadows of the believer's ability to succeed when facing present challenges. Their past faithfulness is the proving ground for meeting the present need.

---

11. For a discussion of this issue see Steinmann, *Ezra and Nehemiah*, 172.

12. Warren W. Wiersbe, *Be Determined (Nehemiah): Standing Firm in the Face of Opposition,* Kindle ed., BE Series Commentary (Colorado Springs: David C. Cook, 2010), 101.

II. Priorities of Nehemiah's Calling

A. The Praise of God (7:1)

Derek Kidner states that Jerusalem's raison d'être, its reason for being, was worship.[13] This assertion appears to bear out in this passage. Both sections of this chapter point to the prominence of temple personnel. Those associated with Israel's worship—the gatekeepers, singers, and Levites—are an important part of Jerusalem's security force. As they are all around the city, they serve not only to provide the people with a sense of security but also as a reminder for Jerusalem's purpose—the worship of Yahweh. In the book of genealogy, a significant section is dedicated to the temple personnel. Again, it communicates the pronounced importance of worship to the people of God in Jerusalem. The priests, Levites, and temple servants all return to Jerusalem with the purpose of rebuilding the city and its temple to lead the people of God in worshiping God for the glory of God.

B. The Principles of God (7:2–3)

One of the overarching principles delineated in the Scriptures is God's desire for the leaders of his people to be godly. This principle is important to Nehemiah as he assigns leaders to help him administrate the city of Jerusalem. Hananiah's spiritual credentials are at least as important as his practical abilities when it comes to his qualifications for leading the people of God. If leadership is having an influence on others, then having leaders who fear the Lord is necessary if the goal is to have a people who fear the Lord.

Another principle is closely akin to the saying Benjamin Franklin popularized in his *Poor Richard's Almanack* in 1736: "God helps those who help themselves."[14] I have actually met people who thought this is a verse in the Bible. While it is not, and while God more often "helps" those who cannot help themselves, as in our salvation, the statement is true when it comes to believers. God helps those who cannot help themselves, but he rarely, if ever, helps those who can help themselves and refuse or neglect to do so. One might respond by saying it is impossible for one to help oneself apart from God, and that is true. However, he has already helped us and continues to do so. At creation, God equipped us

---

13. Derek Kidner, *Ezra and Nehemiah*, Tyndale Old Testament Commentaries 12 (Downers Grove, IL: IVP Academic, 1979), 111.

14. Benjamin Franklin, *Poor Richard's Almanack* (1736).

to think and act with prudence and diligence. The fall has affected us, but it has not totally eradicated these things. We can take sensible action, as the book of Proverbs suggests:

> He who tills his land will have plenty of bread,
> But he who pursues worthless things lacks sense. (Prov 12:11)

> The soul of the sluggard craves and gets nothing,
> But the soul of the diligent is made fat. (Prov 13:4)

God has given New Testament believers bodies, intellect, and the help of the Holy Spirit so that we can take sensible action. There has been such a mistaken belief that works somehow assist in our being saved that many believers overcompensate this wrong by diminishing the importance of the grace God has given us to serve him. In fact, in Ephesians 2:8–10, the apostle Paul indicates that doing God's work is evidence of the grace of God in our lives. He highlights both the grace of salvation that is completely apart from works and the grace God has bestowed on those who are saved to do good works. So, even though Nehemiah has continually demonstrated his dependence on God to help and protect him and the people, once again he does what he knows to do while trusting God to do for him and the people what they cannot do. And that which Nehemiah knows to do is evidence of the grace of God in his life. Acting with good sense is a spiritual endeavor when it is done unto the Lord's purposes.

C. The People of God (7:4–73)

From the beginning of the book, Nehemiah's concern for the people of Jerusalem is apparent. He is distraught when he hears of their distress and reproach. In Nehemiah 1, his initial prayer centers on the people of Jerusalem and not its walls. So it is no surprise that Nehemiah understands that the people are essential to the revitalization of the city. In fact, the rebuilding of the walls of Jerusalem is not the main point of the book of Nehemiah. It is the rebuilding of the people of God for the continued purposes of God for the glory of God. Nehemiah's list of workers in Nehemiah 3 and the list of the returnees here in Nehemiah 7 point to the centrality of the people of God and the spiritual renewal that is happening among them. Therefore, they are to be a holy people. Some who are priests are excluded from service because they are unable to show they are truly descendants of Aaron. By the grace of God, they are included among the people of God, but they cannot serve at the altar according to God's law (v. 64). It is a reminder that one may approach the throne of God his way or no way at all. He is a holy God. Therefore, his people must personify holiness themselves.

The grace of God is further demonstrated by the people who are unable to prove they were even descendants of Israel (v. 61). Still they are part of the community of faith. The people of Judah are a section of a long line of people with whom God established a covenant to be a blessing to the nations. The inclusion of this small group of possible gentiles is but a taste of what is to come with the New Testament. The people of God include people from various walks of life—again a foretaste of the new creation.

D. The Purpose of God (7:1–73)

As the seed of Abraham, the people of Judah are God's covenant people, chosen to be a blessing to the nations (see Gen 12:1–3; 18: 16–19; Isa 41:8). God uses Nehemiah's ministry as part of his continued fulfillment of that purpose. Ultimately, God fulfills his promises to Abraham and David concerning the throne of Israel, through the Lord Jesus Christ. And Zerubbabel in verse 7 is the same Zerubbabel that Matthew records in the genealogy of Jesus the Messiah (Matt 1:12–13). To today's reader, these lists may appear tedious and even meaningless if we fail to read them in light of the promises of God and their ultimate fulfillment in the Lord Jesus Christ. The painstaking work of Nehemiah pales in the face of God's meticulously and wondrously weaved tapestry of his work of redemption through his Son. God's word shows he fulfills his promises down to the most miniscule detail. Though there are numerous obstacles and challenges, nothing can thwart God's purpose. Derek Thomas states, "It would be difficult, therefore, to imagine a better way to underline this truth of the Jews' covenantal status as the people of God than to remind them of the names of those who had returned almost ninety years before. Had they perhaps begun to forget the point behind their return?"[15] Their purpose is to display the power and glory of God to the nations by faithful obedience to Yahweh their God. The restoration of Jerusalem and the people of God serve as a foreshadowing of the new creation to come in Christ.

---

15. Derek W. Thomas, *Ezra & Nehemiah*, Reformed Expository Commentary (Phillipsburg, NJ: P&R, 2016), 319.

CONCLUSION

Nehemiah 7 is much more than a list of people who returned from Babylonian exile. It is a record of God's faithfulness to his promises to restore Jerusalem and his people. It is a reminder that God's work concerns much more than brick and mortar. He saves his people so that the nations and all of creation might look in wonder. By his grace he uses his people to do his good work. The book of genealogy serves as an example of a group of people who are faithful servants of the Lord. They were an example for the people in Nehemiah's day to follow. Let it serve us in the same way, so that we too might be an example to those who follow us of a people who were faithful to God's call on our lives.

FINAL THOUGHTS

1. How should practicality and good sense fit into one's spiritual life?
2. Why is godly leadership so important to the community of faith?
3. How should a believer demonstrate the centrality of worshiping the Lord today?
4. How pliable are you to God's will for your life, and how predictable is your faithful obedience to God's will?
5. What kind of spiritual legacy are you leaving for the next generation?

THE CENTRALITY OF
THE WORD OF GOD

Nehemiah 8:1–18

INTRODUCTION

Over the years, I have asked many believers whether they think we need a spiritual renewal in the church. Without exception, all have said, "Yes." I would not presume Nehemiah 8 is a recipe for spiritual renewal, since a revival of the people of God is not some recipe that any of us could manufacture or whip up. It is of God and not of ourselves. Nevertheless, Nehemiah 8 shows what happens when the people of God come together seeking to know God's word, repent of sin, and then humbly and joyfully obey God's word. Their response to God's word reveals their hearts. Thus Nehemiah 8 provides an example of what the hearts of the people of God should be in the community of faith.

STRUCTURE

Structurally, Nehemiah 8 is divided into two main sections: the initial gathering of the people on the first day of the month of the seventh month (8:1–12), and the gathering of leaders on the next day that initiated the celebration of the Feast of Booths (8:13–18).[1] However, there are parallel conclusions to the subsections of 8:1–8 and 8:9–12, in which both indicate the people "understood" what was read to them. Also, 8:1–8 focuses on the reading of God's law, and 8:9–12 focuses on the people's reaction to that reading. Therefore, I have chosen to follow the three movements of the passage. Verses 1–8 describe how Ezra and others with him read and explain the law, verses 9–12 show how the people respond to it, and verses 13–18 focus on the second day's events of further instruction and the reestablishment of observing the Feast of Booths.

---

1. H. G. M. Williamson, *Ezra, Nehemiah*, Word Biblical Commentary (Nashville: Thomas Nelson, 1985), 281.

SUMMARY OF THE PASSAGE

Nehemiah 8 highlights the centrality of the word of God to those who are the faithful people of God.

OUTLINE OF THE PASSAGE

I. The Reading of God's Word (8:1–8)

    A. The people are unified in their desire to hear the word of God (8:1)

    B. Everyone who can understand God's word comes to listen to God's word (8:2)

    C. The people listen to God's word attentively (8:3)

    D. The people prepared for the reading of God's word (8:4)

    E. The leaders demonstrate their desire to hear God's word (8:4)

    F. The people show respect for God's word (8:5)

    G. Worshiping the Lord and the reading of his word go together (8:6)

    H. The reading of God's word is accompanied by an explanation of its meaning (8:7–8)

    I. The reading of God's word and the worship of God is led by a godly man of integrity (8:1–18)

II. The Reception of God's Word (8:9–12)

    A. The people weep when they hear God's word (8:9)

    B. The leaders encourage the people (8:10–11)

    C. The people rejoice because they understand God's Word (8:12)

III. The Response to God's Word (8:13–18)

    A. The leaders want to gain more insight into God's word (8:13)

    B. The people eagerly obey God's word (8:14–18)

    C. The people rejoice as they obey God's word (8:17–18)

DEVELOPMENT OF THE EXPOSITION

I. The Reading of God's Word (8:1–8)

> [1] And all the people gathered as one man at the square which was in front of the Water Gate, and they asked Ezra the scribe to bring the book of the law of Moses which the LORD had given to Israel. [2] Then Ezra the priest brought the law before the assembly of men, women and all who *could* listen with understanding, on the first day of the seventh month. [3] He read from it before the square which was in front of the Water Gate

from early morning until midday, in the presence of men and women, those who could understand; and all the people were attentive to the book of the law. ⁴ Ezra the scribe stood at a wooden podium which they had made for the purpose. And beside him stood Mattithiah, Shema, Anaiah, Uriah, Hilkiah, and Maaseiah on his right hand; and Pedaiah, Mishael, Malchijah, Hashum, Hashbaddanah, Zechariah *and* Meshullam on his left hand. ⁵ Ezra opened the book in the sight of all the people for he was standing above all the people; and when he opened it, all the people stood up. ⁶ Then Ezra blessed the LORD the great God. And all the people answered, "Amen, Amen!" while lifting up their hands; then they bowed low and worshiped the LORD with *their* faces to the ground. ⁷ Also Jeshua, Bani, Sherebiah, Jamin, Akkub, Shabbethai, Hodiah, Maaseiah, Kelita, Azariah, Jozabad, Hanan, Pelaiah, the Levites, explained the law to the people while the people *remained* in their place. ⁸ They read from the book, from the law of God, translating to give the sense so that they understood the reading.

A. The People Are Unified in Their Desire to Hear the Word of God (8:1)

In Psalm 133, David writes,

> Behold, how good and how pleasant it is
> For brothers to dwell together in unity!
> It is like the precious oil upon the head,
> Coming down upon the beard,
> *Even* Aaron's beard,
> Coming down upon the edge of his robes.
> It is like the dew of Hermon
> Coming down upon the mountains of Zion;
> For there the LORD commanded the blessing—life forever.

It is probably difficult to really appreciate the unity of the people of God until one has experienced disunity among the people of God. In much of ancient Israel's history there is disunity, such as during the divided monarchy, for instance.[2] In

---

2. The ten northern tribes of Israel split away from the tribes of Judah and Benjamin in the south with the death of Solomon in 931 BC; the northern kingdom was called Israel, and the southern kingdom was called Judah.

both Testaments, the Bible records several occasions where the people of God are divided. In fact, there are much fewer instances where the people of God appear to be united "as one man." Except for a couple of exceptions in the Old Testament, in the meager nine times the phrase "as one man" appears in the Old Testament, it inherently points to the unity of God's people.[3]

The apostle Paul contends with the problem of disunity in the church in his first letter to the Corinthians. At the beginning of the letter he writes, "Now I exhort you, brethren, by the name of our Lord Jesus Christ, that you all agree and that there be no divisions among you, but that you be made complete in the same mind and in the same judgment" (1 Cor 1:10). So Paul encourages them to be in unity with one another. Nevertheless, later in the letter Paul indicates there will be factions when there are those who obey God while at the same time there are those within the church who do wrongly (1 Cor 3; 11). Therefore, the Bible does not advocate unity at the cost of truth and righteousness. So what is the unity Paul is advocating? He continues in the letter to inform his readers that this unity is in Christ—in the purposes and will of Christ.

The unity described in Nehemiah 8 is an Old Testament picture of the kind of unity of which Paul writes. The word "people" occurs fifteen times in this chapter, and the phrase "all the people" appears in ten of those occurrences. As God's chosen people, they all gather together in the square in front of the Water Gate seeking to know God's purposes and will for them through his word. What a loss and waste of opportunity it is when the people of God fail to do this, and what a tremendous blessing it is when they do. Every member of the community of faith needs to unite in seeking to know and obey God's purposes and will for the church by attentively listening to the word of God. Spiritual renewal does not happen apart from the centrality of the word of God.

B. Everyone Who Can Understand God's Word
Comes to Listen to God's Word (8:2)

So who are all these people who gather together at the Water Gate to listen to the word of God? It is everyone who is old enough to listen and understand. Kidner makes an astute observation concerning the purpose of God for his people: "The law had always envisaged 'a wise and understanding people,' taught

---

3. Numbers 14:15 and Judg 6:16 appear to have somewhat different nuances in how "as one man" is used in the text. The other references are Judg 20:1, 8, 11; 1 Sam 11:7; 2 Sam 19:14; Ezra 3:1, Neh 8:1.

from childhood not only the words of God but what the words and rituals meant (Exod. 12:26f; Deut. 4:6; 6:6ff; 31:12f)."[4]

Several years ago I visited a prominent church to learn about its ministry. The first session was a worship service. It was amazing, but I wished I had left after that. I learned that the inclusion of children up to the age of twelve years old in the services was discouraged. Instead, they put them in activity rooms to play games. Biblical education for children and senior adults was virtually nonexistent. Way too many churches have adopted this practice. By purposely targeting a certain group, they were purposely excluding others. It is a travesty and not the picture of spiritual education anywhere in the Bible. The Bible still envisages a people who are taught the word of God from childhood and who have an understanding of what it means. Timothy is a great example of such.

The picture in the Scriptures is of all people of every age who are able to understand, and every gender and race who are in the community of faith all coming together to listen to the word of God and worship the Lord. I was eight years old, sitting next to my thirty-four-year-old mother, surrounded by a variety of people of all ages and backgrounds, when I heard the gospel and realized my need for salvation. Is there a place for graded education in the church? Of course. Is there a place for corporate worship where all the people of God who are able to listen and understand should come together to hear the proclamation of God's word? Most definitely. We must not undervalue the importance of hearing God's word together.[5] Among other things, it helps us all remember the breadth of God's work of salvation and how we are all members of one another in Christ, needful of one another in the body of Christ.

C. The People Listen to God's Word Attentively (8:3)

Literally, the Hebrew texts reads "and the ears of all the people were to the scroll of instruction." In other words, they give full attention to listening to God's word as it is read. Moreover, they do this from dawn to midday.[6] Years ago I remember a World War II story in which an expert in London gave directions to a soldier surrounded by the enemy on how to dismantle an explosive. The soldier hung

---

4. Derek Kidner, *Ezra and Nehemiah*, Tyndale Old Testament Commentaries 12 (Downers Grove, IL: IVP Academic, 1979), 114.

5. J. G. McConville, *Ezra, Nehemiah, and Esther* (Louisville: Westminster John Knox, 1985), 117.

6. Andrew E. Steinmann, *Ezra and Nehemiah*, Concordia Commentary (St. Louis: Concordia, 2010), , 502.

on every word because his life depended on it. The people gathered at the Water Gate hang on every word they hear from God's word because they realize their lives depend on it. They realize what God's law already taught.

> So you shall keep My statutes and My judgments, by which a man may live if he does them; I am the LORD. (Lev 18:5)

> Now, O Israel, listen to the statutes and the judgments which I am teaching you to perform, so that you may live. (Deut 4:1)

And the New Testament carries on the message of how essential God's word is to the believer.

> So Jesus was saying to those Jews who had believed Him, "If you continue in My word, *then* you are truly disciples of Mine; and you will know the truth, and the truth will make you free." (John 8:31–32)

> Therefore, putting aside all filthiness and *all* that remains of wickedness, in humility receive the word implanted, which is able to save your souls. (Jas 1:21)

Like the assembly of people who gathered at the Water Gate, we too need to recognize our lives also are dependent on God's word. Therefore, we should do everything we can to be able to attentively listen to God's word. Anything that would impede that should be graciously addressed.

D. The People Prepared for the Reading of God's Word (8:4)

The term "wooden podium" is literally "tower of wood" in Hebrew. Here appears to be the only instance the word is used as a "podium" instead of a tower, and it is the only time one is described as wooden. That they built a podium for Ezra to use as he reads not only serves a practical purpose to assist him as he reads, but it also shows the forethought they gave to what was to transpire. The Hebrew word for "had made" is in the past passive aspect of the verb. Therefore, they made the podium and platform in preparation for the reading of God's word. Furthermore, it serves as a focal point for the people as they listen. Verse 5 indicates Ezra is on a platform in the sight of all the people. It may seem like a small thing, but practical steps to enhance one's ability to focus on listening to God's word are important. The way the people of God treat the reading and teaching of God's word speaks volumes about their spiritual condition.

E. The Leaders Demonstrate Their Desire to Hear God's Word (8:4)

Ezra was a priest and scribe who received permission from Artaxerxes I to lead a group of about three thousand from exile back to Jerusalem in 458/457 BC. His mandate from the king was to reestablish God's law while upholding the king's law in the land (see Ezra 7:11–28). There is quite a bit of ambiguity concerning exactly who the thirteen men are in Nehemiah 8:4 who stand on both sides of Ezra as he reads from the law. Some even question whether there were thirteen. They may have been priests, Levites, laity, or a mixture of the three.[7] In the end, what matters is that these are leaders who publicly display their desire to hear God's word to all the people. Spiritual leaders must never be reticent when it comes to conveying to others the importance of hearing and obeying God's word. Godly leaders not only will encourage others to listen to God's word, but they will also gladly submit themselves to it. Practically speaking, an example of this is a husband and father who is the spiritual leader of his home who will himself enthusiastically submit to the teaching of God's word as he takes his family to corporate worship and small group Bible study in the local church. A sign of mature spiritual leadership is a desire to receive instruction from others as they teach God's word.

F. The People Show Respect for God's Word (8:5)

Verse 5 indicates that when Ezra opens the book in the sight of all the people, "all the people stood up." In that culture, standing up was a sign of extreme respect. Years ago I taught at a Christian school where the students in the classroom were taught to stand when an adult walked into the classroom as a sign of respect for the elder. Often standing ovations are given as a demonstration of respect for an individual. The point is that they display a deep reverence for God's law. No doubt, we do not live in the same culture as the people in Jerusalem did that day. However, is it possible we sometimes may use that as an excuse for our lack of respect for the things of God? How often do people check out during the public reading of God's word or spend that time looking at texts and emails? People who recognize the character of God and the grace he has shown by the giving of his word will readily show their respect to God by demonstrating respect for his word.

---

7. For a discussion of the issues see Williamson, *Ezra, Nehemiah*, 288–89.

G. Worshiping the Lord and the Reading of His Word Go Together (8:6)

Raymond Brown writes,

> In this meeting, the people made no distinction between the exposition of Scripture and the offering of worship. Exposition and adoration belonged together, each flowing naturally into the other. ... We adore God as much by faithful exposition as by wholehearted singing. ... Lively, relevant, biblical exposition ought to promote genuine adoration, just as inspired singing can create a longing for more of the truth we have been exalting.[8]

I have heard pastors say something like, "After we worship, we will look to the reading and teaching of God's word." A cursory reading of Psalm 119 (the longest chapter in the Bible) should be enough to convince us that listening to God's word, when done in humble submission to it, is an act of worship, and Nehemiah 8:6 helps substantiate such a claim. What can demonstrate how much one esteems the Lord any more than one's yearning to listen to and obey his word? Does that not communicate the uttermost worth of our God? And as Brown so aptly observes, do not our songs of praise lead us to want to hear God's word, and does not our hearing of God's word result in our desire to praise him? As Ezra blesses the Lord, the people also affirm their desire to bless him. A desire to hear God's word is one way of blessing him. They stand up in respect for God's word and then bow low in worshipful submission to it. What they do is an outward expression of their readiness to submit to him by listening to and obeying his word.

H. The Reading of God's Word Is Accompanied by an Explanation of Its Meaning (8:7–8)

There has been some debate over the meaning of verses 7 and 8. It surrounds the Hebrew words *mĕbînîm*, meaning "to cause to understand," and *mĕpōrāš*, which comes from the root meaning "to make distinct or clear." Some scholars believe these words refer to the Levites "interpreting" the Hebrew text for people who had been in Babylon either for all their lives or for the last seventy years of their lives. The notion is that the returned exiles no longer knew Hebrew as their primary language. Therefore, as they heard the law read to them in Hebrew,

---

8. Raymond Brown, *The Message of Nehemiah*, The Bible Speaks Today (Downers Grove, IL: InterVarsity Press, 1998), 130–31.

they needed someone to translate it.[9] Others believe it means the Levites clearly articulated it so that it followed the traditional scribal pointing of the text.[10] Still others believe these words mean the Levites actually explained it and provided an exposition of the text like a teacher or pastor would do.

While all three explanations are possible, the first and third seem to be most plausible. While there *may* be hints of proto-Masoretic work going on back to the time of Ezra, it is difficult to prove that was the concern here.[11] Nonetheless, it is possible many of the returned exiles were deficient in Hebrew. However, as Kidner points out, the fact that Nehemiah was appalled by the discovery of people speaking Aramaic and not Hebrew upon his return to Jerusalem twelve years later after he went to report back to the king in Susa implies ignorance of Hebrew was not an issue when he first came to Jerusalem.[12] What the text is stating is that the Levites do what was necessary to make sure the people understand what is being read along with its implications. Surely they want to clearly articulate and, if need be, translate what is said, but they also want to clearly explain what it means. The people's reception of it and response to it bears this out in the following verses. Packer describes what happened this way: "The natural supposition is that Ezra would read a section and then pause while the Levites translated and explained: then he would read a further section, and so on. All this had been planned out and rehearsed in advance, and it worked well. The Levites labored to teach, the crowd labored to learn, and, as 8:12 says, everybody 'understood.'"[13] Throughout the Scriptures, one discovers not only the proclamation of the word of God, but also someone explaining its meaning. Both are necessary. If they were not, there would be no need for teaching. We would just read the Bible and be done with it. But God has provided for his people priests and Levites in the Old Testament and pastors and elders in the New Testament to "cause the people to understand" the Scriptures.

------

9. F. Charles Fensham, *The Books of Ezra and Nehemiah*, New International Commentary on the Old Testament (Grand Rapids: Eerdmans, 1982), 225.

10. Joseph Blenkinsopp, *Ezra-Nehemiah: A Commentary*, Old Testament Library (Philadelphia: Westminster, 1988), 288.

11. As previously mentioned, the Masoretic Text is the completed Hebrew text that sought to preserve the Hebrew Bible through a system of accents, vocalizations, and notes called the Masorah, compiled by scribes called the Masoretes from about AD 600 to 900. The term "proto-Masoretic" refers to scribal work that laid the foundation for the Masoretes.

12. Kidner, *Ezra and Nehemiah*, 116 (Neh 13:1–24).

13. J. I. Packer, *A Passion for Faithfulness: Wisdom from the Book of Nehemiah* (Wheaton, IL: Crossway, 1995), 153.

I. The Reading of God's Word and the Worship of
God Is Led by a Godly Man of Integrity (8:1–18)

If the people of God are central to Nehemiah 8, then so is the man of God. Ezra's leadership is prominent throughout the chapter. The text indicates he is a scribe and a priest. Ezra 7:10 provides a telling description of the kind of man he is. It states, "For Ezra had set his heart to study the law of the LORD and to practice *it*, and to teach *His* statutes and ordinances in Israel." History is replete with people who have studied God's word. However, he not only studies it, but he practices it. He lives it out in his daily life. It is his commitment to learn God's law and to obey it that makes him especially qualified to lead the events that take place in Nehemiah 8 and instruct the people. All three are essential to godly leadership: the study of God's word, obedience to God's word, and the teaching of God's word.

A deficiency in any one of these areas is serious. There are far too many people who know God's word intellectually as a result of intense study and are willing to tell others what it says, yet they really do not *know* God's word experientially because they fail to submit their lives to it. It comes off as hypocrisy. On the other hand, there are those who have concluded it is a waste of time to give serious thought to the teachings of Scripture and advocate that application is where our main attention should be. Yet these people are deceived because they often are applying their own ideas of what they think the Scriptures should say as opposed to what the actual teaching of the word of God is, and as they teach others it becomes the blind leading the blind. Still more, there are those who study God's word and apply it to a point, but fail to communicate it to others. Inherent to the mission of the church is not only to study God's word and obey it, but it is also to make disciples by proclaiming it to others and instructing them in the way of the Lord. Complete application of God's word will include actively proclaiming it to others in whatever circumstance one finds oneself. Ezra is an example of the kind of leader the community of faith desperately needed then and still needs today—a man of spiritual integrity.

II. THE RECEPTION OF GOD'S WORD (8:9–12)

> [9] Then Nehemiah, who was the governor, and Ezra the priest *and* scribe, and the Levites who taught the people said to all the people, "This day is holy to the LORD your God; do not mourn or weep." For all the people were weeping when they heard the words of the law. [10] Then he said to

them, "Go, eat of the fat, drink of the sweet, and send portions to him who has nothing prepared; for this day is holy to our Lord. Do not be grieved, for the joy of the LORD is your strength." [11] So the Levites calmed all the people, saying, "Be still, for the day is holy; do not be grieved." [12] All the people went away to eat, to drink, to send portions and to celebrate a great festival, because they understood the words which had been made known to them.

A. The People Weep When They Hear God's Word (8:9)

When the people hear God's law they weep. It would be speculative to guess how many times they had heard it before, but in this instance it speaks to them as if it is the first time they hear it. I cannot remember a time in my life I was not at least familiar with the gospel, yet when I received God's gracious gift of salvation it was as if I had just heard the gospel for the first time. No doubt, all of this was the work of the Holy Spirit. It is when the light of God's word shines on them that they begin to recognize the darkness in their own hearts. It is impossible for sinners to catch a glimpse of a perfect God and not be convicted of their own sin. When they hear God's holy law, they begin to see the holy God of that law. Therefore, as in Josiah's day, they weep in remorse of their disobedience and with hearts of repentance (2 Kgs 22:11–13, 19). The Pentateuch relates several times when people fail to obey God and suffer as a result. Upon hearing the law, these sinful people who have gathered together corporately recognize their dire standing before God and are convicted of their sin.[14] They experienced physical release from Babylonian captivity, but at the Water Gate they experience spiritual release from the bondage of sin as they repent of it before God.[15] Just as their sin had led them into Babylonian captivity, it had led them into spiritual captivity too. And just as God mercifully and graciously freed them from the Babylonian captivity, so he is ready to free them from their spiritual captivity.

---

14. Jacob M. Myers, *Ezra, Nehemiah*, Anchor Bible 14 (New York: Doubleday, 1965), 154.

15. Mervin Breneman, *Ezra, Nehemiah, Esther*, NAC 10 (Nashville: Broadman & Holman, 1993), 227.

B. The Leaders Encourage the People (8:10–11)

Because of God's readiness to forgiven those who repent, Nehemiah, Ezra, and the Levites encourage the people to cease their weeping and instead to commence celebrating. Moreover, the first day of the seventh month is the first day of the Feast of Trumpets, the beginning of the Jewish civil new year and a ten-day celebration. According to the law, it is to be a day of rejoicing (Lev 23:23–25; Deut 16:15). This day represents a new day in Jerusalem. The people focus on only one part of the message. They see their sin but fail to see God's mercy and grace. The word of God not only shines a light on the hearts of sinners, but it also points to God, who is ready to forgive the person who repents of her sin. Leaders who expound God's word with integrity will make sure the people know the entirety of the message. Moreover, that which is holy unto the Lord should result in joy because the Lord himself is the true source of joy and gladness. It is God's cleansing that makes the sinner right before God, and it is this righteousness that results in the joy of the Lord, and it is the joy of the Lord that strengthens the righteous and gives them hope. As Proverbs 10:28 observes, "The hope of the righteous is gladness, But the expectation of the wicked perishes."

C. The People Rejoice Because They Understand God's Word (8:12)

Rejoicing is the natural response of the people of God when they hear and understand the word of God. Several psalms testify to this truth. Note the following examples:

> But his delight is in the law of the LORD,
> And in His law he meditates day and night. (Ps 1:2)

> The precepts of the LORD are right, rejoicing the heart;
> The commandment of the LORD is pure, enlightening the eyes. (Ps 19:8)

> I have inherited Your testimonies forever,
> For they are the joy of my heart. (Ps 119:111)

> I rejoice at Your word,
> As one who finds great spoil. (Ps 119:162)

Paul writes to Timothy, "But we know that the Law is good, if one uses it lawfully" (1 Tim 1:8). When the law is properly used as it was intended to be used, then it is a good thing. It shows us God's standard of holiness and our failure to live up to that standard, and points us to the holy God who is ready to mercifully and graciously forgive repenting sinners (Gal 3:24).

This is the reason the message of salvation is called the "gospel"—"good news." When believers recognize the mercy and grace God has shown us by forgiving us and saving us, good news and rejoicing are the response. Steinmann writes,

> The Word of God contains both Law and Gospel. While the reading of
> Moses' Teaching contained Law, which always accuses the hearers of
> their sins and brings them sorrow and contrition, the Pentateuch also
> contains magnificent Gospel promises of forgiveness and the Messiah,
> which bring joy to the penitent sinner. It is joy in the Gospel that is the
> believer's ultimate strength. Nehemiah's encouragement, reinforced by
> the Levites (8:11), pointed the people to the comforting Gospel, so that
> the joy of Yahweh overcame their sorrow, and they celebrated the day
> (Neh. 8:12).[16]

Perhaps those of us believers who seldom experience joy in our lives do so because we fail to truly understand the salvation we have in the Lord Jesus Christ. The gospel message is not just for unbelievers, but every believer needs to embrace the gospel, its meaning, and its implications every day. It is our daily strength. Surely, then, we too would rejoice and perhaps be more apt to share the gospel with others. David writes, "How blessed is he whose transgression is forgiven, Whose sin is covered! How blessed is the man to whom the LORD does not impute iniquity, And in whose spirit there is no deceit. ... Be glad in the LORD and rejoice, you righteous ones; And shout for joy, all you who are upright in heart" (Ps 32:1–2, 11).

III. The Response to God's Word (8:13–18)

> [13] Then on the second day the heads of fathers' *households* of all the people,
> the priests and the Levites were gathered to Ezra the scribe that they
> might gain insight into the words of the law. [14] They found written in
> the law how the LORD had commanded through Moses that the sons of
> Israel should live in booths during the feast of the seventh month. [15] So
> they proclaimed and circulated a proclamation in all their cities and in

---

16. Steinmann, *Ezra and Nehemiah*, 512.

Jerusalem, saying, "Go out to the hills, and bring olive branches and wild olive branches, myrtle branches, palm branches and branches of *other* leafy trees, to make booths, as it is written." [16] So the people went out and brought *them* and made booths for themselves, each on his roof, and in their courts and in the courts of the house of God, and in the square at the Water Gate and in the square at the Gate of Ephraim. [17] The entire assembly of those who had returned from the captivity made booths and lived in them. The sons of Israel had indeed not done so from the days of Joshua the son of Nun to that day. And there was great rejoicing. [18] He read from the book of the law of God daily, from the first day to the last day. And they celebrated the feast seven days, and on the eighth day *there was* a solemn assembly according to the ordinance.

A. The Leaders Want to Gain More Insight into God's Word (8:13)

Once the men of the city experience the joy of hearing and understanding God's word, they come back the next day for more. These heads of households want to lead their families in the way of the Lord. This is the true picture of being the spiritual head of a home. It is not that of some tyrannical Neanderthal bullying his spouse and children. It is the picture of one who humbly submits to the teaching of God's word and then leads his family in joyful obedience to it. It is a strong and confident dependence on God that seeks to know and do God's will. They are growing in an appreciation and understanding of God's law that David expresses in Psalm 119. The more one knows God's word, the more one wants to know it even more.

B. The People Eagerly Obey God's Word (8:14–18)

When the men hear more of the law and realize it is the time for the Feast of Booths, they immediately send word to every city with instructions to commence preparation for its observance. The Feast of Booths or Tabernacles (Lev 23:33–36; Deut 16:13) is the third of three feasts the men are required to observe annually by making a pilgrimage to Jerusalem. The first two are Passover and the Feast of Weeks (Pentecost in the NT). The Feast of Booths begins on the fifteenth day of the seventh month, which is Tishri, shortly after the observance of the Day of Atonement, which falls on the tenth day. The feast lasts for seven days. It is associated with the end of Israel's agricultural calendar (Exod 34:22). The first and eighth days of the festival are marked by a cessation from all activity, after which burnt offerings are presented to the Lord. Leviticus 23:39–43 provides details for the festival. The foliage of "beautiful trees" is to be gathered on the first day of the feast, along with palm branches, willow branches, and boughs from trees in full leaf. From these, shelters or booths are constructed, in which the people live for the week of the feast. Every seventh year the observances are marked by a public reading of the provisions of the Sinai covenant, to which the Israelites had committed themselves, a practice designed to remind them of the obligations as well as the blessings of the covenant relationship.[17] Their eagerness to observe the Feast of Booths is reminiscent of Israel's observance of the Passover when Joshua led them into the promised land.[18]

An indicator of true repentance is an immediate desire to obey God's word, so when they hear it is time for the Feast of Booths, they take action. There is no negotiating or delay. Way too often, people in the church equate a serious desire to obey God's word with legalism. Certainly, there are those who substitute works for grace. However, Paul and James under the inspiration of the Holy Spirit both emphasize the importance of obedience to God's word in the believer's life. Doing the will of Christ is evidence of the grace of God in our lives (Eph 2:10; Jas 2:14–26). Moreover, Jesus says, "If you love Me, you will keep My commandments" (John 14:15). Just because people do disgusting things on the internet probably does not mean you have stopped using it yourself. Hopefully, you have decided to use it in a way that is upright before God. Similarly, just because some people misuse God's word by legalism should not lead to our ignoring its demands on our lives. Instead, it hopefully means we will obey God's word in the Spirit of Christ. Jesus was obedient to the Father unto death. For the believer to ignore Christ's commandments because the believer is "under grace" is to deny the grace that Christ has given. When a "believer" does this, it is a repugnant excuse for disobedience, based on a self-centered misuse of God's word every bit as much as legalism is, and it is just as repulsive.[19]

---

17. R. K. Harrison, "Feasts and Festivals of Israel," in *Baker Encyclopedia of the Bible* (Grand Rapids: Baker Book House, 1988), 1:787.

18. Steinmann, *Ezra and Nehemiah*, 517–18.

19. See Derek Thomas's insightful comments on legalism and antinomianism: Thomas, *Ezra & Nehemiah*, Reformed Expository Commentary (Phillipsburg, NJ: P&R, 2016), 343–45.

C. The People Rejoice as They Obey God's Word (8:17–18)

The first day of hearing and obeying God's word continues with more reading of God's word, continued obedience, and literally "great joy" in the following days. All of these actions are done throughout the entire community, and on the eighth day the people gather together again to worship the Lord. It is a picture of what the community of faith is to be in relationship to one another, in service to God, and as a testimony to unbelievers (Deut 4:6–8).

CONCLUSION

Nehemiah 8 demonstrates what happens when the people of God get serious about listening to and obeying the word of God. So many Christians today say we need a spiritual renewal in the church. No such revival has ever taken place among the people of God apart from the centrality of the word of God in their lives, which leads me to believe no such revival will take place today unless we corporately seek to know and obey God's word. The good news is that if, like the people at the Water Gate, we seek God's word and humbly repent of sin and joyfully obey, then we could see such a movement of the Spirit of God among us today. Let us pray God would put such desires into our hearts.

FINAL THOUGHTS

1. What evidence points to your desire to intimately know God's word?
2. What does the centrality of the word of God in Nehemiah 8 communicate about corporate worship?
3. Why is ignoring Christ's commandments (antinomianism) just as wrong as trying to use them as a way to earn or keep salvation (legalism)?
4. Why is active involvement in the community of faith, the church, so important to one's spiritual life?
5. What can we learn about spiritual leadership in the home and church from Nehemiah 8?

HOW TO ASK GOD FOR HELP

Nehemiah 9:1–37

INTRODUCTION

Our prayers in desperate times reveal much about us. When I was a boy, I enjoyed climbing trees. We had a weeping willow tree in our front yard, which I especially enjoyed climbing. One day when I was no more than six years old I climbed it, but I slipped and got wedged between two branches. No matter what I did, I was unable to free myself. The longer I failed to free myself the more distraught I became. Finally, I cried out as loud as I could, "Help me, Jesus! Help me!" I desperately cried out to God as earnestly then as I ever have in my entire life. My mother heard my cry and came and rescued me. I have always believed to this day she was God's "angel" sent to save me in my time of great need. God hears the cries of his children. Nehemiah 9:1–37 is the longest recorded prayer in the Bible outside the Psalms. It is the people's plea for help. However, its focus is more on God's mighty deeds on behalf of his people throughout history than it is on the people themselves. A knowledge of the history of the people of God and his activity in history lays a foundation for one's theology in the present. Much of God's revelation of himself comes in the genre of historical narrative.

Furthermore, the prayer communicates the deep sorrow and confession of sin of the people and of their forefathers. They humbly communicate their renewed loyalty to Yahweh. As the prayer for God's deliverance develops, it shows how the people recognize just how mightily God has acted on their behalf and how amazingly good and compassionate he has been especially in light of their repeated unfaithfulness to him. Their prayer shows how they understand once again that they need God to mercifully and graciously intervene on their behalf. Their prayer reveals their belief in the faithful God of their fathers, who is still good and mighty to save them from their present crisis should he choose to do so.

STRUCTURE

Nehemiah 9:1–37 relates how the people of God come together to ask for his deliverance from their difficult situation. The chapter is divided into two sections. The first, verses 1–5, describes how the people come together first to confess their sins to God. The second, much larger section, verses 6–37, is the prayer of deliverance they utter to the Lord. Its subdivisions focus mostly on the great acts of God on behalf of his people throughout their history, concluding with a plea for God to act on their behalf once again.

SUMMARY OF THE PASSAGE

In worshipful and humble confession of sin, the people of God come before him and plead for his deliverance out of their present crisis. This prayer serves as a model for all believers on how we should approach the Lord in prayer as we seek his help.

OUTLINE OF THE PASSAGE

I. The Prayer of Confession (9:1–5)
   A. They express their humility before God (9:1)
   B. They profess their loyalty to God (9:2)
   C. They stress the importance of the word of God (9:3)
   D. They confess their sins against God (9:3)
   E. They bless the name of their God (9:4–5)
II. The Prayer for Salvation (9:6–37)
   A. The power of God in creation (9:6)
   B. The power of God in election (9:7–8)
   C. The power of God in redemption (9:9–11)
   D. The power of God in provision (9:12–25)
   E. The power of God in compassion (9:26–35)
   F. The power of God in supplication (9:36–37)

DEVELOPMENT OF THE EXPOSITION

I. THE PRAYER OF CONFESSION (9:1–5)

[1] Now on the twenty-fourth day of this month the sons of Israel assembled with fasting, in sackcloth and with dirt upon them. [2] The descendants of Israel separated themselves from all foreigners and stood and confessed their sins and the iniquities of their fathers. [3] While they stood in their place, they read from the book of the law of the LORD their God for a fourth of the day; and for *another* fourth they confessed and worshiped the LORD their God. [4] Now on the Levites' platform stood Jeshua, Bani, Kadmiel, Shebaniah, Bunni, Sherebiah, Bani *and* Chenani, and they cried with a loud voice to the LORD their God. [5] Then the Levites, Jeshua, Kadmiel, Bani, Hashabneiah, Sherebiah, Hodiah, Shebaniah *and* Pethahiah, said,

> "Arise, bless the LORD your God forever and ever!
> O may Your glorious name be blessed
> And exalted above all blessing and praise!"

A. They Express Their Humility before God (9:1)

When the people assemble on the twenty-fourth day of the month to worship the Lord, they come "with fasting, in sackcloth and with dirt upon them." Fasting, sackcloth, and ashes or dirt on the head are connected to mourning and repentance and a way to demonstrate humility and desperation to God in the Scriptures.[1] Desperately desiring God's attention and help, the people humbly come expressing their mourning over their sin and their confession of it. Such public expressions only truly have meaning when they are matched by a personal reality. However, when they are, it sends a powerful message. The people are truly sorry for their sin, are submitted to their God, and are serious in their plea for God's help.

---

1. H. G. M. Williamson, *Ezra, Nehemiah*, Word Biblical Commentary (Nashville: Thomas Nelson, 1985), 310. See, for example, Josh 7:6; 1 Sam 4:12; 2 Sam 1:2; Ezra 8:23; Esth 4:3; Job 2:12; Isa 22:12; Job 1:13–14; Jonah 3:5.

B. They Profess Their Loyalty to God (9:2)

Rather than being an act of arrogance, the people's separating themselves "from all foreigners" is a public profession of their loyalty and obedience to the Lord and of their desire for purity. Steinmann explains the term used well, stating that its references "do not refer to a physical removal of absence of dirt, but to a theological state of purity before God that he imputes to his people through liturgical rites and sacrifices he prescribed. This vocabulary is part of the Old Testament theological terminology of justification and sanctification."[2] In God's law in Leviticus 20:23–26, God commands Israel to do the following:

> Moreover, you shall not follow the customs of the nation which I will drive out before you, for they did all these things, and therefore I have abhorred them. Hence I have said to you, "You are to possess their land, and I Myself will give it to you to possess it, a land flowing with milk and honey." I am the LORD your God, who has separated you from the peoples. You are therefore to make a distinction between the clean animal and the unclean, and between the unclean bird and the clean; and you shall not make yourselves detestable by animal or by bird or by anything that creeps on the ground, which I have separated for you as unclean. Thus you are to be holy to Me, for I the LORD am holy; and I have set you apart from the peoples to be Mine.

Ezra writes of the concern for separation from the impurity of the nations in Ezra 6:21, "The sons of Israel who returned from exile and all those who had separated themselves from the impurity of the nations of the land to *join* them, to seek the LORD God of Israel, ate *the Passover*." As soon as he enters Jerusalem, Ezra encounters the people's sin of failing to separate themselves from the foreigners and instead marrying them and allowing their sons to marry them (Ezra 9:1–4). This practice leads to idolatry, and therefore it is a serious matter. So the people's standing apart from the foreigners is their way of professing allegiance to Yahweh and their desire for purity. Paul gives the same kind of instruction to the Corinthians in 2 Corinthians 6:14–18:

> Do not be bound together with unbelievers; for what partnership have righteousness and lawlessness, or what fellowship has light with

---

2. Andrew E. Steinmann, *Ezra and Nehemiah*, Concordia Commentary (St. Louis: Concordia, 2010), 592–93.

darkness? Or what harmony has Christ with Belial, or what has a believer
in common with an unbeliever? Or what agreement has the temple of
God with idols? For we are the temple of the living God; just as God said,

> "I WILL DWELL IN THEM AND WALK AMONG THEM;
> AND I WILL BE THEIR GOD, AND THEY SHALL BE MY
> PEOPLE.
> "Therefore, COME OUT FROM THEIR MIDST AND BE SEPA-
> RATE," says the Lord.
> "AND DO NOT TOUCH WHAT IS UNCLEAN;
> And I will welcome you.
> "And I will be a father to you,
> And you shall be sons and daughters to Me,"
> Says the Lord Almighty.

Paul exhorts believers to be separate from the world so that they might guard
and profess their loyalty to Christ and in so doing remain pure. The Lord Jesus
Christ voices this concern for his followers as he prays in John 17:14–19:

> I have given them Your word; and the world has hated them, because
> they are not of the world, even as I am not of the world. I do not ask You
> to take them out of the world, but to keep them from the evil *one*. They
> are not of the world, even as I am not of the world. Sanctify them in the
> truth; Your word is truth. As You sent Me into the world, I also have sent
> them into the world. For their sakes I sanctify Myself, that they them-
> selves also may be sanctified in truth.

Jesus states just how powerful and essential the word of God is to sanctification,
the process of our becoming more Christlike and less worldly. Therefore, it is
no surprise the role God's word plays in the gathering of the people of God in
Nehemiah 9.

C. They Stress the Importance of the Word of God (9:3)

For six hours the people listen as the word of God is read to them, demonstrating how utterly important it is to them as they worship the Lord and seek his
help. People who are serious about repentance, confessing sin, and living pure

lives for the Lord will prioritize the intake of his word. The psalmist indicates this truth in Psalm 119:9–12:

> How can a young man keep his way pure?
> By keeping *it* according to Your word.
> With all my heart I have sought You;
> Do not let me wander from Your commandments.
> Your word I have treasured in my heart,
> That I may not sin against You.
> Blessed are You, O LORD;
> Teach me Your statutes.

Why would believers do this? Because they recognize the truth of Paul's words to Timothy in 2 Timothy 3:16–17: "All Scripture is inspired by God and profitable for teaching, for reproof, for correction, for training in righteousness; so that the man of God may be adequate, equipped for every good work." It is the Scriptures that teach believers what is correct thinking, what is incorrect thinking, what is incorrect behavior, and what is correct behavior. The one who truly repents and confesses his sin is concerned with thinking and behaving in a way that honors Christ.

D. They Confess Their Sins against God (9:3)

Just as reading and listening to God's word is central to the people's assembly, so is the humble confession of their sins. The Hebrew text literally states, "they confessed and bowed down." So they confess their sins and bow before the Lord for another six hours. For twelve hours, the people respectfully stand and listen to the word of God, and then humbly bow themselves down and, prostrate before the Lord, confess their sins to him. It is the word of God that serves as the catalyst for their confession of their sins.[3] What difference would it make in the lives of believers today if we spent as much time in prayer and confession in response to the preaching and teaching of God's word as the time we spend actually listening to preaching and teaching?[4] Just as all of Scripture points to the grace of God, it all has a convicting element that requires his grace.

---

3. J. G. McConville, *Ezra, Nehemiah, and Esther* (Louisville: Westminster John Knox, 1985), 124.

4. It is similar to the man who looks at the mirror in Jas 1:22–25.

E. *They Bless the Name of Their God (9:4–5)*

As the passage transitions to the people's plea for God's deliverance, the Levites lead the people in blessing the name of the Lord. The wording "May Your glorious name be blessed and exalted above all blessing and praise" is unique to this passage in the Old Testament. Steinmann suggests that while the people have identified with the sins of their forebears, it also sets them apart, saying they will not disobey like their forebears did.[5] It is good to seek God's blessing before ever asking for his blessing because he is the only one truly deserving of blessing. Yet it is for that very reason we can approach him with our requests for blessing. The first prayer I memorized as a child went like this: "God is good. God is great. Thank you for the food. Amen." It is because God is both good and great that his children can confidently go to him for help in time of need. Blessed be the name of the Lord!

II. THE PRAYER FOR DELIVERANCE (9:6–37)

[6] "You alone are the LORD.
You have made the heavens,
The heaven of heavens with all their host,
The earth and all that is on it,
The seas and all that is in them.
You give life to all of them
And the heavenly host bows down before You.
[7] "You are the LORD God,
Who chose Abram
And brought him out from Ur of the Chaldees,
And gave him the name Abraham.
[8] "You found his heart faithful before You,
And made a covenant with him
To give *him* the land of the Canaanite,
Of the Hittite and the Amorite,
Of the Perizzite, the Jebusite and the Girgashite—
To give *it* to his descendants.
And You have fulfilled Your promise,

---

5. Steinmann, *Ezra and Nehemiah*, 533.

For You are righteous.

[9] "You saw the affliction of our fathers in Egypt,

And heard their cry by the Red Sea.

[10] "Then You performed signs and wonders against Pharaoh,

Against all his servants and all the people of his land;

For You knew that they acted arrogantly toward them,

And made a name for Yourself as *it is* this day.

[11] "You divided the sea before them,

So they passed through the midst of the sea on dry ground;

And their pursuers You hurled into the depths,

Like a stone into raging waters.

[12] "And with a pillar of cloud You led them by day,

And with a pillar of fire by night

To light for them the way

In which they were to go.

[13] "Then You came down on Mount Sinai,

And spoke with them from heaven;

You gave them just ordinances and true laws,

Good statutes and commandments.

[14] "So You made known to them Your holy sabbath,

And laid down for them commandments, statutes and law,

Through Your servant Moses.

[15] "You provided bread from heaven for them for their hunger,

You brought forth water from a rock for them for their thirst,

And You told them to enter in order to possess

The land which You swore to give them.

[16] "But they, our fathers, acted arrogantly;

They became stubborn and would not listen to Your commandments.

[17] "They refused to listen,

And did not remember Your wondrous deeds which You had

    performed among them;

So they became stubborn and appointed a leader to return to their

    slavery in Egypt.

But You are a God of forgiveness,

Gracious and compassionate,

Slow to anger and abounding in lovingkindness;

And You did not forsake them.

¹⁸ "Even when they made for themselves

A calf of molten metal

And said, 'This is your God

Who brought you up from Egypt,'

And committed great blasphemies,

¹⁹ You, in Your great compassion,

Did not forsake them in the wilderness;

The pillar of cloud did not leave them by day,

To guide them on their way,

Nor the pillar of fire by night, to light for them the way in which they
were to go.

²⁰ "You gave Your good Spirit to instruct them,

Your manna You did not withhold from their mouth,

And You gave them water for their thirst.

²¹ "Indeed, forty years You provided for them in the wilderness *and*
they were not in want;

Their clothes did not wear out, nor did their feet swell.

²² "You also gave them kingdoms and peoples,

And allotted *them* to them as a boundary.

They took possession of the land of Sihon the king of Heshbon

And the land of Og the king of Bashan.

²³ "You made their sons numerous as the stars of heaven,

And You brought them into the land

Which You had told their fathers to enter and possess.

²⁴ "So their sons entered and possessed the land.

And You subdued before them the inhabitants of the land, the
Canaanites,

And You gave them into their hand, with their kings and the peoples of
the land,

To do with them as they desired.

²⁵ "They captured fortified cities and a fertile land.

They took possession of houses full of every good thing,

Hewn cisterns, vineyards, olive groves,

Fruit trees in abundance.

So they ate, were filled and grew fat,

And reveled in Your great goodness.

[26] "But they became disobedient and rebelled against You,

And cast Your law behind their backs

And killed Your prophets who had admonished them

So that they might return to You,

And they committed great blasphemies.

[27] "Therefore You delivered them into the hand of their oppressors who
       oppressed them,

But when they cried to You in the time of their distress,

You heard from heaven, and according to Your great compassion

You gave them deliverers who delivered them from the hand of their
       oppressors.

[28] "But as soon as they had rest, they did evil again before You;

Therefore You abandoned them to the hand of their enemies, so that
       they ruled over them.

When they cried again to You, You heard from heaven,

And many times You rescued them according to Your compassion,

[29] And admonished them in order to turn them back to Your law.

Yet they acted arrogantly and did not listen to Your commandments
       but sinned against Your ordinances,

By which if a man observes them he shall live.

And they turned a stubborn shoulder and stiffened their neck, and
       would not listen.

[30] "However, You bore with them for many years,

And admonished them by Your Spirit through Your prophets,

Yet they would not give ear.

Therefore You gave them into the hand of the peoples of the lands.

[31] "Nevertheless, in Your great compassion You did not make an end of
       them or forsake them,

For You are a gracious and compassionate God.

[32] "Now therefore, our God, the great, the mighty, and the awesome
       God, who keeps covenant and lovingkindness,

Do not let all the hardship seem insignificant before You,

Which has come upon us, our kings, our princes, our priests, our
       prophets, our fathers and on all Your people,

From the days of the kings of Assyria to this day.

[33] "However, You are just in all that has come upon us;

For You have dealt faithfully, but we have acted wickedly.

[34] "For our kings, our leaders, our priests and our fathers have not kept Your law

Or paid attention to Your commandments and Your admonitions with which You have admonished them.

[35] "But they, in their own kingdom,

With Your great goodness which You gave them,

With the broad and rich land which You set before them,

Did not serve You or turn from their evil deeds.

[36] "Behold, we are slaves today,

And as to the land which You gave to our fathers to eat of its fruit and its bounty,

Behold, we are slaves in it.

[37] "Its abundant produce is for the kings

Whom You have set over us because of our sins;

They also rule over our bodies

And over our cattle as they please,

So we are in great distress.

A. *The Power of God in Creation (9:6)*

As the people begin to extol the power of God, they begin by recognizing the wondrous might God exhibited when he created the heavens, the earth, and the seas, and all that is in them. Couched by the statements "You alone are the Lord" and "And the heavenly host bows down before You," they voice not only their recognition of Yahweh's mighty power but also his all-encompassing authority over all his creation. It is recognition of his sovereignty. He is the source and sustainer of life; there is no one else. As they make their request to God, it is to the one true God, the one who is able to answer their request and the one who has sovereign authority over all of his creation to do so.

As New Testament believers, we must recognize who our Lord Jesus Christ is. He is God; he is the Creator. John writes, "All things came into being through Him, and apart from Him nothing came into being that has come into being" (John 1:3). And speaking of the Lord Jesus Christ the apostle Paul writes, "He is the image of the invisible God, the firstborn of all creation. For by Him all things were created, *both* in the heavens and on earth, visible and invisible, whether thrones or dominions or rulers or authorities—all things have been created through Him and for Him. He is before all things, and in Him all things hold together" (Col 1:15–17).So, as we make our supplications to God and pray in the name of Jesus, we should be mindful we are praying to the Creator in the name of the Creator, and our Lord Jesus Christ has all authority and power to answer our prayers. Such authority and might belong to him alone.

B. The Power of God in Election (9:7–8)

The people recognize the Lord God is the one who graciously chose Abram to bring into covenant relationship with him. By faith, Abram left his home and followed God's direction to a new land, a land that God promised would belong solely to his descendants. So God changed his name from Abram, "exalted father," to Abraham, "father of a multitude." The record of God's initiating a covenant with Abraham is in his first recorded words to Abram, in Genesis 12:1–3. The passage begins with God telling Abraham to leave his land and go to the land that the Lord will show him. It is in this passage God promises to make Abraham a great nation, to bless him, and to make his name great. Also, it is there where God first reveals his purpose in making the covenant with Abraham. It is so that Abraham himself will be a blessing, which is emphatically stated twice. Who is Abraham to bless? "All the families (ethnic groups) of the earth." God also promises Abraham, "I will bless those who bless you, and the one who curses you I will curse," a promise that lays a foundation for the people's prayer here in Nehemiah 9 as they seek deliverance from their enemy. Genesis 15 indicates God promised to take full responsibility for the fulfillment of this covenant, Genesis 17 indicates it is an eternal covenant, and Genesis 18 and 22 reveal it will continue through Abraham's descendants.

Genesis 18:17–19 clarifies God's purpose in making a covenant with Abraham: "The LORD said, 'Shall I hide from Abraham what I am about to do, since Abraham will surely become a great and mighty nation, and in him all the nations of the earth will be blessed? For I have chosen him, so that he may command his children and his household after him to keep the way of the LORD by doing righteousness and justice, so that the LORD may bring upon Abraham what He has spoken about him.'" Christopher Wright writes that this passage answers three important questions about the Abrahamic Covenant:

Who is Abraham? The one whom God has chosen and come to know in personal friendship (**election [God's choice]**).

Why did God choose Abraham? To initiate a people who would be committed to the way of the Lord and his righteousness and justice, in a world going the way of Sodom (**ethics [faithful obedience]**).[6]

For what purpose should the people of Abraham live according to that high ethical standard [in faithful obedience to God]? So that God can fulfill his mission of bringing blessing to the nations (**mission**).[7]

Paul writes the following concerning the Abraham and believers today in Galatians 3. The italicized portions highlight the connection of New Testament believers to Abraham and God's promises to him:

> *Be sure that it is those who are of faith who are sons of Abraham.* The Scripture, foreseeing that God would justify the Gentiles by faith, preached the gospel beforehand to Abraham, saying, "In you shall all the nations be blessed!" So then, those who have faith are blessed with faithful Abraham. ... *In Christ Jesus the blessing of Abraham comes upon the Gentiles*, that we might receive the promise of the Spirit *through faith*. ... There is neither Jew nor Greek, there is neither slave nor free, there is neither male nor female; for you are all one in Christ Jesus. *And if you are Christ's, then you are Abraham's offspring (seed), heirs according to the promise*. (Gal 3:7–9, 14, 28, 29)

We can draw at least four conclusions from what Paul writes:

1. Those who are of faith are children of Abraham (v. 7).
2. The gospel of salvation was first preached to Abraham (v. 8).
3. In Christ Jesus the blessing of Abraham comes upon the Gentiles ... through faith (v. 14).
4. And if you are Christ's, then you are Abraham's offspring (seed), heirs according to the promise (v. 29).

---

6. Wright uses the word "ethics," but it is such a loaded term, meaning all sorts of things according to the context, that "faithful obedience" does better at getting to the heart of what he means. "Faithful obedience" speaks of both the behavior of doing what God has commanded, obedience, and the motive for doing it, faithfulness to God.

7. Christopher J. H. Wright, *The Mission of God's People: A Biblical Theology of the Church's Mission* (Grand Rapids: Zondervan, 2010), 93.

Part of inheriting the promise to Abraham is not only life in Christ but also the calling of being a blessing to others by proclaiming the gospel of the Lord Jesus Christ, which was first preached to Abraham.

C. The Power of God in Redemption (9:9–11)

The motif of the exodus is a major pattern throughout the Bible in describing God's work of redemption.[8] When God calls Moses to go to Egypt he instructs him, saying,

> Say, therefore, to the sons of Israel, "I am the LORD, and I will bring you out from under the burdens of the Egyptians, and I will deliver you from their bondage. I will also redeem you with an outstretched arm and with great judgments. Then I will take you for My people, and I will be your God; and you shall know that I am the LORD your God, who brought you out from under the burdens of the Egyptians. I will bring you to the land which I swore to give to Abraham, Isaac, and Jacob, and I will give it to you *for* a possession; I am the LORD." (Exod 6:6–7)

Fisher observes there are four elements to the pattern of the exodus redemption:

1. It was a redemption accomplished by God. God is central to the message of salvation.
2. It was a redemption from bondage and oppression into the freedom and dignity of sonship.
3. It was a redemption which God accomplished through a man. God raised up, preserved, chose, called, commissioned and empowered Moses to lead the Israelites out of the bondage of Egypt and into covenant relationship with Yahweh.
4. It was a redemption which created a lasting relationship between God and Israel, a relationship of both privilege and responsibility.[9]

---

8. Fred L. Fisher, "The New and Greater Exodus: The Exodus Pattern in the New Testament," Preaching Source, http://preachingsource.com/journal/the-new-and-greater-exodus-the-exodus-pattern-in-the-new-testament/ (accessed February 23, 2018).

9. Fisher, "New and Greater Exodus."

However, a fifth element should be added to the pattern set forth in the exodus.

5. It was a redemption which put an end to the enemies of God and his people.

Moses conveys this in the song of Exodus 15:

"At the blast of Your nostrils the waters were piled up,
The flowing waters stood up like a heap;
The deeps were congealed in the heart of the sea.
"The enemy said, 'I will pursue, I will overtake, I will divide the spoil;
My desire shall be gratified against them;
I will draw out my sword, my hand will destroy them.'
"You blew with Your wind, the sea covered them;
They sank like lead in the mighty waters.
"Who is like You among the gods, O LORD?
Who is like You, majestic in holiness,
Awesome in praises, working wonders?
"You stretched out Your right hand,
The earth swallowed them.
"In Your lovingkindness You have led the people whom You have redeemed;
In Your strength You have guided *them* to Your holy habitation."

In Nehemiah 9:10–11 the people pray, "Then You performed signs and wonders against Pharaoh, Against all his servants and all the people of the land; For You knew that they acted arrogantly toward them. … And their pursuers You hurled into the depths, Like a stone into raging waters." The defeat of the enemy is an essential part of God's salvation of his people.

Williamson writes, "God's revealed character and abiding reputation ('name'), therefore, is not just that of mighty creator (v. 6) or gracious promise-maker (vv. 7–8) but of a savior of his people, one who has acted in concrete terms to bring his word to realization."[10] The people of God can look back to the time God tangibly redeemed them. It is not some dreamed-up myth to pacify a people. It is an actual event that demonstrated to them they can trust the Lord, who is mighty

---

10. Williamson, *Ezra, Nehemiah*, 313.

to save. It is this memory that gives them the confidence to approach the Lord in this time of need.

D. The Power of God in Provision (9:12–25)

In verses 12–25, the people recount Yahweh's "great goodness" by all the things God provided for them:

1. God's presence and guidance (vv. 12, 19)
2. Instruction (vv. 13–14, 20)
3. Food and water (vv. 15, 20–21)
4. Patience, forgiveness, and compassion (vv. 16–19)
5. God's Spirit to instruct them (v. 20)
6. Clothing (v. 21)
7. Land (v. 22)
8. Strength of numbers (v. 23)
9. Victories in battle (v. 24)
10. Fortified cities, homes, and abundance (v. 25)

The temptation for many believers is to forget or doubt God's great goodness when we find ourselves in a tight spot. However, it is when we find ourselves in difficult circumstances that it is crucial we remember God's great goodness. Many years ago I heard this statement, and it has stuck with me and served to encourage me throughout the years: "Never forget in the darkness what God has shown you to be true in the light." The God who has been faithfully good to us in the past is the same God who is faithfully good to his children in the present and forevermore.

E. The Power of God in Compassion (9:26–35)

One of the great mysteries about God is the reality of the simultaneous coexistence of his righteous judgment and merciful compassion. When the Israelites time and time again respond to God's great goodness with rebellion and disobedience, he repeatedly disciplines them but at the same time repetitively shows them mercy and compassion. God's patience with them is incomprehensible. All along he is attentive to them, even though they deserve God's punishment. Numbers 23:19 states, "God is not man, that he might lie, or a son of man, that he might change his mind. Does he speak and not act, or promise and not fulfill?" (HCSB). Israel's God is "the great, the mighty, and the awesome God, who keeps covenant and lovingkindness" (Neh 9:32). God's faithfulness to his covenant with Israel is truly amazing in light of their repeated unfaithfulness to their covenant with him.

Asaph writes that God's response to Israel's unfaithfulness was to raise up David his servant in order to shepherd his people (Ps 78:71–72). Of course, the greatest display of the simultaneous coexistence of God's righteous judgment and merciful compassion is at Golgotha through the Son of David. It was there the Lord Jesus Christ bore the wrath of God, God's righteous judgment of sin. Yet at the same time, God showed his mercy and compassion on sinners. It is the great exchange. The righteous Son of God became sin for us, so that we who are sinners might become the righteousness of God through faith in the person and work of Christ Jesus (2 Cor 5:21). Unlike the kings and priests before him, Jesus is the King and Priest who faithfully obeyed his heavenly Father. It is this risen Son of David who now shepherds a people who were once his enemies. Not only is this a great mystery, but it is a glorious one.

F. The Power of God in Supplication (9:36–37)

The people are trusting in the promise God made to Solomon in 2 Chronicles 7:14, "If … My people who are called by My name humble themselves and pray and seek My face and turn from their wicked ways, then I will hear from heaven, will forgive their sin and will heal their land." Not only is God powerful in creation, election, salvation, provision, and compassion, but he is also the God who is near to his people when they call to him. Like a mother who is attentive to the cries of her precious child, God demonstrates his power in response to the supplications and pleas of his children. God hears and answers the prayers of his children.

God did not act on behalf of his people since the very beginning for it to end with them in bondage once again. As the people of God, they know that only the Lord himself is to rule over them—not these foreign kings who set themselves up in the place of God over God's holy people and city. Although God gave them great success in rebuilding the walls of Jerusalem and much of their reproach has been lifted, they long for God to finish what he began in and through them. They long for their distress to be completely removed. It is like the believer who has tasted the saving grace of the Lord Jesus Christ in salvation and now longs for the day when she sees the Savior face to face and is made like him. We praise God for his forgiveness and the removal of the reproach that was on us, but we long for the day when the distress of our sinful nature will be completely eradicated. God is faithful to complete what he has begun (Phil 1:6).

CONCLUSION

The prayer of Nehemiah 9 is a reminder that God listens to the confession of his people and can be trusted to save his people. It provides an example of what the confession of sin looks like and sounds like. The prayer of deliverance demonstrates how important it is for believers to remember who God is and what he has done. It is especially essential for believers to remember the "great goodness" of God when facing trials. Moreover, because God is good, God saves his children when they cry out to him in need and despair.

FINAL THOUGHTS

1. What does this passage teach concerning the need of believers to confess sin?
2. How should we approach God when confessing sin?
3. How does one's memory of the mighty acts of God play a role in seeking God's help?
4. What mighty acts have you witnessed God do in your life?
5. What impact does knowledge of God's nearness to believers in hearing and answering their prayers have on you?

THE PEOPLE'S COMMITMENT TO GOD

Nehemiah 9:38–10:39

INTRODUCTION

There are certain principles concerning commitments that even secular society recognizes to be true. In his article "Make a Public Commitment to Your Goals and Work toward Them Every Day," psychologist Tom Muha writes,

> To be successful, studies show, people benefit from writing down their goals. It's important to set specific objectives that include a timeline detailing exactly what you want to achieve and when you want to achieve it. After writing down your action plan, it's essential to share it with others. Publicly committing to pursuing positive outcomes is far more powerful than simply dreaming about doing something.
>
> Writing down goals along with specific steps to success and a list of supportive relationships makes it easier to see a positive outcome is possible. An action plan ignites passion, fosters teamwork, and generates optimism—three essential ingredients needed to overcome the obstacles that you'll face on your path to success.[1]

In Nehemiah 9:38–10:39, Nehemiah and the leaders of Jerusalem lead the people in a solemn public ceremony to make an oath to God to keep his covenant. They assemble together to sign a written document promising to be faithful to Yahweh by submitting to his law. The passage details exactly what actions they intend to take in order to accomplish their pledge to God and one another. The gravity of the occasion is marked by who the participants are and by what they commit to do.

---

1. Tom Muha, "Make a Public Commitment to Your Goals and Work toward Them Every Day," Propel Principles, https://www.thepropelprinciples.com/2016/01/03/make-a-public-commitment-to-your-goals-and-work-toward-them-every-day/ (accessed June 8, 2018).

STRUCTURE

Nehemiah 9:38–10:39 has a straightforward structure. The first section (9:38–10:29) contains a record of the people who participate in making this solemn agreement with the Lord and one another, and the second section (10:30–39) describes the specifications of the agreement.

SUMMARY OF THE PASSAGE

Having listened to the word of God and confessing their sins to God, all of the people who are committed to separating themselves from the nations and devoting themselves to the Lord make a solemn written agreement to submit and obey God's law in their families, their commerce, and their worship.

OUTLINE OF THE PASSAGE

I. Who Makes This Solemn Commitment to God (9:38–10:29)?
  A. The national leadership (10:1)
  B. The religious leadership (10:2–13)
    1. The priests (10:2–8)
    2. The Levites (10:9–13)
  C. The local leadership (10:14–27)
  D. The rest of the people (10:28–29)
II. What Is Their Solemn Commitment to God (10:30–39)?
  A. They promise to submit to God in their family activities (10:30)
  B. They promise to submit to God in their business activities (10:31)
  C. They promise to submit to God in their religious activities (10:32–39)
    1. By financially supporting the work of the house of God
    2. By financially supporting the workers in the house of God

DEVELOPMENT OF THE EXPOSITION

I. WHO MAKES THIS SOLEMN COMMITMENT TO GOD (9:38–10:29)?

38 "Now because of all this
We are making an agreement in writing;
And on the sealed document *are the names of* our leaders, our Levites
  and our priests."

The statement "In view of all this" refers to the events of the previous two chapters. In Nehemiah 8, the people approach Ezra and ask him to publicly read the book of the law. All of the people who are old enough to understand it gather at the Water Gate to attentively listen to him. It becomes a time of weeping over their sin and at the same time a celebration of the marvelous grace of God. As a result, they observe the Feast of Booths according to God's commandment. In Nehemiah 9, the people continue listening to the reading of God's law, which results in their confessing their sin and continued worship. Their leaders remind them of God's continued goodness to Israel from the very beginning of creation. They recognize God's goodness to them before they even existed and his faithfulness to them to the present time. In order to demonstrate their loyalty to Yahweh, the people gather together to make a "binding agreement in writing" containing the names of their leaders, Levites, and priests to represent all of the people as they commit themselves to live according to God's word. It is interesting that the word 'ămānâ ("agreement") appears here instead of the usual word, bĕrît (covenant). It possibly is because they are making a solemn pledge to keep the already-existing covenant between God and Israel that the law stipulated. What they are committing to is not new. Instead, it is a promise to keep that which God had already established with Israel at Mount Sinai through his servant Moses.

Why such a public display? First of all, it sends a message to all the surrounding peoples that those making this solemn agreement will be serving Yahweh, the God of Israel, the God who created the heavens, the earth, the seas, and all that is in them (9:6). Just as the Lord publicly identified himself with Israel as his treasured possession, so they are publicly identifying with him as their one and only God. Second, the public nature of this binding agreement invites accountability not only to God but to one another. It emphasizes the corporate commitment of the people. Today many believers refer to their "personal relationship with Christ" as if it is different from everyone else's relationship with Christ. Rest assured, everyone's relationship to Christ is personal. The rejection of Christ and life of rebellion against him is personal to him every bit as much as the faith and obedience of one who follows him. However, the emphasis of the Scriptures in both Testaments is the corporate commitment of the people of God. It appears that the vast majority of believers today resist the necessity of corporate accountability in the community of faith. We seem to be okay with other believers telling us what is right as long as they do not cross a line by meddling in our lives and holding us accountable to do what is right. The person who says that we are only accountable to God and not to one another in the body of Christ has either neglected the reading of the Scriptures or has chosen to ignore or disregard them. Surely, such an unwillingness to invite and embrace accountability within the community of faith is a major reason for the prevalence of anemic Christians and dying congregations today. Those who are serious about their following Christ will desire the accountability that comes within the body of Christ, which serves to purify them and conform them more into the image of Christ.

Speaking to his disciples, Jesus teaches the following: "If your brother sins, go and show him his fault in private; if he listens to you, you have won your brother. But if he does not listen *to you*, take one or two more with you, so that BY THE MOUTH OF TWO OR THREE WITNESSES EVERY ACT MAY BE CONFIRMED. If he refuses to listen to them, tell it to the church; and if he refuses to listen even to the church, let him be to you as a Gentile and a tax collector" (Matt 18:15–17). The phrase "tell it to the church" indicates believers are accountable to the community of faith and that we are to hold one another accountable so that, using the words of Nehemiah, we will no longer be a reproach. Paul's instruction in 1 Corinthians 5 supports this truth too.[2] The solemn agreement of Nehemiah 10 highlights the people's accountability to their leaders, to one another, and to God.

A. The National Leadership (10:1)

[1] Now on the sealed document *were the names of*: Nehemiah the governor, the son of Hacaliah, and Zedekiah,

As the Persian governor of Yehud or Judah, Nehemiah's name appears first. Zedekiah was an official who worked alongside Nehemiah and was the scribe who was responsible for actually producing this document. His abbreviated name, Zadok, appears in Nehemiah 13:13.[3] This document is a testament not only to Nehemiah's organizational capabilities but also to his spiritual leadership in the public arena. Obviously, Nehemiah worked closely with the religious leadership, as the following names attest, but he was as committed to using his place of influence to spiritually lead the people as much as any of the priests or Levites were

---

2. Bethlehem Church staff, "The Meaning of Membership and Church Accountability," is especially helpful: Desiring God, https://www.desiringgod.org/articles/the-meaning-of-membership-and-church-accountability (accessed April 10, 2018).

3. Andrew E. Steinmann, *Ezra and Nehemiah*, Concordia Commentary (St. Louis: Concordia, 2010), 557.

in their positions. While people today might understand Nehemiah's position to have been secular, he saw it as a divine calling on his life to lead the people to Yahweh and to remove the reproach that had been associated with them for so long.

B. The Religious Leadership (10:2–13)

[2] Seraiah, Azariah, Jeremiah, [3] Pashhur, Amariah, Malchijah, [4] Hattush, Shebaniah, Malluch, [5] Harim, Meremoth, Obadiah, [6] Daniel, Ginnethon, Baruch, [7] Meshullam, Abijah, Mijamin, [8] Maaziah, Bilgai, Shemaiah. These *were* the priests. [9] And the Levites: Jeshua the son of Azaniah, Binnui of the sons of Henadad, Kadmiel; [10] also their brothers Shebaniah, Hodiah, Kelita, Pelaiah, Hanan, [11] Mica, Rehob, Hashabiah, [12] Zaccur, Sherebiah, Shebaniah, [13] Hodiah, Bani, Beninu.

1. The Priests (10:2–8)

Nehemiah 10:2–8 lists at least fifteen ancestral families of the priests who participate in the solemn occasion who are also original returnees from Babylon. The other names are most likely those of individuals who had become heads of these houses. It accounts for the reason Ezra's name is absent from the list, because he was from the family of Seraiah (Ezra 7:1–5; 1 Chr 6:3–14).[4] Most importantly, the priests and their families are active and prominent participants in this commitment ceremony. These spiritual leaders lead by example.[5] The Lord Jesus Christ was the perfect example of this with his disciples. Not only did he tell his disciples they needed to be servants, but he took the lead, showing them what he meant by serving them. Hans Finzel observes, "Jesus demonstrated servant leadership by taking off His robe, picking up a towel, and washing His disciples' feet."[6]

I am often amazed by seminary students preparing for ministry who fail to realize this concept. For instance, someday they may be pastors of local congregations where they will be encouraging the church to be actively involved in the

---

4. Derek Kidner, *Ezra and Nehemiah*, Tyndale Old Testament Commentaries 12 (Downers Grove, IL: IVP Academic, 1979), 125.

5. For a discussion of the responsibilities of priests in the Old Testament see T. J. Betts, *Ezekiel the Priest: A Custodian of Tora*, Studies in Biblical Literature 74 (New York: Peter Lang, 2005), 17–45.

6. Hans Finzel, *The Top Ten Leadership Commandments* (Colorado Springs: David C. Cook, 2012), 92.

ministry of the church, yet these students have little to no participation of service in their churches as they prepare for leadership positions in the church. It may really hit home with them when they urge their future congregations to give generously from their financial resources to support the work of the ministry in the church when these future ministers themselves give a small percentage or nothing at all of their income to the work of the church. If they reap what they have sown, it could be very difficult for them. Effective spiritual leaders recognize the importance of leading by example. Just as the "do as I say not as I do" approach to leadership in the home fails with parenting children, it fails in the family of God as well. Spiritual leaders should not ask the congregation to do any more than what they themselves are doing or are willing to do, and these leaders should not ask the congregation to do any less than what is God's will for all believers.

2. The Levites (10:9–13)

The list of Levites who participate in the ceremony is either a list of names of individuals or a combination of individual and family names.[7] The Levites served as associates to the priests, assisting the priests in their various duties (see Num 1:47–54; 3:1–39). Six or seven of them participated in the instruction of God's law in Nehemiah 8. So, along with the priests, these Levites stand beside them as spiritual leaders in this commitment ceremony. These men lead the people by following their spiritual leaders, the priests. Such submission to spiritual leadership can have as great or even greater influence on others than the impact of more prominent leaders, such as the priests in this instance.

C. The Local Leadership (10:14–27)

[14] The leaders of the people: Parosh, Pahath-moab, Elam, Zattu, Bani, [15] Bunni, Azgad, Bebai, [16] Adonijah, Bigvai, Adin, [17] Ater, Hezekiah, Azzur, [18] Hodiah, Hashum, Bezai, [19] Hariph, Anathoth, Nebai, [20] Magpiash, Meshullam, Hezir, [21] Meshezabel, Zadok, Jaddua, [22] Pelatiah, Hanan, Anaiah, [23] Hoshea, Hananiah, Hasshub, [24] Hallohesh, Pilha, Shobek, [25] Rehum, Hashabnah, Maaseiah, [26] Ahiah, Hanan, Anan, [27] Malluch, Harim, Baanah.

---

7. Steinmann, *Ezra and Nehemiah*, 558; Kidner, *Ezra and Nehemiah*, 125.

The first twenty-one names of the local leaders are similar to the list of names in Ezra 2:3–30 and Nehemiah 7:8–27. The list also contains some of the names of people listed in Nehemiah 3 who participated in rebuilding the wall. The remaining names may be branches of these families, the names of newer arrivals, or possibly the names of families who were in Judah during the entire period of the exile and have reunited with those who have returned from Babylon.[8] Importantly, these lay leaders are just as committed as any of the other leaders to publicly pledging to sign and keep this solemn oath to the Lord.

D. The Rest of the People (10:28–29)

> [28] Now the rest of the people, the priests, the Levites, the gatekeepers, the singers, the temple servants and all those who had separated themselves from the peoples of the lands to the law of God, their wives, their sons and their daughters, all those who had knowledge and understanding, [29] are joining with their kinsmen, their nobles, and are taking on themselves a curse and an oath to walk in God's law, which was given through Moses, God's servant, and to keep and to observe all the commandments of GOD our Lord, and His ordinances and His statutes;

Every child and adult who can understand and who has separated themselves from the surrounding peoples in order to obey God's law joins their leaders in making a solemn oath to carefully live by God's law. It is reminiscent of Deuteronomy 29:10–13, which states,

> You stand today, all of you, before the LORD your God: your chiefs, your tribes, your elders and your officers, even all the men of Israel, your little ones, your wives, and the alien who is within your camps, from the one who chops your wood to the one who draws your water, that you may enter into the covenant with the LORD your God, and into His oath which the LORD your God is making with you today, in order that He may establish you today as His people and that He may be your God, just as He spoke to you and as He swore to your fathers, to Abraham, Isaac, and Jacob.

---

8. Mervin Breneman, *Ezra, Nehemiah, Esther*, NAC 10 (Nashville: Broadman & Holman, 1993), 245.

These people follow the example of God's covenant with Israel to reestablish their commitment to this covenant. True dedication to God will always be rooted in a knowledge of and submission to God's word.

Separation from the nations means separation from their ungodliness. In our vernacular it means living for Christ and being separated from the world—being in the world but not of it (see 1 John 2:15–17). It means conforming to the will of God, communicated to us through the Scriptures. It means obedience to his word and conforming to Christ. God's word shapes who we are and what we do. The participants in this ceremony recognize that knowing who was the Source of the law and knowing its contents is insufficient. True repentance to God demonstrates itself by obedience to the word of God. Knowing God's word is good, but knowing God's word and carefully submitting one's life to it in obedience is what counts. In fact, the person who thinks he knows God's word but lives in disobedience to it really does not know the Scriptures after all. True knowledge of God's word comes through submissive obedience to it, and it is this submissive obedience to God's word that leads to a deeper knowledge of and intimacy with God. Moreover, the people are so committed to being held accountable to keep this promise that they put themselves under a curse should they fail to fulfill the solemn oath to "walk in God's law … to keep and observe all the commandments of GOD [Yahweh] our Lord." They again follow the pattern of God's covenant with Israel in Deuteronomy, which contains both blessings and curses, evidence of just how seriously they are taking God's law (Deut 27:1–26; 29:14–28; 30:19).

II. WHAT IS THEIR SOLEMN COMMITMENT TO GOD (10:30–39)?

A. They Promise to Submit to God in Their Family Activities (10:30)

> ³⁰ and that we will not give our daughters to the peoples of the land or take their daughters for our sons.

True commitment to the Lord will be reflected in the home. This truth is purported in the law: "You shall love the LORD your God with all your heart and with all your soul and with all your might. These words, which I am commanding you today, shall be on your heart. You shall teach them diligently to your sons and shall talk of them when you sit in your house and when you walk by the way and when you lie down and when you rise up" (Deut 6:5–7).

In the Old Testament, God's word warns of the danger of intermarriage with the peoples of the land leading to spiritual adultery and eventually destruction and exile (Exod 34:15–16; Deut 7:3–4; 29:26–28; Josh 23:11–13; 1 Kgs 11:1–6). If these Judeans are going to faithfully remain separated from the nations, then it surely means their children will only marry other Israelites and not foreigners, as taught in the law (Exod 34:11–16; Deut 7:1–4; 20:10–18). Joseph Blenkinsopp points out that in this instance, the phrase "the peoples of the land" contemporizes the law of Deuteronomy, where it refers to seven nations.[9] Therefore, they are using the law as a paradigm for comprehension and application in this new context. This is not a racially motivated commitment but a spiritual one. Rahab and Ruth were both foreigners who were under God's curse, but both were received into the community of faith because of their faith in Yahweh. This principle is reiterated in the New Testament by Paul in his second letter to the Corinthians: "Do not be bound together with unbelievers; for what partnership have righteousness and lawlessness, or what fellowship has light with darkness?" (2 Cor 6:14; see 6:14–7:1). Parents who are committed to the Lord will teach their children what it means to follow Christ, and inherent to following Christ is eschewing anything that threatens one's faithfulness to Christ. Such truths should be communicated by both practice and instruction.

B. They Promise to Submit to God in Their Business Activities (10:31)

> [31] As for the peoples of the land who bring wares or any grain on the sabbath day to sell, we will not buy from them on the sabbath or a holy day; and we will forego *the crops* the seventh year and the exaction of every debt.

Most likely, the people making this oath kept the Sabbath by abstaining from working on it. However, it appears merchants from the surrounding foreign people groups saw the Israelite Sabbath as an opportunity to do business without Judean competition. While the law does not directly forbid buying goods and

---

9. Joseph Blenkinsopp, *Ezra-Nehemiah: A Commentary*, Old Testament Library (Philadelphia: Westminster, 1988), 315.

merchandise from foreigners on the Sabbath, the activity appears to be inconsistent with the principle of rest instructed in the law concerning the Sabbath. Isaiah seems to support the idea of abstaining from shopping on the Sabbath in Isaiah 58:13–14:

> If because of the sabbath, you turn your foot
> From doing your *own* pleasure on My holy day,
> And call the sabbath a delight, the holy *day* of the LORD honorable,
> And honor it, desisting from your *own* ways,
> From seeking your *own* pleasure
> And speaking *your own* word,
> Then you will take delight in the LORD,
> And I will make you ride on the heights of the earth;
> And I will feed you *with* the heritage of Jacob your father,
> For the mouth of the LORD has spoken.

Therefore, the people who participate in making this solemn oath appear to be paradigmatically applying the law pertaining to the Sabbath in a new context as well. Furthermore, just as circumcision is a sign of the covenant God made with Israel at Sinai, so the Sabbath also is a sign of the covenant (Exod 20:12; 31:13). What kind of testimony could they have had to the other nations concerning the holiness of Yahweh if the people conducted themselves in a way that undermined the holiness of the Sabbath, the day set apart from normal daily affairs and dedicated to Yahweh?

The law concerning the Sabbatical Year is found in Exodus 21:2–6; 23:10–11; and Deuteronomy 15:1–18. Both Exodus and Deuteronomy address the issue of canceling the debt of indentured slaves in the Sabbatical Year along with other debts. The people's commitment in these areas demonstrates the necessity of believers to be conscious of conducting themselves in a way that honors God's word in their social and business environments no matter how inconvenient or difficult it may be to do so. Having integrity in one's social and business communities begins with having integrity before God by daily putting into practice the teachings and demands of God's word. Failure in regard to God's word will eventually certainly expose itself in the way of moral failure in every other venue.

Obeying these laws pertaining to the Sabbath also demonstrates their trust in God. To allow their farm land to lie untouched for a year and to cancel debts owed to them has to stretch their faith in God's provision for them, because from a human business perspective obeying these laws appears less than prudent. However, they realize the land belongs to the Lord and that the Lord is the source of their provision. Therefore, to obey the Lord in these matters is the wisest decision they can make.

C. They Promise to Submit to God in Their Religious Activities (10:32–39)

³² We also placed ourselves under obligation to contribute yearly one third of a shekel for the service of the house of our God: ³³ for the showbread, for the continual grain offering, for the continual burnt offering, the sabbaths, the new moon, for the appointed times, for the holy things and for the sin offerings to make atonement for Israel, and all the work of the house of our God.

³⁴ Likewise we cast lots for the supply of wood *among* the priests, the Levites and the people so that they might bring it to the house of our God, according to our fathers' households, at fixed times annually, to burn on the altar of the LORD our God, as it is written in the law; ³⁵ and that they might bring the first fruits of our ground and the first fruits of all the fruit of every tree to the house of the LORD annually, ³⁶ and bring to the house of our God the firstborn of our sons and of our cattle, and the firstborn of our herds and our flocks as it is written in the law, for the priests who are ministering in the house of our God. ³⁷ We will also bring the first of our dough, our contributions, the fruit of every tree, the new wine and the oil to the priests at the chambers of the house of our God, and the tithe of our ground to the Levites, for the Levites are they who receive the tithes in all the rural towns. ³⁸ The priest, the son of Aaron, shall be with the Levites when the Levites receive tithes, and the Levites shall bring up the tenth of the tithes to the house of our God, to the chambers of the storehouse. ³⁹ For the sons of Israel and the sons of Levi shall bring the contribution of the grain, the new wine and the oil to the chambers; there are the utensils of the sanctuary, the priests who are ministering, the gatekeepers and the singers. Thus we will not neglect the house of our God.

1. By Financially Supporting the Work of the House of God

Much of what the people promise to do to support the work of the temple is not explicitly stated in the law. However, it is closely connected to it. For instance, the law does not specify a tax for the maintenance of the temple. Nevertheless, the law indicates the people need to give to support "the service of the tent of meeting" (Exod 30:16; see 30:11–16; 38:25–26). Even though there are differences between these passages, the action in this instance is certainly based on a midrashic interpretation of the passages in Exodus to provide for daily duties of the priests and Levites in the temple as well as its maintenance.[10] Likewise, the law states that a fire should continually burn on the altar (Lev 6:12–13), but it does not specify how the wood for the fire is to be supplied. So the people take it on themselves to set up a system to ensure the priests have the necessary supply of wood to fulfill this law along with performing all the other required sacrifices according to the law. Spirituality embraces practicality in order to do God's work. The bottom line is that the people accept responsibility in providing for the work of the house of God and do what was necessary to make it happen. It is a shining example for believers today to be mindful and responsible for the needs of the church to carry out the work of the gospel.

2. By Financially Supporting the Workers in the House of God

Not only are the people concerned about the physical needs of the daily operation of the temple, but they also are attentive to the needs of the priests and temple servants. The law stipulates the people are to provide for the needs of the priests and Levites through their tithes and offerings (Exod 23:19; 34:26; Num 18:8–13, 21–24; Deut 26:1–19).[11] Consequently, their solemn oath to submit to the Lord and keep his law includes the promise to take care of their spiritual leaders. As they say, "We will not neglect the house of God." Their actions demonstrate that an authentic commitment to God will necessarily include a commitment to support the "house of God." Neglect in this area calls into question one's genuine commitment to God.

---

10. H. G. M. Williamson, *Ezra, Nehemiah*, Word Biblical Commentary (Nashville: Thomas Nelson, 1985), 335–36.

11. Williamson suggests the mention of consecrating the firstborn males in Neh 10:36 may be to show that Num 18:12–13, where the priests eat the offered firstlings, takes precedence over Deut 15:19–20, where the firstlings are to be eaten by the owner at the temple (*Ezra, Nehemiah*, 337).

CONCLUSION

The people's commitments reveal how they apply the law. Rather than being locked into a legalistic, word-for-word reading of the law, which lends itself to loopholes, they understand it is to be used paradigmatically. According to Merriam-Webster, a paradigm is an "example, pattern; especially: an outstandingly clear or typical example or archetype."[12] It is a rubric or perspective on how to approach a situation. They focus on the spirit of or the intention of the law. For instance, instead of saying, "The law only forbids us to marry people from the exact seven nations mentioned in the law," they realize in their contemporary situation it means "the peoples of the land."[13]

Raymond Brown observes three aspects of this covenant renewal ceremony itself. First, the people's commitment is personal. The listing of the people's names and description of their actions point to this fact. Second, the people's commitment is public. It is put on display as an encouragement to one another and a witness to outsiders. Third, their commitment is practical.[14] Their commitment is not merely theoretical, ambiguous staging and lip service. They are specific about the actions they are to do. Continuing in the same vein as Brown, fourth, the people's commitment is powerful. It has an impact on every aspect of the people's lives. Fifth, the people's commitment is proper. It is appropriate for them to do this since they and the forebears were unfaithful to the covenant Yahweh made with them. Sixth, their commitment to God is principled. It is based on the principles of God's word. And finally, their commitment to Yahweh is prudent. My father used to tell me to "do the right thing because it is the right thing to do." The people commit their lives to Yahweh because it was the right thing for them to do. They realized the truth Jim Elliot, a missionary who was martyred for the cause of Christ in Ecuador, came to realize, "He is no fool who gives what he cannot keep to gain what he cannot lose."[15]

---

12. "Paradigm," merriam-webster.com, https://www.merriam-webster.com/dictionary/paradigm (accessed June 8, 2018).

13. J. G. McConville, *Ezra, Nehemiah, and Esther* (Louisville: Westminster John Knox, 1985), 133.

14. Raymond Brown, *The Message of Nehemiah*, The Bible Speaks Today (Downers Grove, IL: InterVarsity Press, 1998), 173–74.

15. Elisabeth Elliot, *Shadow of the Almighty: The Life and Testament of Jim Elliot* (San Francisco: HarperCollins, 1989), 15.

FINAL THOUGHTS

1. How should one's commitment to Christ affect one's way of life in the home?

2. How should one's commitment to Christ affect one's business practices?

3. How should one's commitment to Christ affect one's relationship to the work of the church?

4. What can one learn from this passage concerning how to practically apply the commands of Scripture in one's contemporary environment?

5. Considering the way the people go about making their solemn oath to God in Nehemiah 10, what can we learn about how we should go about making a commitment to the Lord?

A PLACE FOR EVERYONE TO SERVE

Nehemiah 11:1–36

INTRODUCTION

When I was a young pastor I heard a statement concerning the people of God that has since affected my perspective on the church: "Not everyone can do everything, but everyone can do something." Believers are not gifted to do everything in the ministry of the church. However, we are all called and gifted to serve within the church in some capacity. We are the body of Christ, many various members joined together and working together in Christ to perform specific functions so that as a whole we might glorify him (see 1 Cor 12:1–31). When I first attended seminary, it was not long before I was taught the Pareto Principle, or what others call the 80/20 Rule, which when concerning the church states that "twenty percent of the people do eighty percent of the work." What a travesty if this is true! The greatness of a church is not measured by the size of its budget, facilities, pastoral staff, or membership and attendance. It is measured by the percentage of that congregation who have answered God's call to faithfully serve him in the body of Christ.

At least two challenges arise in the church regarding this truth. The first is for every believer to recognize that when he was called to Christ in salvation it was also a call to ministry. For a few, it was a call to ministry as one's occupation, but for the vast majority it was to a ministry in which one also has a "secular" job that provides an income apart from a ministerial position in a local church, or church-related, or parachurch organization. Just as every member of the human body is expected to perform a function, so is every member of the body of Christ (1 Cor 12:12–27). For example, the person who serves families by serving in the nursery of the church is carrying out an admirable ministry in the name of Christ.

The second challenge is when believers desire or even covet the ministries of other believers. We may fail to be content with our calling to a particular place of ministry. It appears Paul dealt with a similar issue in the church at Corinth

(1 Cor 12:14–18). Peter also seems to have struggled with this idea concerning John (John 21:18–23). The proverb Paul wrote to Timothy stating "Godliness with contentment is great gain" is certainly apropos in this instance (1 Tim 6:6). At times we may be tempted to believe what God has called us to do is either too difficult or on the other hand quite insignificant compared to the ministries of others. However, it takes an extraordinary faith and commitment to God to be a faithful foot washer, someone whose greatest pleasure in serving others comes from knowing that it is service to Christ. It helps to remember the words of Christ when he said, "Truly I say to you, to the extent that you did it to one of these brothers of Mine, even the least of them, you did it to Me" (Matt 25:40). When it comes to fulfilling God's will for our lives concerning our calling to minister, it is well that we joyfully and faithfully learn to stay in our lane. It entails being willing to go where God calls us to go and being willing to stay where he wants us to stay.

Nehemiah 11 explains how the city of Jerusalem is repopulated. The construction project of rebuilding the wall is complete, but its present population is insufficient for the city to thrive. Nehemiah 7:4 describes the situation when the wall is finally completed: "Now the city was large and spacious, but the people in it were few and the houses were not built." Why is this the situation? First of all, it is because most of the people who once lived in Jerusalem had been taken away into Babylonian exile, and the majority of them appear to have remained there. Also, perhaps a number of them passed away while in exile, and Jerusalem was not home to their children. Second, those who did return found Jerusalem to be a city of ruins, so much so that arguably it was mostly uninhabitable without significant manpower and effort to remove the debris. Third, given the difficulties that Ezra records that the people encountered when they first arrived, and considering the obstacles the people encountered both from within and without while restoring Jerusalem under Nehemiah's leadership, it surely was easier for them to build settlements away from the city when they returned from exile (see Ezra 4).

Nehemiah 11 provides an example of the people of God's willingness to live and serve wherever God wants them to serve. Some have to move from elsewhere and live and serve in Jerusalem, while others stay where they are outside the city and minister in the surrounding region. Some serve as priests and Levites, and others serve as craftsmen and farmers. However, the places of service and types of service to which individuals are called is essential to the overall purposes of God for his people as a whole. The passage displays how all this is done in an orderly fashion, how the people cooperate with one another, and how it is for the purpose of building up of one another and for the glory of God.

STRUCTURE

There are two sections in this passage. The first section (11:1–24) lists the families that repopulate Jerusalem. The second section (11:25–36) lists the towns and areas in the regions of Judah and Benjamin where the rest of the people live.

SUMMARY OF THE PASSAGE

In light of the people's recommitment to Yahweh in Nehemiah 10, Nehemiah 11 records the organized, voluntary repopulation of Jerusalem, "the holy city," the place of God's manifest presence with his people and the place of worship for his people.

OUTLINE OF THE PASSAGE

I. The Repopulation of Jerusalem (11:1–24)
    A. What does the repopulation of Jerusalem involve (11:1–2)?
        1. Administration
        2. Dedication
        3. Organization
        4. Cooperation
        5. Consecration
        6. Affirmation
    B. Who Does the Repopulation of Jerusalem Involve (11:3–24)?
        1. The lay families (11:3–9)
        2. The priests (11:10–14)
        3. The Levites, gatekeepers, and temple servants (11:15–24)
II. The Repopulation of Judah and Benjamin (11:25–36)

DEVELOPMENT OF THE EXPOSITION

I. THE REPOPULATION OF JERUSALEM (11:1–24)

Although the construction of the walls is complete, Jerusalem is still vulnerable to attack because there are not enough people inhabiting it to man those walls. Usually in ancient times, the farmers who lived in the surrounding vicinity of a city fled to the city when they spotted an approaching enemy. They often sounded the first alarms of encroaching danger. If the city and its inhabitants were to survive an attack, they needed trained, professional soldiers to lead in its defense. Walled cities were especially targets of would-be invaders because these cities were located in strategic locations that served as centers of influence over a region. To lose Jerusalem would mean the loss of all of Judah. The Persians would have had similar concerns. Even though the Persians were uninterested in the people's theological motives to restore and protect Jerusalem, they were concerned about having a strong fortification in the area as long as its inhabitants were loyal to the Persian king. Reinforcing Jerusalem with troops would have been an expectation of the Persians in this situation.[1]

Moreover, during peacetime, ancient cities served as centers of commerce. Craftsmen and farmers traveled there to sell their goods, and people from all over the region came to shop. They were the original farmers markets, much like those scattered across the Midwestern United States, where I reside. Buying local was not only good for the economy, but for most it was the only option. An economically thriving Jerusalem meant an economically thriving Judah. Therefore, the repopulation of Jerusalem became as important as the rebuilding of its walls had been. Of course, the Persians had concerns about the economy of their empire. A thriving economy in Judah would mean more tax revenues for the king. Pleasing the Persians in this respect was a win-win scenario.

A. What Does the Repopulation of Jerusalem Involve (11:1–2)?

[1] Now the leaders of the people lived in Jerusalem, but the rest of the people cast lots to bring one out of ten to live in Jerusalem, the holy city, while nine-tenths *remained* in the *other* cities. [2] And the people blessed all the men who volunteered to live in Jerusalem.

1. Administration

Several years ago, I attended a conference where I heard John Maxwell say, "Everything rises and falls on leadership."[2] It is noteworthy that the leaders of the people of Judah already live in Jerusalem before taking action to bring 10

---

1. Joseph Blenkinsopp, *Ezra-Nehemiah: A Commentary*, Old Testament Library (Philadelphia: Westminster, 1988), 323.
2. John Maxwell was then (1990) the founder and leader of INJOY Life Club and pastor of Skyline Church in San Diego.

percent of Judah's population to relocate to Jerusalem.[3] They are already ahead of the people they lead. They understand the principle of leadership espoused by General Longstreet at Gettysburg, who said, "You can't lead from behind." They are men who have witnessed the great work God accomplished through his people in rebuilding the wall, and they believe that Jerusalem can once again become a thriving city and no longer be a reproach.

It is often easier to follow a leader one can see than to take action based only on an idea, no matter how noble, right, and good for you that idea may be. Weight Watchers has had millions of people join based on this concept of leadership. Mathematically speaking, weight loss is a "simple" matter of numbers—calorie intake versus calories burned. However, most of us who have tried to trim down have discovered there is nothing simple about it. The Mayo Clinic states, "According to research, having friends or family members who are supportive of your healthy eating and exercise goals is important for long-term weight-loss success."[4] Weight Watchers employs a leader in its meetings who is a role model who has lost weight in the program and kept it off. The leader provides encouragement, suggestions, instruction, and an incarnate example based on experience as they stand alongside their members in their sessions. They are living proof it can be done as they continue applying what they have learned themselves to keep off the weight.[5]

The leaders in Nehemiah's day employ the same principle. They already live in Jerusalem. They assume their roles as leaders by taking on the responsibility that goes with being a leader. They are hands-on administrators and living proof the repopulating of Jerusalem should and can be done. They make themselves examples for the people to follow for the strengthening of Jerusalem and for glory to God. It reminds me of Paul's words to the Corinthians: "Be imitators of me, just as I am of Christ" (1 Cor 11:1).

---

3. The use of "Judah" here refers to the entire Persian province of Yehud, which included areas of the tribal allotments left to Judah and Benjamin.

4. "Social Support: A Necessity for Weight Loss," Mayo Clinic, http://diet.mayoclinic.org/diet/motivate/social-support-for-weight-loss?xid=nl_MayoClinicDiet_20151021 (accessed June 15, 2018).

5. "Weight Watchers Diet," US News and World Report, https://health.usnews.com/best-diet/weight-watchers-diet (accessed June 15, 2018).

2. Dedication

Verse 2 refers to Jerusalem literally in Hebrew as "the city of holiness," which translates easily to "the holy city." Almost 100 percent of the time when I ask seminary students, "What does it mean to be holy in the Old Testament?" their response is "to be set apart." This is the definition I was always given growing up in church. However, there is an important element to the Hebrew word qōdeš, "holy" in English, which many miss, according to several Hebraists. For example, Peter Gentry argues that central to the meaning of "holy" in the Old Testament is that which is "dedicated, devoted, or committed."[6] Jackie Naudé maintains, "Separateness is often thought to be the basic meaning of holiness, but it is more its necessary consequence. Consecration is a separation to God rather than a separation from the world."[7] Thus, the ideas of being "set apart" or having "moral uprightness" are implicit in the meaning of holiness as one carries out one's devotion.

The motif of marriage that forms a longitudinal theme throughout the Scriptures depicting God's relationship to Israel and Christ's relationship to the church illustrates this truth. The people of God are to be devoted to him. Implicit in this devotion is exclusiveness. They are forbidden to worship any other gods. In other words, their devotion to Yahweh involves separation from anything associated with other gods. Furthermore, to be faithful to Yahweh includes moral blamelessness. To be unfaithful and commit adultery against Yahweh is to be morally defiled. This notion of holiness being both separation and devotion is highlighted in the solemn covenant renewal ceremony in Nehemiah 10:28, which identifies the participants as "all those who had separated themselves from the peoples of the lands to the law of God." Here it speaks of both separation "from the peoples of the lands," and of devotion "to the law of God." Their separation is a necessary consequence of devotion to Yahweh. Without the separation, faithful devotion would be impossible.

So if Jerusalem is supposed to be devoted to Yahweh and set apart from all other cities on the face of the earth as the "holy city," how is it to be devoted to him? It is dedicated to being the place for the people of God to worship him. It began many years earlier with Abraham on Mount Moriah, when God supplied

---

6. Peter J. Gentry, "The Meaning of 'Holy' in the Old Testament," *Bibliotheca Sacra* 170, no. 677–80 (2013): 400–417.

7. Jackie A. Naudé, "קדשׁ," in *New International Dictionary of Old Testament Theology and Exegesis*, ed. W. VanGemeren (Grand Rapids: Zondervan, 1997), 3:885.

him with a substitute to sacrifice in the place of his son Isaac (Gen 22:1–19). It was there it was called, "On the mountain of Yahweh, he will be seen."[8] This statement prophetically anticipates the manifest presence of Yahweh, high and lifted up in his temple. The lists of priests and Levites serving in Jerusalem in Nehemiah 11:10–24 attest to the city's holy purpose of worshiping the Lord with their sacrifices. Ultimately, the statement anticipates Jerusalem as the holy city because it is there "on the mountain of Yahweh, he will be seen" offering his only Son for our sins.

Moreover, the holy city requires a holy people, a people devoted to worshiping the Lord and serving God in whatever capacity is required to remove its reproach and see it thrive once again. Consequently, the notion that they are a "tithe" of the people is noteworthy.[9] Just as the tithe is dedicated to the service of Yahweh at the temple in Jerusalem, these people who consist of the 10 percent of the population who relocate to Jerusalem devote themselves to the revitalization of the holy city. Certainly, it is a sacrifice. Nevertheless, it is a special privilege and sacred calling.

3. Organization

Everyone needs to know their place of service and responsibilities when they get there. It is also well for them to know where everyone else is serving and what they are doing. Therefore, the organization of this endeavor is imperative. These lists provide such information and organization. Having 10 percent of the overall population in Jerusalem and 90 percent of it dispersed throughout the remaining areas appears to be the best way to promote the strength of Jerusalem in particular and the people of God as a whole. Having 10 percent of the population come to Jerusalem probably has a theological connection to the solemn oath of recommitment to their covenant with Yahweh just made in Nehemiah 10, where the people promise to bring their tithes to the temple in Jerusalem.[10]

The text does not indicate the person or persons who make the calculation and decide this is the most appropriate solution. Perhaps it is Nehemiah. What

---

8. This is my translation. The construct beginning with its preposition lends itself to "On the mountain of Yahweh," and the third-person masculine singular passive Niphal stem reads "he will be seen." A number of translations translate *yērāʾe*, "to see," as "provide," but the word literally means "to see or appear." While "provide" fits the context, it is unnecessary to translate the phrase in this way to understand the meaning of the text.

9. Blenkinsopp, *Ezra-Nehemiah*, 323.

10. Blenkinsopp, *Ezra-Nehemiah*, 323.

is clear is that without such organization, the situation would be chaotic, and the few who live in the city and people at large would suffer. The practical steps to organize the people of God to do the work of God can be as spiritually important as anything we can do if these steps aid in carrying out the work in the best way possible. There are those people who act as if it is unspiritual to plan anything pertaining to the Christian life or the life of the church, and I have often wondered whether such notions are more a smokescreen for laziness than anything else. Thank God for those who labor in organizing the work of the people of God so that the endeavor will be done in a way that blesses the people of God and brings honor to God.

4. Cooperation

In verse 2, the participle *hammitnaddĕbîm*, "volunteered," demonstrates that the people who are chosen by the lots to relocate to Jerusalem volunteer to do so. There are no draft dodgers. What would happen in the church today if all of us readily stepped up and volunteered to do whatever we could to build up the body of Christ?

5. Consecration

Also, the root of the Hebrew word *hammitnaddĕbîm* is closely associated with the freewill offering in the Old Testament. In the context of the holy city and of a tithe of the people who are chosen to relocate, it is fitting to recognize the people freely offer themselves up as an offering to God to serve him in this consecrated endeavor. The apostle Paul conveys this mind-set when he encourages the believers in Rome to do the same when he writes, "Therefore I urge you, brethren, by the mercies of God, to present your bodies a living and holy sacrifice, acceptable to God, *which is* your spiritual service of worship. And do not be conformed to this world, but be transformed by the renewing of your mind, so that you may prove what the will of God is, that which is good and acceptable and perfect" (Rom 12:1–2).

It is probable the casting of lots is performed by the high priest using the Urim and Thummim (see Neh 7:65).[11] The Urim and Thummim were part of the high priest's apparel and were used to cast as lots as a means of communicating

---

11. Blenkinsopp, *Ezra-Nehemiah*, 323.

the will of Yahweh to the people.[12] If this is how the casting of lots happens, then it further demonstrates and emphasizes how the Lord uses a holy priest to choose a holy people in a holy city to perform a holy service to their holy God.

6. Affirmation

The people affirm those who have offered themselves to serve the Lord by relocating to Jerusalem by pronouncing a blessing on them. It most likely is a scene where they kneel down as the people pray corporately for God's blessing on them. The idea of kneeling being associated with blessing "derives from the assumption that the person who was to be blessed knelt to receive the benediction."[13] Such a display demonstrates the healthy practice of the people of God publicly appreciating, encouraging, affirming, and blessing those who have voluntarily given themselves, and sometimes their families, for the sole purpose of serving the Lord in a specific capacity.

B. Who Does the Repopulation of Jerusalem Involve (11:3–24)?

[3] Now these are the heads of the provinces who lived in Jerusalem, but in the cities of Judah each lived on his own property in their cities—the Israelites, the priests, the Levites, the temple servants and the descendants of Solomon's servants. [4] Some of the sons of Judah and some of the sons of Benjamin lived in Jerusalem. From the sons of Judah: Athaiah the son of Uzziah, the son of Zechariah, the son of Amariah, the son of Shephatiah, the son of Mahalalel, of the sons of Perez; [5] and Maaseiah the son of Baruch, the son of Col-hozeh, the son of Hazaiah, the son of Adaiah, the son of Joiarib, the son of Zechariah, the son of the Shilonite. [6] All the sons of Perez who lived in Jerusalem were 468 able men.

[7] Now these are the sons of Benjamin: Sallu the son of Meshullam, the son of Joed, the son of Pedaiah, the son of Kolaiah, the son of Maaseiah, the son of Ithiel, the son of Jeshaiah; [8] and after him Gabbai *and* Sallai, 928. [9] Joel the son of Zichri was their overseer, and Judah the son of Hassenuah was second in command of the city.

12. T. J. Betts, *Ezekiel the Priest: A Custodian of Tora*, Studies in Biblical Literature 74 (New York: Peter Lang, 2005), 20.

13. William C. Williams, "בָּרַךְ," in *New International Dictionary of Old Testament Theology and Exegesis*, ed. W. VanGemeren (Grand Rapids: Zondervan, 1997), 1:755.

¹⁰ From the priests: Jedaiah the son of Joiarib, Jachin, ¹¹ Seraiah the son of Hilkiah, the son of Meshullam, the son of Zadok, the son of Meraioth, the son of Ahitub, the leader of the house of God, ¹² and their kinsmen who performed the work of the temple, 822; and Adaiah the son of Jeroham, the son of Pelaliah, the son of Amzi, the son of Zechariah, the son of Pashhur, the son of Malchijah, ¹³ and his kinsmen, heads of fathers' *households*, 242; and Amashsai the son of Azarel, the son of Ahzai, the son of Meshillemoth, the son of Immer, ¹⁴ and their brothers, valiant warriors, 128. And their overseer was Zabdiel, the son of Haggedolim.

¹⁵ Now from the Levites: Shemaiah the son of Hasshub, the son of Azrikam, the son of Hashabiah, the son of Bunni; ¹⁶ and Shabbethai and Jozabad, from the leaders of the Levites, who were in charge of the outside work of the house of God; ¹⁷ and Mattaniah the son of Mica, the son of Zabdi, the son of Asaph, who was the leader in beginning the thanksgiving at prayer, and Bakbukiah, the second among his brethren; and Abda the son of Shammua, the son of Galal, the son of Jeduthun. ¹⁸ All the Levites in the holy city *were* 284.

¹⁹ Also the gatekeepers, Akkub, Talmon and their brethren who kept watch at the gates, *were* 172.

²⁰ The rest of Israel, of the priests *and* of the Levites, *were* in all the cities of Judah, each on his own inheritance. ²¹ But the temple servants were living in Ophel, and Ziha and Gishpa were in charge of the temple servants.

²² Now the overseer of the Levites in Jerusalem was Uzzi the son of Bani, the son of Hashabiah, the son of Mattaniah, the son of Mica, from the sons of Asaph, who were the singers for the service of the house of God. ²³ For *there was* a commandment from the king concerning them and a firm regulation for the song leaders day by day. ²⁴ Pethahiah the son of Meshezabel, of the sons of Zerah the son of Judah, was the king's representative in all matters concerning the people.

1. The Lay Families (11:3–9)

The families who relocate to Jerusalem are made up of "able men" or men of valor. James Hamilton writes, "What is valiant and valorous about these people is their willingness to risk their necks for the kingdom of God. They courageously chose to dwell in Jerusalem for the sake of God's name. That's valorous. That's valiant."[14] Such valor is needed today. The Lord has called believers to various places and occupations all over the world so that we would be valiant in our witness of the transforming work of the gospel through our Lord Jesus Christ. Wherever we go and whatever we do should be undergirded by our desire and prayer to be courageous for the cause of Christ.

2. The Priests (11:10–14)

Among the priests is its leader, the high priest, and other leaders along with the rest who are committed to performing the work of the temple, offering sacrifices and instructing the people in God's law. Some of these priests are "valiant warriors." They not only faithfully serve in the temple but also are ready and able to protect it. It contradicts the stereotypical picture some have of meek and weak ministers today. It was as one of my martial arts instructors used to say, "Don't mistake kindness for weakness."

3. The Levites, Gatekeepers, and Temple Servants (11:15–24)

The Levites and temple servants consist of those who assist the priests with their duties in the temple. There are also gatekeepers, who take care of needed security for the city. Some of the Levites are responsible for leading in thanksgiving prayer. Others serve by leading in singing praises to the Lord (vv. 22–23). These spiritual leaders place a priority on prayer and worship through song for the people of God.

However, a number of the Levites have the responsibility of being "in charge of the outside work of the house of God." It is an important task. The way we take care of the things of God is a reflection of how much we truly value him, and this is surely communicated to nonbelievers, who for the most part connect value and worth to how well one takes care of oneself and the things one possesses. And while we may deny it, we believers most often do the same. We must not forget that one of Nehemiah's deepest concerns in Susa where he first heard the report about the condition of Jerusalem was that the people were a reproach with the wall of Jerusalem broken down and its gates burned with fire (1:3). The statement believers make about taking care of the things dedicated to God's use,

---

14. James M. Hamilton Jr., *Exalting Jesus in Ezra-Nehemiah*, Kindle ed., Christ-Centered Exposition Commentary (Nashville: Holman Reference, 2014), 204.

such as church buildings and grounds, is more than just a statement indicating we like things to look nice. It points to a God who is worthy of our best. Who can respect believers who care for themselves and their things more than they do the things of God? When David sought to build a house for the Lord, the Lord indicated he did not need a temple, but his response also indicates he was pleased by David's desire to bless him by promising to bless David. David lived in a nice house, while the things of God were in a tent. David believed God deserved better than what David possessed for himself, and so should we (2 Sam 7).

At times, some of us may be prone to take advantage of God's grace in this area. Since we need to do nothing to earn God's love, we may be tempted to do nothing to express our love for him. For instance, we hopefully do not need to earn our spouse's love, but at the same time, hopefully, we do acts of kindness for them because we love them. We want them and everyone else to know we love them, and one of the ways we do this is by adorning them with valuable things. Most of the time it begins with an engagement ring and then moves on from there. It is a symbol of our affection for our spouses, both to them and the world. One might argue, "God knows my heart, so I don't need to do that." This is true, but the world does not know what is in our hearts. What's more, God is blessed by our outward expressions of adoration when they are a true reflection of our love and adoration for him within. With all this said, the Levites who take care of the outside of the temple have an essential and noble responsibility to communicate God's worth both in Judah and to the surrounding peoples, and to ensure the work of the temple is able to be carried out.

II. The Repopulation of Judah and Benjamin (11:25–36)

[25] Now as for the villages with their fields, some of the sons of Judah lived in Kiriath-arba and its towns, in Dibon and its towns, and in Jekabzeel and its villages, [26] and in Jeshua, in Moladah and Beth-pelet, [27] and in Hazar-shual, in Beersheba and its towns, [28] and in Ziklag, in Meconah and in its towns, [29] and in En-rimmon, in Zorah and in Jarmuth, [30] Zanoah, Adullam, and their villages, Lachish and its fields, Azekah and its towns. So they encamped from Beersheba as far as the valley of Hinnom. [31] The sons of Benjamin also *lived* from Geba *onward*, at Michmash and Aija, at Bethel and its towns, [32] at Anathoth, Nob, Ananiah, [33] Hazor, Ramah, Gittaim, [34] Hadid, Zeboim, Neballat, [35] Lod and Ono, the valley of crafts-men. [36] From the Levites, *some* divisions in Judah belonged to Benjamin.

Chuck Swindoll refers to the people in this chapter as the "willing unknowns ... the lesser lights, the forgotten heroes, the unknowns, the 'nobodies' who paved the way for the 'somebodies.'"[15] The real willing unknowns are the people who live throughout the areas of Judah and Benjamin who are not even mentioned by name. The preceding lists at least contain the names of most of the people in mind. But in the list of the 90 percent of the population living outside Jerusalem, only the place names of the areas where they live are noted. Nevertheless, without these 90 percent who are composed of craftsmen, priests, Levites (v. 20), farmers, and so on, there would be no thriving city of Jerusalem. Everyone is essential to the revitalization of Jerusalem. Thank God for those within the body of Christ who faithfully serve without any concern for recognition.

Not everyone can do everything, but everyone can do something (and is called by the Lord to do so).

CONCLUSION

As we study Nehemiah 11, composed of long lists of foreign names that are difficult to pronounce, we must remind ourselves of their lasting significance and application for believers today. First, the lists should remind us that while we may find it challenging to relate to these people from over two millennia ago in history, God remembers the joyful obedience of his people, and he is eternally blessed by them. It should give us pause to consider whether we would be on such lists that recall the names of the people who were faithful servants of the Lord in their day.

My brother has a keen interest in our family's genealogy. Recently he discovered the membership roll and record of business meetings from the church where our great-grandfather was pastor in Wilburn, Arkansas, around 1905. The membership roll included a number of my relatives, and the records of the business meetings recounted various actions of that church. It reminds me of a heritage of believers who laid a spiritual foundation for my family many years before I was ever born. This lends itself to recognizing a second reason lists such as these in Nehemiah 11 are important for us today. We should be grateful for the faithful who have gone before us. These lists remind us that God was doing a great work through his people long before we came on the scene. These people provide an example for us and should encourage us to strive to leave the same kind of legacy for our brothers and sisters in Christ who will follow us after we are long gone.

---

15. Charles R. Swindoll, *Hand Me Another Brick* (Nashville: Thomas Nelson, 1978), 169.

Likewise, third, the lists should remind us other people are important to God. The lists include the names of people with a variety of gifts and responsibilities: leaders, servants, warriors, singers, teachers, craftsmen, and so on. Such lists of faithful believers should challenge our preoccupation with self-importance and the narrow-minded thinking that what we are doing is the only significant thing happening within the body of Christ. They remind us to beware of thinking too highly of ourselves while at the same time encouraging us to recognize that what we do in the name of Christ has eternal significance. Even if what we do in our Lord's service is mundane, it is substantial to God. When it comes to God's call on our lives to serve him, we must at the same time be both specialists and generalists: specialists who give keen attention to diligently carrying out the particular work to which he has called us but also generalists who have a general knowledge of what others are doing in kingdom work so that we might know how we can work together and support one another.

FINAL THOUGHTS

1. What are ways you can lead others to serve Christ more faithfully?

2. What do you think would happen if every believer stepped up and volunteered to faithfully serve somewhere in the church? What impact would it have on the church? What impact would it have on the community and beyond?

3. How are you volunteering your service to Christ and his church?

4. How does it benefit the cause of Christ when believers are unconcerned about getting credit for what they do?

5. What kind of legacy of commitment to Christ and his church do you desire to leave to those who come after you? What are you presently doing to fulfill that hope?

DOCUMENTATION AND DEDICATION

Nehemiah 12:1–13:3

INTRODUCTION

Recently I had the privilege of attending a service where three men in our church were designated as deacons emeriti. Together these men had faithfully served as deacons in the church for over one hundred and fifty years. One of them alone served as a deacon in our church since 1958. They were men who served our church during its many highs and lows, and given what I know about the history of the church, were it not for their servant leadership this local church might not exist today. When my sons were still at home, these godly men were examples to whom I was able to point and tell my sons that they should aspire to grow up to be men like these three men. It was good to be in a service where the people of God joined together to recognize how God has blessed us with such godly men and to be reminded that we are in debt to their faithful service to the church. During that same service we ordained a twenty-eight-year-old man to serve as a deacon in the church. I have known him quite well since he was a little boy. This man grew up in the church and has shown himself to be a godly man who is willing to serve the church as best he can. Our prayer for him is that someday he too will finish well, just as these other three are doing in their later years of life. So, while we remembered what God has done in the past through three godly men, we also looked to the future as a new man committed himself to serving the people of God. It was a reminder that while God has done great things, he is doing great things and will continue to do great things going forward.

What happened in our ordination service is similar to what is recorded in Nehemiah 12. The chapter begins by recognizing the spiritual leaders who diligently served the Lord and the people of God as priests and Levites. Many of them were the ones who were willing to make the long trek back to Jerusalem out of exile in order to seek the rebuilding and revitalization of the temple and

Jerusalem. With the dedication of the temple in Nehemiah's day, it was good to recall those who sacrificed and dedicated themselves to this day even though they did not live long enough to see it with their own eyes. It is humbling and good for us to remember that long before we ever came on the scene, God had a people for himself and used them for the building of his kingdom, laying a foundation for those who would come after them to continue what they had so faithfully committed to God.

I was recently reminded of this truth when I had the privilege of going to Tambo, Ecuador, to provide biblical training for pastors and lay leaders of churches in that region. While there, I learned the intricate hardwood floor I walked on was laid years earlier by missionaries from our church. The bunk beds we slept on were built by others on another mission trip from our church. The gas tanks that provided us with hot water for showers in that chilly environment were installed by still others on a previous mission trip, and the list goes on. The point should be obvious. The team of which I was a part was able to carry out its mission because others before us had laid a foundation for us to do so. Hopefully, we did the same for future missionaries to the region.

Like the ordination service I attended, the dedication of the wall is much more than a memorial service. While those attending the dedication look back at what God had done, they are looking forward to what is yet to come. Their rejoicing stems from a view to the past, present, and future. Therefore, Nehemiah 12 should remind believers we need an eternal perspective, one that goes in both directions. It should remind us that all that we see God doing in our time is part of the grand work of his redemption to save a people to himself from every nation. What God is doing now has always been in his heart, and it will declare his glory throughout all eternity. It should give rise both to rejoicing over what God has done and rejoicing for what he is doing and is going to do in the future. In truth, the dedication of the wall is really the people's dedicating themselves to protect the things of God and carry out his purposes.

STRUCTURE

There are three sections in this passage. The first section (12:1–26) provides important documentation of the priests and Levites who serve in Jerusalem. The second section (12:27–47) describes what happens at the dedication of the wall of Jerusalem. And the third section (13:1–3) shows how, upon hearing the reading of God's law, the people separate themselves from foreigners by excluding foreigners from their community.

SUMMARY OF THE PASSAGE

Nehemiah 12:1–13:3 demonstrates the importance of recognizing the centrality of worship in the community of faith. Everything the people of God did in this passage, from acknowledging those who led in worship to dedicating the product of their work as an act of worship and living in purity to offer themselves to God as an expression of worship, revealed the centrality of worship among the people of God.

OUTLINE OF THE PASSAGE

I. The Documentation of Spiritual Leadership (12:1–26)
   A. The priests who first returned (12:1–7)
   B. The Levites who first returned (12:8–9)
   C. The line of high priests (12:10–11)
   D. The priests under Joiakim's leadership (12:12–21)
   E. The priests and Levites who served until the reign of Darius the Persian (12:22–23)
   F. The Levites under Joiakim's leadership (12:24–26)
II. The Dedication of the Wall of Jerusalem (12:27–47)
   A. It is a time of rejoicing and singing
   B. It is a time of cleansing and purifying
   C. It is a time of organizing and giving
III. The Disengagement of the People (13:1–3)

DEVELOPMENT OF THE EXPOSITION

I. THE DOCUMENTATION OF SPIRITUAL LEADERSHIP (12:1–26)

A. The Priests Who First Returned (12:1–7)

¹ Now these are the priests and the Levites who came up with Zerubbabel the son of Shealtiel, and Jeshua: Seraiah, Jeremiah, Ezra, ² Amariah, Malluch, Hattush, ³ Shecaniah, Rehum, Meremoth, ⁴ Iddo, Ginnethoi, Abijah, ⁵ Mijamin, Maadiah, Bilgah, ⁶ Shemaiah and Joiarib, Jedaiah, ⁷ Sallu, Amok, Hilkiah and Jedaiah. These were the heads of the priests and their kinsmen in the days of Jeshua.

As noted earlier, there were three separate times exiles returned to Jerusalem: the first was led by Zerubbabel in 537/36 BC, the second was led by Ezra in 458/57 BC, and the third was led by Nehemiah in 445/44 BC. Nehemiah 12 looks back to those who first returned to Jerusalem with Zerubbabel. This list contains the names of twenty-two priestly families. Originally David established twenty-four family divisions to carry out the work at the sanctuary (1 Chr 24:7–19). Scholars suggest two of the family names were omitted by an error in copying the text, or that the full rotation was not yet reestablished, or it may be that two of the families did not initially return from exile with the others.[1] What is significant about this list is that every name represents a man of God who returned home from seventy years of exile to the debris of a destroyed temple and city in order to reestablish the worship of Yahweh in his holy city, Jerusalem. Ezra recounted that time: "Then the heads of fathers' *households* of Judah and Benjamin and the priests and the Levites arose, even everyone whose spirit God had stirred to go up and rebuild the house of the LORD which is in Jerusalem" (Ezra 1:5). Even though they were in grave danger from the peoples surrounding them, they were the ones who built the altar of the God of Israel to offer continual burnt offerings to the Lord. They were the ones who encouraged the people to give so that the foundation of the temple could be rebuilt. And they were the ones who began the work of reestablishing "the work of the house of the Lord" (Ezra 3:1–11).

Thank God for those who are willing to get their hands dirty and serve the Lord in difficult places. I mentioned earlier that I had the opportunity to minister to church leaders in Ecuador. At no time during my stay did I believe my life was in danger. However, I was fully aware of the sacrifice Jim Elliot and four others with him made as they were martyred for their willingness to go into a hostile environment to share the gospel. They paved the way for missions in Ecuador, and many have come to saving faith in Christ because of their sacrifice.

Years ago, a friend of mine had recently moved into a well-established neighborhood. I remember his saying that he wanted to be in a neighborhood with large trees in the yards. I remember thinking it is good to enjoy the beautiful trees, but it is also good there were those who first built those homes and had the foresight of planting those trees. They were willing to move into a barren

---

1. See Derek Kidner, *Ezra and Nehemiah*, Tyndale Old Testament Commentaries 12 (Downers Grove, IL: IVP Academic, 1979), 133; Andrew E. Steinmann, *Ezra and Nehemiah*, Concordia Commentary (St. Louis: Concordia, 2010), 582.

place and plant the saplings so that they could become strong, beautiful shade trees for the hot and humid days of Louisville summers. The church needs more Jim Elliots, more people who are willing to plant the saplings and possibly never live long enough to see them grow to maturity but joyfully do so because of their faith in God. Their joy is not in what is seen, but it is in the substance of what is not yet seen. As the writer of Hebrews penned, "Now faith is the assurance of things hoped for, the conviction of things not seen" (Heb 11:1). This truth was personified in the priests and others with them who first returned to Jerusalem with Zerubbabel. It has been personified throughout history by men and women such as Jim Elliot. May it be personified in us as well today. These names of priests listed in Nehemiah 12 may not mean much to us, but they are forever recorded in God's eternal word as men who faithfully served the Lord in a difficult time. Obviously, they are significant to God, and in the end that is all that really matters.

B. The Levites Who First Returned (12:8–9)

> [8] The Levites *were* Jeshua, Binnui, Kadmiel, Sherebiah, Judah, *and* Mattaniah *who was* in charge of the songs of thanksgiving, he and his brothers. [9] Also Bakbukiah and Unni, their brothers, stood opposite them in *their* service divisions.

Nehemiah 12:8–9 provides a list of the Levitical families who returned with Zerubbabel. This is a fuller list of names than what Ezra provides (Ezra 2:40). These men are worship leaders in songs of thanksgiving and antiphonal singing, alternate singing by two choirs. It highlights the importance of singing in the worship of Yahweh. Singing praises and songs of thanksgiving to the Lord is prevalent in both Testaments of the Bible. The longest book of the Bible, the book of Psalms, is composed of 150 songs of worship. Jeffrey Kranz proposes there are about 185 songs in the entire Bible.[2] Singing was certainly important to the apostles and the early church because it was an important way for believers to profess their faith in Christ and to attribute to him the worship he alone deserves. Furthermore, there will be singing in heaven (see Rev 15:2–3).

---

2. Jeffrey Kranz, "All the Songs in the Bible," overviewbible.com, https://overviewbible.com/bible-songs/ (accessed July 11, 2018). See this page for a comprehensive listing of the songs in the Bible.

C. *The Line of High Priests (12:10–11)*

[10] Jeshua became the father of Joiakim, and Joiakim became the father of Eliashib, and Eliashib became the father of Joiada, [11] and Joiada became the father of Jonathan, and Jonathan became the father of Jaddua.

The list of high priests in these verses includes the names of the high priests from the first return of exiles up to the high priest who served during the rule of Darius the Persian.[3] Jeshua was the high priest when the first exiles returned to Judah with Zerubbabel in about 537/36 BC. He was the high priest during the rebuilding and completion of the temple in 515 BC at the coaxing of the prophets Haggai and Zechariah.[4] Joiakim bridged the gap between the first return and the time of Nehemiah. Therefore, it appears he possibly was the high priest at the time of the second return of exiles to Judah led by Ezra in 457 BC. Eliashib was high priest when Nehemiah led the third return to Jerusalem in 445/44 BC. All of this information recognizes the continuity of the high-priestly line and the responsibilities that came with this office during these years of the postexilic era.

D. *The Priests under Joiakim's Leadership (12:12–21)*

[12] Now in the days of Joiakim, the priests, the heads of fathers' *households* were: of Seraiah, Meraiah; of Jeremiah, Hananiah; [13] of Ezra, Meshullam; of Amariah, Jehohanan; [14] of Malluchi, Jonathan; of Shebaniah, Joseph; [15] of Harim, Adna; of Meraioth, Helkai; [16] of Iddo, Zechariah; of Ginnethon, Meshullam; [17] of Abijah, Zichri; of Miniamin, of Moadiah, Piltai; [18] of Bilgah, Shammua; of Shemaiah, Jehonathan; [19] of Joiarib, Mattenai; of Jedaiah, Uzzi; [20] of Sallai, Kallai; of Amok, Eber; [21] of Hilkiah, Hashabiah; of Jedaiah, Nethanel.

Joiakim's service as high priest bridged the time of Jeshua, the high priest during the first return and the rebuilding of the temple, and the time of Eliashib, the high priest during the third return and the rebuilding of the wall of Jerusalem

---

3. Which Persian king Darius the Persian refers to is unclear and up for debate. It is most likely Darius II or Darius III. For discussions on the issue see H. G. M. Williamson, *Ezra, Nehemiah*, Word Biblical Commentary (Nashville: Thomas Nelson, 1985), 364; Kidner, *Ezra and Nehemiah*, 136; Steinmann, *Ezra and Nehemiah*, 584.

4. Eugene H. Merrill, *A Commentary on 1 & 2 Chronicles*, Kregel Exegetical Library (Grand Rapids: Kregel Academic, 2015), 507–8.

led by Nehemiah. This list recognizes the service of the priests who served during the intermediate period between these two significant events. They were most likely serving when Ezra returned with a mandate from King Artaxerxes to "teach anyone who is ignorant" of the laws of Ezra's God. Moreover, the king dictated that anyone who did not observe God's law should be severely punished (Ezra 7:25–26).

These priests served during a perilous time, when several men including priests and Levites had married foreign wives, retaking steps that once before led Israel into idolatry and ultimately exile (see Ezra 9:5–15; 10:18–24). When Ezra and his cohort arrived in Jerusalem, he confronted the people with their sin. Before Ezra arrived, it was a period of compromise among the people, including some of their spiritual leaders. It was a layperson named Shecaniah who stepped forward in repentance and suggested everyone take an oath to put away their foreign wives and children. It is possible his own father was guilty.[5] Ezra 10:5 states, "Then Ezra rose and made the leading priests, the Levites and all Israel, take oath that they would do according to this proposal; so, they took the oath."

There are several observations one can make from the incident recorded in Ezra 9–10. First, it was a period when the spiritual leadership compromised God's law and set a dangerous example for the rest of the people to follow. Second, after some time God raised up a spiritual leader, namely Ezra, to confront the sin. Third, before confronting the people, Ezra turned to God in prayer. Fourth, it was a layperson who first stepped up to confess the people's sin and do what was right to correct it. Fifth, Ezra began with the spiritual leadership when he called the people to repentance. Sixth, almost everyone repented, but not everyone did. And finally, this record indicates that the compromise of the priests and Levites before the arrival of Ezra did not destroy their offices. A number of the spiritual leaders among the priests and Levites compromised and sinned against God's law, but not all of them did. All through history, there have been those in the office of spiritual leadership who have fallen, but in every era, God has continued to raise up those who have proved to be his faithful servants.

---

5. Mervin Breneman, *Ezra, Nehemiah, Esther*, NAC 10 (Nashville: Broadman & Holman, 1993), 157.

E. The Priests and Levites Who Served until the
Reign of Darius the Persian (12:22–23)

> [22] As for the Levites, the heads of fathers' *households* were registered in the
> days of Eliashib, Joiada, and Johanan and Jaddua; so *were* the priests in
> the reign of Darius the Persian. [23] The sons of Levi, the heads of fathers'
> *households*, were registered in the Book of the Chronicles up to the days
> of Johanan the son of Eliashib.

The "Book of the Chronicles" mentioned in verse 23 should not be confused with
the biblical book of Chronicles (later split into 1 Chronicles and 2 Chronicles).
The book in reference here is an archival document kept in the temple.[6]

F. The Levites under Joiakim's Leadership (12:24–26)

> [24] The heads of the Levites *were* Hashabiah, Sherebiah and Jeshua the son
> of Kadmiel, with their brothers opposite them, to praise *and* give thanks,
> as prescribed by David the man of God, division corresponding to divi-
> sion. [25] Mattaniah, Bakbukiah, Obadiah, Meshullam, Talmon *and* Akkub
> *were* gatekeepers keeping watch at the storehouses of the gates. [26] These
> *served* in the days of Joiakim the son of Jeshua, the son of Jozadak, and
> in the days of Nehemiah the governor and of Ezra the priest *and* scribe.

Hashabiah and Sherebiah, along with his sons and brothers, were part of the
group that answered Ezra's call for Levites to join him in his return to Jerusalem
(Ezra 8:15–20). For whatever reason, they initially were not in the group. However,
when they received Ezra's personal request to go with him to minister at the house
of God in Jerusalem, they uprooted their families and answered the call. Ezra
made the appeal for the Levites to join him when he realized they would be
needed to help the priests as they ministered in the temple. These Levites were
the ones who saw to all the physical needs of the temple, helped the priests with
their duties, and supported Ezra the priest as he confronted the existing priests
and Levites and people with their sin of intermarriage. Just like Ezra and just like
Moses needed help holding up his arms in the battle with Amalek (Exod 17:11–13),
spiritual leaders need the support of faithful servants of the Lord around them.

---

6. F. Charles Fensham, *The Books of Ezra and Nehemiah*, New International Commentary on
the Old Testament (Grand Rapids: Eerdmans, 1982), 253.

Many of us in the church aspire to be leaders, but the Lord has instructed his disciples that our true aspiration should be to serve one another. One's greatness will be measured by one's becoming a servant (Matt 20:20–28). This list of Levites is a list of men whom God ordained to spend their lives serving Yahweh by serving others (Num 1:47–53; 8:19; Deut 10:8–9).

II. THE DEDICATION OF THE WALL OF JERUSALEM (12:27–47)

²⁷ Now at the dedication of the wall of Jerusalem they sought out the Levites from all their places, to bring them to Jerusalem so that they might celebrate the dedication with gladness, with hymns of thanksgiving and with songs *to the accompaniment* of cymbals, harps and lyres. ²⁸ So the sons of the singers were assembled from the district around Jerusalem, and from the villages of the Netophathites, ²⁹ from Beth-gilgal and from *their* fields in Geba and Azmaveth, for the singers had built themselves villages around Jerusalem. ³⁰ The priests and the Levites purified themselves; they also purified the people, the gates and the wall.

³¹ Then I had the leaders of Judah come up on top of the wall, and I appointed two great choirs, the first proceeding to the right on top of the wall toward the Refuse Gate. ³² Hoshaiah and half of the leaders of Judah followed them, ³³ with Azariah, Ezra, Meshullam, ³⁴ Judah, Benjamin, Shemaiah, Jeremiah, ³⁵ and some of the sons of the priests with trumpets; *and* Zechariah the son of Jonathan, the son of Shemaiah, the son of Mattaniah, the son of Micaiah, the son of Zaccur, the son of Asaph, ³⁶ and his kinsmen, Shemaiah, Azarel, Milalai, Gilalai, Maai, Nethanel, Judah *and* Hanani, with the musical instruments of David the man of God. And Ezra the scribe went before them. ³⁷ At the Fountain Gate they went directly up the steps of the city of David by the stairway of the wall above the house of David to the Water Gate on the east.

³⁸ The second choir proceeded to the left, while I followed them with half of the people on the wall, above the Tower of Furnaces, to the Broad Wall, ³⁹ and above the Gate of Ephraim, by the Old Gate, by the Fish Gate, the Tower of Hananel and the Tower of the Hundred, as far as the Sheep Gate; and they stopped at the Gate of the Guard. ⁴⁰ Then the two choirs took their stand in the house of God. So did I and half of the officials with me; ⁴¹ and the priests, Eliakim, Maaseiah, Miniamin, Micaiah, Elioenai,

Zechariah and Hananiah, with the trumpets; [42] and Maaseiah, Shemaiah, Eleazar, Uzzi, Jehohanan, Malchijah, Elam and Ezer. And the singers sang, with Jezrahiah *their* leader, [43] and on that day they offered great sacrifices and rejoiced because God had given them great joy, even the women and children rejoiced, so that the joy of Jerusalem was heard from afar.

[44] On that day men were also appointed over the chambers for the stores, the contributions, the first fruits and the tithes, to gather into them from the fields of the cities the portions required by the law for the priests and Levites; for Judah rejoiced over the priests and Levites who served. [45] For they performed the worship of their God and the service of purification, together with the singers and the gatekeepers in accordance with the command of David *and* of his son Solomon. [46] For in the days of David and Asaph, in ancient times, *there were* leaders of the singers, songs of praise and hymns of thanksgiving to God. [47] So all Israel in the days of Zerubbabel and Nehemiah gave the portions due the singers and the gatekeepers as each day required, and set apart the consecrated *portion* for the Levites, and the Levites set apart the consecrated *portion* for the sons of Aaron.

A. It Is a Time of Rejoicing and Singing

The dedication of the wall is a time of great joy and rejoicing. The English words "joy" and "rejoicing" come from the same Hebrew root. The Hebrew word for joy is *śimḥâ*, and the word for rejoicing is *śāmaḥ*. This Hebrew root is used five times in verses 43–44, emphasizing the rejoicing that occurs. The authors of the Old Testament employ this word in four theological contexts: "joyfulness in relation to Israel's worship calendar [or national gatherings of worship], rejoicing grounded in the character and activity of God, the gloating/joyfulness of the wicked over the affliction of the righteous, and the joyful anticipation of future salvation."[7] Three of these for uses appear to be implied by the text. First, the dedication of the wall is a national gathering where the people offer "great sacrifices and rejoiced." Second, the source of their "great joy" is God. In fact, everyone including the women and children rejoices in the Lord so much that "the joy of Jerusalem was heard from afar." Whether well received or not, what a tremendous testimony it

---

7. Michael A. Grisanti, "שָׂמַח," in *New International Dictionary of Old Testament Theology and Exegesis*, ed. W. VanGemeren (Grand Rapids: Zondervan, 1997), 3:1252.

must have been to others who heard it. And third, the dedication of the wall is a way of putting the past behind them and looking to God's protection moving ahead. The wall is a symbol of restoration and future salvation.

Rejoicing is the mark of a people who truly worship the Lord, acknowledge who he is, what he has done, and trust in his future salvation. The instruction for God's people to be a rejoicing people is throughout the entire Bible. The law instructs the people to rejoice in Jerusalem, stating,

> When you cross the Jordan and live in the land which the LORD your God is giving you to inherit, and He gives you rest from all your enemies around *you* so that you live in security, then it shall come about that the place in which the LORD your God will choose for His name to dwell, there you shall bring all that I command you: your burnt offerings and your sacrifices, your tithes and the contribution of your hand, and all your choice votive offerings which you will vow to the LORD. And you shall rejoice before the LORD your God, you and your sons and daughters, your male and female servants, and the Levite who is within your gates, since he has no portion or inheritance with you. (Deut 12:10–12)

The Psalms call for believers to rejoice more than any other book of the Bible. For instance, "Be glad in the LORD and rejoice, you righteous ones: And shout for joy, all you who are upright in heart" (Ps 32:11). The prophets give reason for the people of God to rejoice: "Rejoice greatly, O daughter of Zion! Shout *in triumph*, O daughter of Jerusalem! Behold, your king is coming to you; He is just and endowed with salvation, Humble, and mounted on a donkey, Even on a colt, the foal of a donkey" (Zech 9:9). Jesus teaches his disciples that even in persecution they have reason to rejoice: "Rejoice and be glad, for your reward in heaven is great; for in the same way they persecuted the prophets who were before you" (Matt 5:12). The apostles instruct believers to rejoice at all times: "Rejoice in the Lord always; again I will say, rejoice" (Phil 4:4)! And Jesus promises his disciples a future of continued joy and rejoicing: "Therefore you too have grief now; but I will see you again, and your heart will rejoice, and no one will take your joy from you" (John 16:22). Moreover, one aspect of the fruit of the Spirit is joy (Gal 5:22). Therefore, one of the characteristics of a faithful follower of Christ will be joy and rejoicing that springs forth from it.

The importance of singing has already been noted, but here it is highlighted in the preparations that are made for the dedication of the wall along with the proceedings themselves. They seek out Levites to lead in songs of thanksgiving and to accompany the singing that is to happen with their cymbals, harps, and lyres. During the dedication service, two "great choirs" proceed from opposite directions to the temple and lead the people in worship. Note that Ezra leads one of the choirs in its processional. It shows us that this great teacher of God's law leads the people to sing praises to the Lord. One could say serving God involves singing to God. They seem to go together. Psalm 48:9–14 appears to communicate what the people sang:

> We have thought on Your lovingkindness, O God,
> In the midst of Your temple.
> As is Your name, O God,
> So is Your praise to the ends of the earth;
> Your right hand is full of righteousness.
> Let Mount Zion be glad,
> Let the daughters of Judah rejoice
> Because of Your judgments.
> Walk about Zion and go around her;
> Count her towers;
> Consider her ramparts;
> Go through her palaces,
> That you may tell *it* to the next generation.
> For such is God,
> Our God forever and ever;
> He will guide us until death.

B. It Is a Time of Cleansing and Purifying

The Hebrew word meaning "to be clean or to purify" is *ṭāhēr*. It is a common word in Old Testament law. As stated earlier, references to purity "do not refer to a physical removal of absence of dirt, but to a theological state of purity before God that he imputes to his people through liturgical rites and sacrifices he prescribed. This vocabulary is part of the Old Testament theological terminology of justification and sanctification."[8] It is theological terminology for New Testament believers also as we are cleansed by the blood of Jesus Christ (Heb 9:14) and

---

8. Steinmann, *Ezra and Nehemiah*, 592–93.

yet also called to purify ourselves in the process of sanctification (1 John 3:3). The people make sure they are right with God before entering into this time of worship and dedication. It should be a reminder to every believer that when we come to worship the Lord "if I regard iniquity in my heart, the Lord will not hear me" (Ps 66:18).

C. It Is a Time of Organizing and Giving

First, Nehemiah organizes the dedication service itself, gathering the right people to lead it and participate in it. Second, men are appointed to organize and supervise the contributions made to the temple so that those who serve in the house of God will be provided for. The people of Judah joyfully give to the temple for the provision of the priests and Levites because these men lead the people in worship and are stewards of the temple. Those who love the Lord will appreciate those who teach them God's word and lead them in worship. They will joyfully seek to bless these godly people because of the blessing of spiritual leadership they have bestowed. Such obedience to God's word and generosity is a sign of spiritual health, just as it is today.

III. The Disengagement of the People (13:1–3)

> ¹ On that day they read aloud from the book of Moses in the hearing of the people; and there was found written in it that no Ammonite or Moabite should ever enter the assembly of God, ² because they did not meet the sons of Israel with bread and water but hired Balaam against them to curse them. However, our God turned the curse into a blessing. ³ So when they heard the law, they excluded all foreigners from Israel.

It is hard to believe there would have been a dedication of the wall of Jerusalem to Yahweh without the reading of God's word. The reference in these verses is to Deuteronomy 23:3–6, which recounts how, when the Israelites were headed to the promised land, the Ammonites and the Moabites had an opportunity to bless Israel with safe passage, but instead chose to curse the people of God. The Ammonites cursed the Israelites by refusing to allow them to purchase needed supplies from Ammonite merchants. The Moabites actually hired the prophet Balaam to pronounce a curse on Israel. Therefore, God's law stated, "No Ammonite or Moabite shall enter the assembly of the LORD." The passage demonstrates the Lord's faithfulness to his eternal promise to Abraham in Genesis 12:1–3 to curse those who curse Abraham. God remembered both the sins of omission and commission the Ammonites and Moabites committed against his people.

Moreover, verse 2 states "God turned the curse into a blessing." It is reminiscent of the garden of Eden when Adam and Eve sinned against God and were cursed with difficulty, affliction, and death. Nevertheless, our Lord Jesus Christ came to earth to live, die, be raised from the dead, and ascend to the right hand of the Father so that the curse would be turned into blessing for those who believe. And just as the Lord did not forget what the Ammonites and Moabites did to his covenant people, so he has not forgotten how the devil deceived Adam and Eve along with all of humanity. The day will come when the devil will reap what he has sown and be thrown into the lake of fire (Rev 20:10).

The people's response to what they hear from the reading of God's law indicates how the people interpret the text as a broader principle pertaining to all foreign people groups and not just the two people groups mentioned in the text. Apparently, they recognize all foreign entanglements threaten their ability to fulfill God's purposes for them. What is so wonderful about this passage is how the people hear God's law and promptly respond in obedience to it. It should be this way for every believer when God's word shines a light on our sin.

CONCLUSION

Nehemiah 12 reminds us of the importance of being ever acknowledging of the truth that we are recipients of the faithful service of generations of believers who have come before us. It should humble us, fill our hearts with gratitude, and prompt us to be mindful of generations to come. We should hope for, pray for, and strive for a legacy that will leave future generations an example of faithful service to Christ. This chapter also provides us with a picture of what the people of God should be doing when we worship the Lord. May others hear our unashamed songs of rejoicing in our Lord and Savior, Jesus Christ, and may we be found faithful in our giving to the church by supporting our spiritual leaders so that the work of God will flourish. Moreover, may we be receptive to God's word, repent of sin, and separate ourselves from any threat of sin. The passage shows how the people of God should be characterized by praise and moral uprightness.[9]

---

9. Ralph Davis, "The Work of Consolidation," Gospel Coalition, https://resources.thegospel-coalition.org/library/ezra-nehemiah-part-19 (accessed July 23, 2018).

FINAL THOUGHTS

1. What priority do you give to worshiping the Lord with song?

2. How can organization in the church be as spiritual an endeavor as other things we do in the church?

3. Why is rejoicing such an important characteristic of a believer?

4. What role does purification or sanctification play in one's preparation for worship?

5. How can believers improve in recognizing those who have and are faithfully serving the body of Christ?

THE NECESSITY OF CORRECTION

Nehemiah 13:4–31

INTRODUCTION

Receiving correction is often difficult, but sometimes being the one to give correction can be just as trying. We are all familiar with a parent telling a child just before disciplining them, "This is going to hurt me more than it is going to hurt you." And any of us who heard those words automatically thought, "Yeah, right." As we grow up we realize parents need to correct their children, and some of us are appalled when we witness parents who fail to correct their children's bad behavior. Who suffers when a child's behaviors are not held in check? The child suffers, the family suffers, and society suffers—schools, churches, and so on. Ultimately everyone suffers, and bad behavior gone uncorrected often leads to tragic consequences now and in the future. Licensed clinical social worker Amy Morin lists ten unhealthy reasons parents avoid correcting or disciplining their children:

1. "I feel sorry for him. He's been under a lot of stress."
2. "He didn't mean to do that."
3. "I haven't spent much time with them lately."
4. "I was too hard on him yesterday."
5. "Kids will be kids."
6. "I don't want him to be upset."
7. "I'm too tired to deal with it."
8. "He won't listen anyway."
9. "He'll think I'm mean."
10. "I always have to be the bad guy."[1]

---

1. Amy Morin, "10 Unhealthy Reasons Parents Avoid Disciplining Children," Very Well Family, https://www.verywellfamily.com/unhealthy-reasons-parents-avoid-disciplining-children-1094778 (accessed July 19, 2018).

Many of the excuses listed above are excuses we may use in the body of Christ for failing to correct one another's sinful behaviors. Many of us would rather go along to get along than to do the difficult work of lovingly confronting others with their sin and taking action to help them correct the problem. It takes time. It takes effort. It is often physically and emotionally draining. And it can make us vulnerable to being misunderstood and misrepresented as we seek to do the right thing. Therefore, it means we must put ourselves under the light of God's word and be willing to accept correction ourselves, because in truth at times we all need correction. It is for this reason Paul writes Timothy concerning the importance of God's word to the believer's life: "All Scripture is inspired by God and profitable for teaching, for reproof, for correction, for training in righteousness; so that the man of God may be adequate, equipped for every good work" (2 Tim 3:16–17). All the Scriptures are "profitable" for teaching us what is right, teaching us what is wrong, correcting our wrong behavior, and training us how to behave rightly, so that we can fulfill God's calling on our lives to glorify him. Showing what is wrong and correcting wrong behavior are fundamental purposes for the word of God in the life of a believer. For this reason Paul goes on to instruct Timothy to

> preach the word; be ready in season *and* out of season; reprove, rebuke, exhort, with great patience and instruction. For the time will come when they will not endure sound doctrine; but *wanting* to have their ears tickled, they will accumulate for themselves teachers in accordance to their own desires, and will turn away their ears from the truth and will turn aside to myths. But you, be sober in all things, endure hardship, do the work of an evangelist, fulfill your ministry. (2 Tim 4:2–5)

Any believer who loves the people of God and seeks the glory of God through his church will "with great patience and instruction" need to correct another brother or sister in Christ at one time or another.

Nehemiah encounters a situation where the people of Judah need to be corrected in a number of areas. Each of the issues is connected to their very reason for existence as the people of God as stated in Exodus 19:5–6: "'Now then, if you will indeed obey My voice and keep My covenant, then you shall be My own possession among all the peoples, for all the earth is Mine; and you shall be to Me a kingdom of priests and a holy nation.' These are the words that you shall speak to the sons of Israel."

God made Judah his own possession among all the nations so that Judah would be a "kingdom of priests" and a "holy nation" unto God—a kingdom of servants of God and a nation devoted to God. God states it this way in the law in Leviticus 20:26: "Thus you are to be holy to Me, for I the LORD am holy; and I have set you apart from the peoples to be Mine."

Nehemiah 13 states how, when Nehemiah returns to Judah after going back to report to the Persian king, he encounters an unholy people who are living in disobedience to God's law. In our day, Nehemiah's actions may seem harsh. But as we look at the passage and witness Nehemiah's actions to correct the appalling state of affairs the people had put themselves in, let us ask the question, "What would have been the results for the people of God and his glory if Nehemiah had ignored the situation or failed to take extreme measures to correct what was happening in Judah?" Believing that living in obedience to the law of God was the only path to blessing for both the people and Yahweh, Nehemiah cares enough about the people of God and the reputation of God among the nations to take action no matter how personally difficult it must be for him to do so. Gary Smith points out Nehemiah is committed to two uncompromising truths:

1. Spiritual leaders need to live holy lives, dedicated to the service of God and those coming to worship God; and

2. The people need to reject the path of sin and provide for the needs of the spiritual leaders.[2]

STRUCTURE

Nehemiah 13 contains four sections: 13:4–9, 10–14, 15–22, 23–31. Each section is a record of how Nehemiah needs to correct the people's disobedience to God's law when he returns to Judah after going to report to the Persian king.

SUMMARY OF THE PASSAGE

The passage shows how, when Nehemiah leaves Jerusalem to go back and report to King Artaxerxes, the people fail to keep their commitments to keeping God's law in Nehemiah 10 in a number of concrete ways. Therefore, when Nehemiah returns, he is compelled to correct the people and reestablish order, lest their sins lead them to the same destruction the sins of their forebears brought about.

---

2. Gary V. Smith, *Ezra-Nehemiah, Esther*, ed. Philip W. Comfort, Cornerstone Biblical Commentary (Carol Stream, IL: Tyndale House, 2010), 208–9.

OUTLINE OF THE PASSAGE

I. Holiness Means Being Faithful in the Responsibilities God Has Given Us (13:4–9)

II. Holiness Means Faithfully Giving to Support God's Work (13:10–14)

III. Holiness Means Keeping Holy That Which God Has Made Holy (13:15–22)

IV. Holiness Means Shunning Anything That Would Damage Our Devotion to God (13:23–31)

DEVELOPMENT OF THE EXPOSITION

I. HOLINESS MEANS BEING FAITHFUL IN THE RESPONSIBILITIES GOD HAS GIVEN US (13:4–9)

> [4] Now prior to this, Eliashib the priest, who was appointed over the chambers of the house of our God, being related to Tobiah, [5] had prepared a large room for him, where formerly they put the grain offerings, the frankincense, the utensils and the tithes of grain, wine and oil prescribed for the Levites, the singers and the gatekeepers, and the contributions for the priests. [6] But during all this *time* I was not in Jerusalem, for in the thirty-second year of Artaxerxes king of Babylon I had gone to the king. After some time, however, I asked leave from the king, [7] and I came to Jerusalem and learned about the evil that Eliashib had done for Tobiah, by preparing a room for him in the courts of the house of God. [8] It was very displeasing to me, so I threw all of Tobiah's household goods out of the room. [9] Then I gave an order and they cleansed the rooms; and I returned there the utensils of the house of God with the grain offerings and the frankincense.

During the time Nehemiah goes back to report to King Artaxerxes, "Eliashib the priest" makes a grave error. There is debate whether this was the high priest who bore this name.[3] Those who argue this passage refers to someone else points out that Eliashib the high priest is called the high priest in Nehemiah (3:1, 20; 13:28). Second, the high priest would not have been involved in managing storerooms, and it would be odd to say he was "appointed over the chambers of the house"

---

3. H. G. M. Williamson, *Ezra, Nehemiah*, Word Biblical Commentary (Nashville: Thomas Nelson, 1985), 386; F. Charles Fensham, *The Books of Ezra and Nehemiah*, New International Commentary on the Old Testament (Grand Rapids: Eerdmans, 1982), 260–61; Derek Kidner, *Ezra and Nehemiah*, Tyndale Old Testament Commentaries 12 (Downers Grove, IL: IVP Academic, 1979), 141.

if it were speaking of the high priest. Nevertheless, even though this Eliashib probably was not the high priest, it is also difficult to believe the high priest was ignorant of what transpired. If he was ignorant of it, then he was at least guilty of negligence for failing to oversee everything that transpired in the temple.

Eliashib provides Tobiah with a sizable warehouse area as living quarters in the temple precincts. Nehemiah 4:1–7 identifies that Tobiah the Ammonite was opposed to the rebuilding of the wall of Jerusalem and joined those who ridiculed and tried to intimidate the builders. Nehemiah 6:10–19 indicates Tobiah joined Sanballat and others in a conspiracy to frighten Nehemiah and lead him into sin so that they could have something with which to disgrace him. Later, Tobiah sent direct letters to Nehemiah to threaten him. The passage also specifies Tobiah was married to a Judean woman who was the daughter of Shecaniah the son of Arah. Tobiah's son also was married to a Judean woman who was the daughter of Meshullam the son of Berechiah. Apparently, Tobiah is a very influential man among the nobles of Judah because of these relationships, and according to Nehemiah 13:4–9, Tobiah's sphere of influence includes Eliashib the priest. The Hebrew word qārôb, translated "related," can refer to familial relations or can mean having a close association with someone. Either way, imagine how a priest of the Most High God had the audacity to move from their appointed place in the house of God "the grain offerings, the frankincense, the utensils and the tithes of grain, wine and oil," items that had been dedicated to the Lord as provisions for the temple servants, Eliashib's very brothers. It may be the reason the Levites are compelled to leave the temple and go to their fields for food, as recorded in verse 10. It calls into question, "Did all of the stored provisions that had been moved out still reach their intended destinations?" Given what we know about Tobiah, it is doubtful.

Certainly, Tobiah's residence in the temple precincts provides him with even more prominence among the inhabitants of Jerusalem and financial benefits. This setup gives an Ammonite who is an outspoken opponent to God's work access to come and go into the temple as he pleases. How ironic, given that the last action recorded in Nehemiah 13:1–3 at the dedication of the temple is to expel the foreigners from the community of Israelites. What's more, even though all the foreigners were removed, Tobiah is from one of the two people groups explicitly mentioned in the text they read from the law (Deut 23:3–6). There is no excuse for what Eliashib does.

Therefore, Nehemiah's reaction upon his probably unexpected return is appropriate. Kidner describes it well, observing, "Unlike the ecclesiastics of the time who could see all sides of a matter, including the side to support, Nehemiah stormed in as violently as, one day, his Master would. Throughout this chapter he stands out from his contemporaries by his refusal to allow for a moment that holiness is negotiable or that custom alone can hallow anything."[4] One must not overlook Nehemiah's directive for the area to be purified. The ritual purity of the temple represents the holiness of God. Therefore, Nehemiah is concerned about the ritual purity of the space just as he is concerned about the moral purity of God's people.

This incident leads to at least seven observations.

1. Compromising relationships usually lead to more compromise.
2. Personal concerns and relationships must not supersede one's obedience to God's word.
3. The people of God have been called to serve the Lord, not to use him to serve our own interests.
4. Unfaithful leaders or the absence of faithful spiritual leadership usually open the door to the sin of others.
5. Godly people are displeased when they learn of sin, either by themselves or by their brothers and sisters in the faith.
6. Correcting a problem includes both confronting the problem and setting or resetting things as they should be.
7. Accountability is essential to everyone in the community of faith, including its leadership.

II. Holiness Means Faithfully Giving to Support God's Work (13:10–14)

> [10] I also discovered that the portions of the Levites had not been given *them*, so that the Levites and the singers who performed the service had gone away, each to his own field. [11] So I reprimanded the officials and said, "Why is the house of God forsaken?" Then I gathered them together and restored them to their posts. [12] All Judah then brought the tithe of the grain, wine and oil into the storehouses. [13] In charge of the storehouses

---

4. Kidner, *Ezra and Nehemiah*, 142.

I appointed Shelemiah the priest, Zadok the scribe, and Pedaiah of the Levites, and in addition to them was Hanan the son of Zaccur, the son of Mattaniah; for they were considered reliable, and it was their task to distribute to their kinsmen. [14] Remember me for this, O my God, and do not blot out my loyal deeds which I have performed for the house of my God and its services.

It is no surprise, given the action of Eliashib the priest clearing out space allotted for the provisions of the priests and Levites in order to give it to Tobiah, that the temple servants are being neglected. Breneman correctly states, "When the spiritual life of leaders diminishes because of sin or carelessness, God's provision for his work also decreases."[5] Therefore, it is appropriate for Nehemiah to reprimand those in charge. Their spiritual neglect leads to the physical neglect of God's servants. Their spiritual failure influences the people they lead to follow the same path. When Nehemiah first returns to Jerusalem, his concern is much more than just rebuilding the wall. He wants to remove the reproach of the people and restore them to a proper relationship to Yahweh, to experience an authentic spiritual revival of faithful obedience and service to God. Numbers 18:21 clearly states the tithes of Israel are to be brought and given to the Levites for their service at the sanctuary. In the commitment service in Nehemiah 9:38–10:39, the people commit to bring the tithes so that they will "not neglect the house of our God" (Neh 10:37–39). And at the dedication of the wall Nehemiah 12:44 states, "On that day men were also appointed over the chambers for the stores, the contributions, the first fruits and the tithes, to gather into them from the fields of the cities the portions required by the law for the priests and Levites; for Judah rejoiced over the priests and Levites who served."

However, when Nehemiah returns from the Persian king, he finds spiritual leaders and a people who are neglecting the house of God—exactly the opposite of what they promised before he left them. Neglecting to faithfully give to support the house of God is a sign of a spiritual drift away from devotion to God, away from holiness. It is amazing how drastically things can change, either for good or for ill. Nehemiah's story is a testament to this truth. When he first received the report from his brother of the condition that Jerusalem was in, the

---

5. Mervin Breneman, *Ezra, Nehemiah, Esther*, NAC 10 (Nashville: Broadman & Holman, 1993), 271.

news grieved him. But God providentially used him to influence a heathen king and receive needed support, to travel hundreds of miles, to organize and rejuvenate a downcast people, and to overcome enemies and obstacles so that in a short time the debris was removed, the wall of Jerusalem was rebuilt, and the people of God experienced spiritual renewal and no longer were a reproach to the nations. God did amazing things with his people.

However, the life of faith requires diligence. As I heard many years ago, "Yesterday's victories do not suffice for today's challenges." The enemies of the faith, the world, Satan, and our own sinful nature will continue to attempt to destroy what God has done in the lives of his people. And no matter how many wonderful things we have witnessed the Lord do in the past, we must be ready to rise to the occasion in the present and future. It is for this reason that the apostle Paul's Letter to the Ephesians includes a section on spiritual warfare and the full armor of God (Eph 6:10–18). Simply put, sin is the result of our arrogant thinking that we can do without God. Our way is better. The "lust of the flesh, the lust of the eyes, and the boastful pride of life" (1 John 2:16) constantly seek to dismantle what the Lord has done and is doing in our lives. The life of faith is marked by a humility that drives us to God's word and down onto our knees in prayer because we realize our total dependence on Christ. This lack of humility leads to the dismal circumstances Nehemiah discovers when he returns to Judah.

The text lends itself to at least seven more observations.

1. Sin is never an isolated incident; it always affects others. There is no sin only unto oneself.

2. Spiritual leaders cannot do God's work if they are not supported by the people of God. In his providence, God has chosen to work through his people.

3. More generally speaking, the sins of the people of God frustrate the work of the people of God.

4. After Nehemiah reprimands the leaders, the people begin bringing their tithes once again. It is courageous of Nehemiah to rebuke the leaders, and it is noble of the leaders to accept his reprimand and lead the people to renew bringing in their tithes.

5. Wisdom calls for selecting reliable people to oversee God's work, even if it requires replacing the unreliable. Eliashib is replaced by reliable men. To some this act may seem unredemptive. If

Eliashib had repented, the Lord would have forgiven him, and the people should have as well (1 John 1:9). However, Eliashib loses the confidence of the people. He has shown himself to be unreliable, and that lost trust will need to be rebuilt. Whenever there is sin, there is loss. Restoration to one's fellowship with God through confession and the forgiveness of sin does not guarantee a restoration to the circumstances that were in place before the sin. Starting with the garden of Eden and moving forward, the Bible demonstrates this reality.

6. Corporately, God's holy people are expected to be devoted to God's holy work. God's law teaches this expectation.

7. Personally, one's highest priority in life should be to glorify and please God. Nehemiah's motive for remedying this situation is to please God and hear the words, "Well done, good and faithful servant."

III. Holiness Means Keeping Holy That Which God Has Made Holy (13:15–22)

[15] In those days I saw in Judah some who were treading wine presses on the sabbath and bringing in sacks of grain and loading *them* on donkeys, as well as wine, grapes, figs and all kinds of loads, and they brought *them* into Jerusalem on the sabbath day. So I admonished *them* on the day they sold food. [16] Also men of Tyre were living there *who* imported fish and all kinds of merchandise, and sold *them* to the sons of Judah on the sabbath, even in Jerusalem. [17] Then I reprimanded the nobles of Judah and said to them, "What is this evil thing you are doing, by profaning the sabbath day? [18] Did not your fathers do the same, so that our God brought on us and on this city all this trouble? Yet you are adding to the wrath on Israel by profaning the sabbath."

[19] It came about that just as it grew dark at the gates of Jerusalem before the sabbath, I commanded that the doors should be shut and that they should not open them until after the sabbath. Then I stationed some of my servants at the gates *so that* no load would enter on the sabbath day. [20] Once or twice the traders and merchants of every kind of merchandise spent the night outside Jerusalem. [21] Then I warned them and said

to them, "Why do you spend the night in front of the wall? If you do so again, I will use force against you." From that time on they did not come on the sabbath. [22] And I commanded the Levites that they should purify themselves and come as gatekeepers to sanctify the sabbath day. *For* this also remember me, O my God, and have compassion on me according to the greatness of Your lovingkindness.

In the Law and the Prophets, the Lord is very clear about his expectations for Israel and the Sabbath:

> Remember the sabbath day, to keep it holy. Six days you shall labor and do all your work, but the seventh day is a sabbath of the LORD your God; *in it* you shall not do any work, you or your son or your daughter, your male or your female servant or your cattle or your sojourner who stays with you. For in six days the LORD made the heavens and the earth, the sea and all that is in them, and rested on the seventh day; therefore the LORD blessed the sabbath day and made it holy. (Exod 20:8–11)

> For six days work may be done, but on the seventh day there is a sabbath of complete rest, a holy convocation. You shall not do any work; it is a sabbath to the LORD in all your dwellings. (Lev 23:3)

> If because of the sabbath, you turn your foot
> From doing your *own* pleasure on My holy day,
> And call the sabbath a delight, the holy *day* of the LORD honorable,
> And honor it, desisting from your *own* ways,
> From seeking your *own* pleasure
> And speaking *your own* word,
> Then you will take delight in the LORD,
> And I will make you ride on the heights of the earth;
> And I will feed you *with* the heritage of Jacob your father,
> For the mouth of the LORD has spoken. (Isa 58:13–14)

> Also I gave them My sabbaths to be a sign between Me and them, that they might know that I am the LORD who sanctifies them. But the house of Israel rebelled against Me in the wilderness. They did not walk in My statutes and they rejected My ordinances, by which, if a man observes them, he will live; and My sabbaths they greatly profaned. Then I resolved

to pour out My wrath on them in the wilderness, to annihilate them. But I acted for the sake of My name, that it should not be profaned in the sight of the nations, before whose sight I had brought them out (Ezek 20:12–14)

The law and the prophets declare how essential it is to Yahweh that Israel remember the Sabbath and keep it holy. It is a day to desist from the human preoccupation of trying to better one's own material condition and turn attention to God, realizing that every good gift comes from him. Yahweh is their true Provider. Keeping the Sabbath demonstrates their faith in God. It is a celebration of rest, of freedom, and of the Savior who delivered Israel from Egyptian bondage. It is essential to their identity and testimony as a kingdom of priests since the Sabbath is a sign of their covenant with the Lord before the nations, who have no such practice. Moreover, God's command for Israel to keep the Sabbath holy comes with the promise of blessing for Israel. Their delight in the Lord will result in greater blessing still.

Therefore, Israel profaning the Sabbath is a great offense against God, and when Nehemiah witnesses the people working on the Sabbath, he is outraged. He is furious for at least two reasons. First, simply put, what they are doing is evil. Second, by profaning the Sabbath they are doing one of the very same things their forebears did that led to the destruction of Jerusalem, the destruction of the temple, and the exile. How can they be so self-centered and so thick-headed? One would think they would have paid attention to what happened to their forebears given the difficulties the returnees encountered when they reached Judah.

Notice what Nehemiah does. Once he sees the problem, he automatically confronts them with their sin. He rebukes the people, he reprimands the leaders who allowed it to happen, and he shuts down the ability for foreigners to bring in their wares during the Sabbath. What's more, he ensures the matter is corrected. There are those who try to circumvent Nehemiah's actions by setting up their shops in the evening just outside the wall. Nonetheless, they flee when Nehemiah threatens to use force to expel them from the city. Nehemiah has the courage to act on his convictions. How is that possible? Because his sole desire is to honor God by keeping holy what God made holy, the Sabbath. Imagine how alienated Nehemiah must feel. He must be tempted to think he is on an island by himself. The Hebrew word ḥûsâ, translated "compassion," is an imperative that carries with it the idea of "have compassion on me and spare me" or "be a refuge over me." Nehemiah probably feels alienated and in danger. Nevertheless, he trusts in Yahweh's ḥesed, the "covenant faithfulness" and "steadfast love" of his God.

IV. Holiness Means Shunning Anything That Would Damage Our Devotion to God (13:23–31)

²³ In those days I also saw that the Jews had married women from Ashdod, Ammon *and* Moab. ²⁴ As for their children, half spoke in the language of Ashdod, and none of them was able to speak the language of Judah, but the language of his own people. ²⁵ So I contended with them and cursed them and struck some of them and pulled out their hair, and made them swear by God, "You shall not give your daughters to their sons, nor take of their daughters for your sons or for yourselves. ²⁶ Did not Solomon king of Israel sin regarding these things? Yet among the many nations there was no king like him, and he was loved by his God, and God made him king over all Israel; nevertheless the foreign women caused even him to sin. ²⁷ Do we then hear about you that you have committed all this great evil by acting unfaithfully against our God by marrying foreign women?" ²⁸ Even one of the sons of Joiada, the son of Eliashib the high priest, was a son-in-law of Sanballat the Horonite, so I drove him away from me. ²⁹ Remember them, O my God, because they have defiled the priesthood and the covenant of the priesthood and the Levites. ³⁰ Thus I purified them from everything foreign and appointed duties for the priests and the Levites, each in his task, ³¹ and I *arranged* for the supply of wood at appointed times and for the first fruits. Remember me, O my God, for good.

The book of Nehemiah concludes with one last incident where Nehemiah needs to confront the people with the egregious sin of marrying foreigners. What makes him curse the men, the fathers and husbands in this patriarchal society, who are responsible, strike some of them, and pull out their hair? A reading of 1 and 2 Kings provides the answer. From the time of Solomon's sins of marrying foreigners (1 Kgs 11:1–10) and constructing altars to worship their gods (2 Kgs 22:13) until the time of the utter destruction of Jerusalem and the exile of the people of Judah to Babylon hundreds of years later, one witnesses a very sad story of what blessings could have been and what sorrow most often prevailed because of Israel's disregard for God and his law. It is tragic. Nehemiah's anger and frustration spill out because no matter what steps forward the people make toward following Yahweh, they fall back into sin. The matter is crucial to the future of the people of God, and as an official under the Persian king's authority and as a man of God it is his responsibility to deal with the problem in a way that communicates how serious it is within their cultural context.

The people are their own worst enemies. They disregard God's law, and that their children cannot understand Hebrew in order to understand the law apparently is of little to no concern for them. What they did was far removed from Deuteronomy 6:6–7, Yahweh's instruction for parents to prioritize the teaching of the law to their children. To make matters worse, one of the high priest's grandsons married the daughter of Sanballat the Horonite. Sanballat is one of the chief leaders who opposed Nehemiah and the people as they rebuilt the wall. The law prohibits the high priest from marrying a foreigner in Leviticus 21:14–15. As he is the grandson of the high priest, it is possible this priest is in line to be the high priest when his father, Joiada, dies.[6] It poses a serious danger. Therefore, Nehemiah expels him from the community.

Some might think Nehemiah's actions are too harsh, but his primary concern is for the glory of God and the welfare of the people of God. I recall having a professor who denounced any corporal punishment as a part of disciplining children in the home. When a student pressed him and asked, "Is there any time at all you would spank your child?" the professor thought a moment and responded something like this, "If my child disobeyed me by running out into a busy street where he or she could be killed, I would spank them then because of the seriousness of the matter." I left that class thinking that the difference between this professor and other parents is their assessment of what is serious and what is not when it comes to raising a child. One's lack of understanding the seriousness of Israel's sin against God and its danger of extinction as a people who were specially raised up and called by God as an instrument of salvation for the nations will lend one to thinking Nehemiah is over the top in his reaction. Such thinking calls into question one's own devotion to God and the people of God. Nehemiah's anger is because of his desire to honor God and to lead the people of Judah to do the same. His anger is not out of selfishness. Today many of us get angry about the wrong things and are passive about what should anger us. What should anger us? Whatever dishonors God and seeks to destroy the body of Christ should anger us, and like Nehemiah, we should be fervent in our desire to glorify Christ and

---

6. Andrew E. Steinmann, *Ezra and Nehemiah*, Concordia Commentary (St. Louis: Concordia, 2010), 611.

protect his church from the wolves within and without that seek to devour the sheep. Such a mind-set is in keeping with that of the Good Shepherd.

So Nehemiah sees to it that the people and the spiritual leadership are purified "from everything foreign," and he sees to it that the work in the house of God is restored to what it is supposed to be. The passage concludes with Nehemiah's praying a third time for God to "remember" him. Concerning these requests, Thomas observes, "They tell us that Nehemiah was a man of prayer. He sought the Lord's blessing on all that he did. 'Remember this also in my favor,' he asks (Neh. 13:22). This is not a request for a prominent place in the kingdom of God (Matt. 20:20–24), but the plea of a man deeply conscious of the subtleties of sin, the allurements of the world, and the malevolence of the evil one."[7] More than anything else, Nehemiah longs to make a difference in the kingdom for God's glory. And should everyone else turn against him, he prays that God will not forget him.

CONCLUSION

The conclusion to the book of Nehemiah is sobering. A romantic might wish the book would have concluded with Nehemiah 13:3, the people listening to and obeying God's law, separating themselves from the world. Instead, it ends with a picture of enemies who appeared to be defeated earlier in the book rising up and continuing to cause trouble for Nehemiah and the people of God. It is the picture of a people who demonstrated wonderful commitment to the Lord who abandon those commitments and apparently forsake their God. The law can never save them from their sin; it never was intended to save. And even though Nehemiah corrects them, it leaves the reader with the sense that if it happened here and so many times in Israel's past, what real hope is there for the future? That is the point! The only hope is in the Lord Jesus Christ, and what more do we need? As the apostle Paul states, "the Law has become our tutor *to lead us* to Christ, so that we may be justified by faith" (Gal 3:24).

The Lord Jesus did for us what we could not do for ourselves. He was born of a virgin, he lived a sinless life, he offered himself as our substitute on the cross, and he died for our sin; conquering death he rose again, and then ascended into heaven to sit at the right hand of the Father, reign as King of kings and Lord of lords, and serve as our High Priest. By God's grace through faith in the Lord

---

7. Derek W. Thomas, H., *Ezra & Nehemiah*, Reformed Expository Commentary (Phillipsburg, NJ: P&R, 2016), 410.

Jesus Christ we are saved from sin and its penalty, death. We have been justified, legally declared righteous by Almighty God, and now we have the Holy Spirit, who helps us in our sanctification, our growing into the image of Christ. Nevertheless, until we experience glorification and are completely the image of Christ, we need correction. We need the correction of God's word, we need the correction of the Holy Spirit, and we need the correction of our brothers and sisters in Christ. Nehemiah does not give up on God's people or on the Lord's work, and neither should we.

Nehemiah's work is not in vain. God uses Nehemiah to restore the wall and gates that will someday welcome the Messiah. God uses Nehemiah to remove the reproach that was on the people of God, to preserve them, and in particular the tribe of Judah, from which the Lion of Judah will come. Nehemiah prays that the Lord will remember and use what he did, and God does so in such an amazing way. Nehemiah's life is an example and encouragement to every believer, showing us what God will do with the life of one of his servants who is zealous for God's glory and for the health and reputation of the people of God.

FINAL THOUGHTS

1. What happens to believers when we are resistant to godly correction? What happens when Christians fail to correct other believers in a loving way?

2. Is it ever right for Christians to be angry? If so, when is it right, and how should it be expressed?

3. What can lead to one's compromising one's walk with God?

4. How does one succeed in being a pleaser of God rather than a pleaser of people?

5. What can we learn from Nehemiah's perseverance in ministering to the people of Judah?

BIBLIOGRAPHY

Ackroyd, Peter R. *Israel under Babylon and Persia*. London: Oxford University Press, 1970.

Albright, William F. *The Biblical Period from Abraham to Ezra*. New York: Harper, 1963.

Altmann, Peter. *Economics in Persian-Period Biblical Texts*. Tübingen: Mohr Siebeck, 2016.

Barber, Cyril J. *Nehemiah: An Expositional Commentary*. Eugene, OR: Wipf & Stock, 1991.

Beaulieu, Paul-Alain. *The Reign of Nabonidus, King of Babylon, 556–539 BC*. New Haven, CT: Yale University Press, 1989.

Betts, T. J. *Ezekiel the Priest: A Custodian of Tora*. Studies in Biblical Literature 74. New York: Peter Lang, 2005.

Blenkinsopp, Joseph. *Ezra-Nehemiah: A Commentary*. Old Testament Library. Philadelphia: Westminster, 1988.

Braun, Roddy. *1 Chronicles*. Word Biblical Commentary 14. Nashville: Thomas Nelson, 1986.

Breneman, Mervin. *Ezra, Nehemiah, Esther*. NAC 10. Nashville: Broadman & Holman, 1993.

Bridges, Jerry. *The Joy of Fearing God*. Colorado Springs: WaterBrook, 1998.

Brisco, Thomas. *Holman Bible Atlas*. Nashville: Broadman & Holman, 1998.

Brown, Raymond. *The Message of Nehemiah*. The Bible Speaks Today. Downers Grove, IL: InterVarsity Press, 1998.

Butler, John G. *Nehemiah: The Wall Builder*. Bible Biography Series 16. Clinton, IA: LBC, 1998.

Canepa, Matthew P. "Achaemenid and Seleucid Royal Funerary Practices and Middle Iranian Kingship." Pages 3–5 in *Commutatio et contention: Studies in the Late Roman, Sasanian, and Early Islamic Near East*, edited by Henning Börm and Josef Wiesehöfer. Düsseldorf: Wellem Verlag, 2010.

Cook, John M. *The Persian Empire*. New York: Schocken, 1983.

Dandamyev, M. "Achaemenid Babylonia." In *Ancient Mesopotamia*, edited by I. M. Diakonoff. Moscow: Nauka, 1969.

Davis, Ralph. "The Work of Consolidation." Gospel Coalition. https://resources.thegospelcoalition.org/library/ezra-nehemiah-part-19. Accessed July 23, 2018.

Deffinbaugh, Bob. "Righteous Anger (Ephesians 4:26–27)." Bible.org. https://Bible.org/seriespage/14-righteous-anger-ephesians-426-27. Accessed August 30, 2017.

Easley, Kendell H. *The Illustrated Guide to Biblical History*. Nashville: Holman Bible, 2003.

Evans, Walwyn. "Stiff-Necked." Biblestudy.com. www.biblestudytools.com/dictionary/stiff-necked/. Accessed August 16, 2017.

Fensham, F. Charles. *The Books of Ezra and Nehemiah*. New International Commentary on the Old Testament. Grand Rapids: Eerdmans, 1982.

Finzel, Hans. *The Top Ten Leadership Commandments*. Colorado Springs: David C. Cook, 2012.

Fisher, Fred L. "The New and Greater Exodus: The Exodus Pattern in the New Testament." Preaching Source. http://preachingsource.com/journal/the-new-and-greater-exodus-the-exodus-pattern-in-the-new-testament/. Accessed February 23, 2018.

Franklin, Benjamin. *Poor Richard's Almanack*. 1736.

Fuller, Russell. *Invitation to Biblical Hebrew Syntax: An Intermediate Grammar*. Grand Rapids: Kregel, 2017.

Garrett, Duane A. *A Commentary on Exodus*. Kregel Exegetical Library. Grand Rapids: Kregel Academic, 2013.

Gentry, Peter J. "The Meaning of 'Holy' in the Old Testament." *Bibliotheca Sacra* 170, no. 677–80 (2013): 400–417.

Gershevitch, I., ed. *The Cambridge History of Iran II: The Median and Achaemenian Periods*. Cambridge: Cambridge University Press, 1985.

Getz, Gene A. *Nehemiah: Becoming a Disciplined Leader*. Men of Character 4. Nashville: B&H, 1995.

———. *When Your Goals Seem Out of Reach: Take a Lesson from Nehemiah*. Biblical Renewal Series. Ventura, CA: Regal Books, 1981.

Grayson, A. Kirk. *Assyrian and Babylonian Chronicles*. Locust Valley, NY: J. J. Augustin, 1975.

Hamilton, James M., Jr. *Exalting Jesus in Ezra-Nehemiah*. Kindle ed. Christ-Centered Exposition Commentary. Nashville: Holman Reference, 2014.

Harper, Henry A. *The Bible and Modern Discoveries*. 5th ed. London: A. P. Watt & Son, Hastings House, 1895.

Harrison, R. K. "Elephantine Papyri." In *The International Standard Bible Encyclopedia*, edited by Geoffrey W. Bromiley. Grand Rapids: Eerdmans, 1986.

———. "Feasts and Festivals of Israel." Page 787 in vol. 1 of *Baker Encyclopedia of the Bible*. Grand Rapids: Baker Book House, 1988.

Henkelman, Wouter F. M. "'Consumed before the King': The Table of Darius, That of Irdabama and Irtaštuna, and That of His Satrap, Karkiš." In *Der Achämenidenhof: Akten des 2. Internationalen Kolloquiums zum Thema "Vorderasien im Spannungsfeld klassischer und altorientalischer Überlieferungen," Landgut Castelen Bei Basel, 23.–25. Mai 2007*, edited by B. Jacobs and R. Rollinger. Wiesbaden: Harrassowitz, 2010.

Hill, Andrew E., and John H. Walton. *A Survey of the Old Testament*. 2nd ed. Grand Rapids: Zondervan, 2000.

Hilprecht, Hermann V., and Albert T. Clay. *Business Documents of Murashu Sons of Nippur Dated in the Reign of Artaxerxes I (464–425 B.C.)*. Babylonian Expedition 9. Philadelphia: University of Pennsylvania Press, 1898.

Hoerth, Alfred J., Gerald Mattingly, and Edwin M. Yamauchi, eds. *Peoples of the Old Testament World*. Grand Rapids: Baker Books, 1994.

"John Huss: Pre-Reformation Reformer." *Christianity Today*. http://www.christianitytoday.com/history/people/martyrs/john-huss.html. Accessed September 13, 2017.

Kaiser, Walter C., Jr. *A History of Israel*. Nashville: Broadman & Holman, 1998.

Kenyon, Kathleen. *Digging Up Jerusalem*. London: Ernest Benn, 1974.

———. *Jerusalem: Excavating 3000 Years of History*. New York: McGraw-Hill, 1967.

Khanbolouki, Mahbod. "Nowruz—The Persian New Year and the Spring Equinox." Ancient-origins.net. https://www.ancient-origins.net/news-general/nowruz-persian-new-year-and-spring-equinox-002808. Accessed February 15, 2019.

Kidner, Derek. *Ezra and Nehemiah*. Tyndale Old Testament Commentaries 12. Downers Grove, IL: IVP Academic, 1979.

Laney, J. Carl. *Ezra and Nehemiah*. Everyman's Bible Commentary. Chicago: Moody, 1982.

Larson, Knute, and Kathy Dahlen. *Ezra, Nehemiah, Ezra*. Holmen Old Testament Commentary 9. Nashville: B&H, 2005.

Levering, Matthew. *Ezra & Nehemiah*. Brazos Theological Commentary on the Bible. Grand Rapids: Brazos, 2007.

Lipschits, Oded, and Joseph Blenkinsopp, eds. *Judah and the Judeans in the Neo-Babylonian Period*. Winona Lake, IN: Eisenbrauns, 2003.

Malamat, A. "Last Kings." *Israel Exploration Journal* 18 (1968).

———. "The Last Years of the Kingdom of Judah." Pages 218–20 in *The Age of the Monarchies: Political History*. Vol. 4 of *World History of the Jewish People*. Jerusalem: Massada, 1979.

McConville, J. G. *Ezra, Nehemiah, and Esther*. Louisville, KY: Westminster John Knox, 1985.

Merrill, Eugene H. *A Commentary on 1 & 2 Chronicles*. Kregel Exegetical Library. Grand Rapids: Kregel Academic, 2015.

———. *A Kingdom of Priests: A History of Old Testament Israel*. Grand Rapids: Baker Books, 1996.

Miller, Walter, trans. *Xenophon in Seven Volumes* Cambridge, MA: Harvard University Press, 1914.

Murray, Andrew. *With Christ in the School of Prayer*. Springdale, PA: Whitaker House, 1981.

Myers, Ben. "On Smiling and Sadness: Twelve Theses." Faith and Theology. http://www.faith-theology.com/2010/11/on-smiling-and-sadness-twelve-theses.html. Accessed February 7, 2017.

Myers, Jacob M. *Ezra, Nehemiah*. Anchor Bible 14. New York: Doubleday, 1965.

Naumann, Rudolf. *Architektur Kleinasiens von ihren Anfangen bis zum Ende der hethitischen Zeit*. Tübingen: Verlag Ernst Wasmuth, 1955.

Newsome, James C. *By the Waters of Babylon*. Atlanta: John Knox, 1979.

Olmstead, A. T. "The Fall of Samaria." *American Journal of Semitic Languages* 21 (1905): 170–82.

———. *History of Assyria*. Chicago: University of Chicago Press, 1975.

———. *History of the Persian Empire*. Chicago: University of Chicago Press, 1948.

Packer, J. I. *A Passion for Faithfulness: Wisdom from the Book of Nehemiah.*
Wheaton, IL: Crossway, 1995.

Page, Sydney H. T. *Powers of Evil: A Biblical Study of Satan and Demons.* Grand
Rapids: Baker, 1995.

Parpola, Simo. "The Murderer of Sennacherib." *Reontre assyrilolgique
internationale* 26 (1980): 171–82.

Paul, Shalom. "Sargon's Administrative Diction in II Kings 17:27." *Journal of
Biblical Literature* 88 (1969).

Piccirillo, Michele. *Mount Nebo.* Jerusalem: Studium Biblicum Franciscanum,
2002.

Plutarch. *Lives: The Translation Called Dryden's.* Corrected from the Greek and
revised by A. H. Clough. 5 vols. Boston: Little Brown, 1906.

Porten, B. "Elephantine Papyri." In *Anchor Bible Dictionary.* New York:
Doubleday, 1992.

Porten, B., and J. C. Greenfield. *Jews of Elephantine and Aramaeans of Syene.*
Jerusalem: Hebrew University Press, 1974.

Pritchard, J. B. *Ancient Near Eastern Texts Relating to the Old Testament.* 3rd ed.
Princeton: Princeton University Press, 1969.

Redford, Donald B. *Egypt, Canaan, and Israel in Ancient Times.* Princeton:
Princeton University Press, 1992.

Roberts, Mark. *Ezra, Nehemiah, Esther.* Mastering the Old Testament 11.
Dallas: Word, 1993.

Sélincourt, Aubrey de, trans. *Herodotus, Histories.* New York: Penguin Books,
2003.

Selman, Martin J. *1 Chronicles.* Tyndale Old Testament Commentaries.
Nottingham, UK: IVP Academic, 1994.

Simonin, Antoine. "The Cyrus Cylinder." Ancient History Encyclopedia.
https://www.ancient.eu/article/166/the-cyrus-cylinder/. Accessed
Febrary 18, 2019.

Smith, Gary V. *Ezra-Nehemiah, Esther.* Edited by Philip W. Comfort.
Cornerstone Biblical Commentary. Carol Stream, IL: Tyndale House,
2010.

Smith, Sidney. *Babylonian Historical Texts Relating to the Capture and Downfall
of Babylon.* London: Methuen, 1924.

Spurgeon, Charles. "December 22 Immediately Present." In *Faith's Checkbook*. 1888. http://www.gbfc-tx.org/Books/Public%20Domain/FAITH'S%20 CHECKBOOK.PDF.

Steinmann, Andrew E. *Ezra and Nehemiah*. Concordia Commentary. St. Louis: Concordia, 2010.

Stern, Ephraim. *Archaeology of the Land of the Bible: The Assyrian, Babylonian, and Persian Periods (732–332 B. C. E.)*. Vol. 2. Anchor Bible Reference Library. New York: Doubleday, 2001.

Stiebing, William H. *Ancient Near Eastern History and Culture*. New York: Addison Wesley Longman, 2003.

Swindoll, Charles R. *Hand Me Another Brick*. Nashville: Thomas Nelson, 1978.

Tarn, W. W. "Xerxes and His Successors: Artaxerxes I and Darius II." In *Macedon 401–301 BC*, edited by J. B. Bury. S. A. Cook, and F. E. Adcock. Vol. 7 of *The Cambridge Ancient History*. Cambridge: Cambridge University Press, 1927.

Thomas, Derek W. *Ezra & Nehemiah*. Reformed Expository Commentary. Phillipsburg, NJ: P&R, 2016.

Throntveit, Mark A. *Ezra-Nehemiah*. Interpretation: A Bible Commentary for Teaching and Preaching. Louisville, KY: Westminster John Knox, 1992.

VanGemeren, W., ed. *New International Dictionary of Old Testament Theology and Exegesis*. Grand Rapids: Zondervan, 1997.

Wallis, Arthur. *God's Chosen Fast*. Fort Washington, PA: Christian Literature Crusade, 1968.

Waters, Matt. *Ancient Persia: A Concise History of the Achaemenid Empire, 550–330 BCE*. New York: Cambridge University Press, 2014.

Weinberg, S. "Postexilic Palestine: An Archaeological Report." *Proceedings of the Israel Academy of Science and Humanities* (1971).

Whitney, Donald S. *Spiritual Disciplines for the Christian Life*. Colorado Springs: NavPress, 1991.

Widengren, Geo. "The Persian Period." In *Israelite and Judean History*, edited by J. H. Hayes and J. M. Miller. London: SCM Press, 1977.

Wiersbe, Warren W. *Be Determined (Nehemiah): Standing Firm in the Face of Opposition*. Kindle ed. BE Series Commentary. Colorado Springs: David C. Cook, 2010.

Williamson, H. G. M. *Ezra, Nehemiah*. Word Biblical Commentary. Nashville: Thomas Nelson, 1985.

Wilson, Robert Dick. *A Scientific Investigation of the Old Testament*. Chicago: Moody, 1959.

Wiseman, D. J. *Chronicles of Chaldaean Kings, 626–556 B. C.* London: British Museum Press, 1956.

———. *Notes on Some Problems in the Book of Daniel*. London: Tyndale, 1956.

Wright, Christopher J. H. *The Mission of God: Unlocking the Bible's Grand Narrative*. Downers Grove, IL: IVP Academic, 2006.

———. *The Mission of God's People: A Biblical Theology of the Church's Mission*. Grand Rapids: Zondervan, 2010.

Xypolia, Illa. "Divide et Impera: Vertical and Horizontal Dimensions of British Imperialism." *Critique* 44 (July 2016).

Yamauchi, Edwin M. "Ezra-Nehemiah." In vol. 4 of *The Expositor's Bible Commentary*, edited by Frank E. Gaebelein. Grand Rapids: Zondervan, 1988.

———. *Persia and the Bible*. Grand Rapids: Baker, 1996.

Young, Rodger C. "When Was Samaria Captured? The Need for Precision in Biblical Chronologies." *Journal of the Evangelical Theological Society* 47, no. 4 (2004): 577–95.

Zeitlin, Solomon. "The Origin of the Synagogue." In *The Synagogue: Studies in Origins, Archaeology, and Architecture*, edited by Joseph Gutmann. New York: Ktav, 1975.

SCRIPTURE INDEX

Old Testament

Old Testament Apocrypha

New Testament